Girl Power?

Girl Power?

A History of Girl-Focused Development from Nairobi

SARAH BELLOWS-BLAKELY

The University of Chicago Press
Chicago and London

The University of Chicago Press, Chicago 60637
The University of Chicago Press, Ltd., London
© 2025 by Sarah Bellows-Blakely
All rights reserved. No part of this book may be used or reproduced in any manner whatsoever without written permission, except in the case of brief quotations in critical articles and reviews. For more information, contact the University of Chicago Press, 1427 E. 60th St., Chicago, IL 60637.
Published 2025
Printed in the United States of America

34 33 32 31 30 29 28 27 26 25   1 2 3 4 5

ISBN-13: 978-0-226-83970-7 (cloth)
ISBN-13: 978-0-226-83972-1 (paper)
ISBN-13: 978-0-226-83971-4 (e-book)
DOI: https://doi.org/10.7208/chicago/9780226839714.001.0001

Library of Congress Cataloging-in-Publication Data

Names: Bellows-Blakely, Sarah, author.
Title: Girl power? : a history of girl-focused development from Nairobi / Sarah Bellows-Blakely.
Other titles: History of girl-focused development from Nairobi
Description: Chicago ; London : The University of Chicago Press, 2025. | Includes bibliographical references and index.
Identifiers: LCCN 2024044583 | ISBN 9780226839707 (cloth) | ISBN 9780226839721 (paperback) | ISBN 9780226839714 (ebook)
Subjects: LCSH: African Women Development and Communication Network. | UNICEF. | World Conference to Review and Appraise the Achievements of the United Nations Decade for Women (1985 : Nairobi, Kenya) | World Conference on Women (4th : 1995 : Beijing, China) | Beijing Platform for Action. | Girls—Developing countries. | Girls—Africa. | Economic development projects—History—20th century. | Capitalism. | Policy networks.
Classification: LCC HQ792.2 .B45 2025 | DDC 362.7082/096—dc23/eng/20241014
LC record available at https://lccn.loc.gov/2024044583

♾ This paper meets the requirements of ANSI/NISO Z39.48-1992 (Permanence of Paper).

Contents

Introduction 1

1 Making Girl Power Neoliberal: Erasing Alternative Visions of African Girlhood 21

2 Pan-African Organizing and the UN World Conference on Women in Nairobi 46

3 Neoliberal Austerity Births Girl-Focused Economic Development at UNICEF 72

4 Girls as a Battlefield over Structural Adjustment Programs at FEMNET 105

5 Crafting International Norms: The Girl Child and the Final UN World Conference on Women in Beijing 124

6 Empowering African Girls through Corporate Sponsorships? The Afterlives of the Beijing Platform for Action 147

Conclusion 164

*Acknowledgments 173
Notes 177
Index 213*

Introduction

There are many studies about the creation of knowledge; comparatively few examine how knowledge disappears. This book begins with a story of how knowledge was created and then selectively erased. In 1990, staff at the United Nations Children's Fund (UNICEF) commissioned a study on the education of girls in Eastern and Southern Africa. Policymakers at the agency wanted to know about girls' participation in schools as an issue of not only gender-based equality but also economic necessity. The study accompanied UNICEF's embrace of the idea that global poverty rates could be dramatically reduced by harnessing the power of girls. The guiding belief was that girls systematically lagged behind boys in access to schooling, and this educational deficit prevented them from fully participating in economic development when they became adults. According to the dominant narrative at UNICEF, encouraging girls' participation in school and empowering them more generally would combat rising inequalities in wealth from below, without fundamentally changing the global economic order from above.

To carry out the study on girls' educational access in Eastern and Southern Africa, UNICEF employees turned to members of the African Women's Communication and Development Network (FEMNET). A Nairobi-based nongovernmental organization (NGO), FEMNET emerged in the 1980s in the context of the United Nations Decade for Women. Its founders, who included Eddah Gachukia and Njoki Wainaina from Kenya, Aida Gindy from Egypt, and Sara Hlupekile Longwe from Zambia, conceived of the NGO as a Pan-African institution intended to advocate around issues related to women and economic development. This was a deliberate effort on their part to decolonize policymaking within the United Nations and organize African women to represent their own interests on the international stage.

FEMNET's founders coordinated among United Nations agencies and hundreds of organizations focused on women and development across Africa. As an institution, FEMNET has enjoyed relatively high status within the United Nations and many of its African member states, and it has had official consultative status to the United Nations Commission on the Status of Women since the 1990s.[1] Its individual members have included current, former, and future members of Parliament, heads of state agencies, and leaders of internationally well-connected NGOs.

Between 1990 and 1992, FEMNET oversaw the creation of eight country studies for the UNICEF project on girls' access to education in Eastern and Southern Africa. More than fifteen researchers from the continent participated in qualitative and quantitative data collection for the reports. FEMNET then compiled the evidence into one volume and sent it to UNICEF for publication. Before staff at UNICEF published and disseminated the study, however, the findings were altered. Multiple sections of data and analysis disappeared or were fundamentally revised.

The result was a reversal of the core conclusions that FEMNET's staff and a team of Africa-based researchers had initially produced. The original version of the report found that gendered disparities in primary school access were minimal in half of the countries studied; in Botswana, for example, girls had long attended school at *higher* rates than boys. Meanwhile, the altered published report claimed that girls everywhere in Africa trailed boys in access to formal education. It maintained that girls were universally oppressed on the continent. The unaltered FEMNET report presented evidence that where wide gender disparities to the detriment of girls did exist, a mix of factors were to blame. This included what one coauthor called the "three C's": capitalism, colonialism, and Christianity. The altered UNICEF version of the report deleted those sections. References to the varied, high-prestige roles that women and girls had occupied in many societies on the continent since precolonial times similarly disappeared.

The contested economic politics of girl-focused policymaking were on full display in the competing versions of the report. FEMNET's original study presented data showing how the turn to neoliberal capitalism—to austerity-mandating structural adjustment programs (SAPs) that required African states to slash state spending on education, health care, and other public services since the 1980s—had uniquely hurt girls and women, exacerbating the feminization of poverty across the continent. The altered UNICEF report removed these sections. It argued not only that neoliberal SAPs were beneficial for girls and women but that they had actually not gone far enough. It also systematically erased evidence and analysis that placed blame for gendered

INTRODUCTION

educational disparities in Africa on an unequal international system forged through the intertwined violences of colonialism and capitalism. African cultures, traditions, and families instead became the primary culprits of girls' universal oppression. Empowering girls to labor in capitalist markets as future women became the source of their salvation.

UNICEF published and disseminated the altered study on girls' educational access in 1992. The original report that FEMNET compiled from the eight country studies was never circulated publicly. Three years later, at the final United Nations World Conference on Women in Beijing, a set of policy frameworks was adopted to guide global action on the intertwined issues of women's rights and economic development, cementing the logic laid out in the altered UNICEF study. The findings in the original FEMNET version of the study are today absent from dominant international policy frameworks, having been suppressed, kept out of circulation, and unadopted. This raises the urgent questions of how and why particular forms of knowledge become institutionalized at high levels of policymaking while other forms are marginalized. It calls for us to examine the bureaucratic politics that underlie these interwoven processes of magnification and erasure.

This story represents one episode in this book's broader narrative of a battle waged over capitalism, colonialism, and their relationships to girls and development within international policymaking. The book charts how, between the 1980s and 1995, officials at FEMNET and UNICEF were at the heart of an international movement that made girls central to efforts to fight poverty and drive economic growth. Yet their political leanings and prescribed solutions were often radically different: some members of both institutions leaned toward socialist, antiracist, decolonial, and intersectional feminist critiques of the international system and neoliberal capitalism. They often called for high-level policy changes to combat the roots of poverty and connected forms of oppression such as patriarchy and racism. Other members of the two institutions, including those belonging to UNICEF's New York City–based leadership, accepted that structural adjustment and broader neoliberal capitalism were here to stay. They tended to favor bottom-up solutions to rising economic inequalities and poverty. Changes at the individual, family, and community levels dominated their policy proposals and advocacy. Still other people within this network advocated for a mix of the two approaches: for structural changes to the global economic system from above and the bottom-up empowerment of girls from below.

All sides of the debate tended to agree that poverty and economic inequalities were intersectional problems—that they disproportionately impacted girls in the Global South, given the interwoven forms of oppression related to gender, generation, race, colonial legacies, and more that many girls experienced. A consensus therefore existed within both FEMNET and UNICEF that development planning should focus on girls in the Global South as a kind of trickle *up* policymaking. What people disagreed on was at which level to advocate for change—put simply, from above (through high-level policy changes), from below (by educating and empowering girls to work their way to prosperity), or through a mix of the two.

The fraught UNICEF-FEMNET relationship at the center of this book was no mere sideshow. It was essential to the creation of global policies and guiding principles on how to eradicate poverty and promote gender equality in Africa and globally. The narrative arc of the book traces how, between the 1980s and 1995, the work between employees at UNICEF and FEMNET grew into a full-fledged lobbying campaign focusing on the urgent need to place girls at the heart of development planning.

This lobbying campaign came to a head in 1995. That year, fifty thousand people from 189 countries convened in Beijing, China, for the final United Nations World Conference on Women. Thousands of journalists attended, broadcasting the convention's dramas and proceedings to audiences around the world through newspapers, radio, television, and the burgeoning internet. Hillary Clinton gave an acclaimed speech on the importance of women's and girls' human rights. Many scholars and activists have noted the importance of the widely celebrated, circulated, and commented-upon conference outputs. Foremost among them were the Beijing Declaration and Platform for Action, which delegates from all attending nations voted to approve. This set the blueprints for the linked movements for women's rights and economic development not only in 1995 but into the present.[2]

Initially, the Beijing conference outputs were not going to include a specific section on girls, and one did not appear in the official draft of the Platform for Action prepared by early 1995. Linda Tarr-Whelan, an official delegate to the UN conference under the administration of US president Bill Clinton, wrote in *Human Rights* in 1995 that the section on the "girl child" in the Beijing Platform for Action was belatedly included due to its "particular importance to African delegates."[3] In reality, the special section on girls was written into the Beijing conference outputs at the eleventh hour due to lobbying from FEMNET and UNICEF representatives.

The section on the girl child, or girls under the age of eighteen, in the Beijing Platform for Action promoted the idea that girls could drive economic development when freed from the burdens of culturally rooted patriarchy. It wrote girl-focused development planning into a set of international norms that would guide not only United Nations policymaking but the work of actors around the world through the popularization, dissemination, and international endorsement of a certain set of ideas about girls and economic growth. While the last-minute inclusion of a special section on girls at the World Conference on Women in Beijing was not solely responsible for making girl-focused development into a dominant logic within powerful international spaces, it represents a crucial step in this process.[4]

Several scholars have dubbed the outputs and aftermath of the Beijing Platform for Action as "neoliberal feminism" or "free-market feminism."[5] Kristen Ghodsee, for example, has defined neoliberalism as a "fetishization of unfettered free markets, emaciated states, and dismantled social safety nets." She and others have called neoliberalism the "dismantling of the welfare state." Ghodsee describes the outcome of the final United Nations World Conference on Women in Beijing as the victory of "a certain brand of liberal, bootstrap-pulling, entrepreneurial feminism" that was "coopted" by neoliberal capitalism. The result, she argues, was a feminism unaccompanied by structural changes to the economic system from above. Instead, it merely provided "certain women equal access to fetishized free markets" and "justified the dismantling of welfare states and social supports."[6] Underpinning much of Ghodsee's analysis is Nancy Fraser's description of neoliberal feminism as the process through which "the dream of women's emancipation is harnessed to the engine of capitalist accumulation."[7]

Racism and colonialism are undertheorized in Ghodsee's work.[8] However, scholars such as Kalpana Wilson and Shirin Rai have shown how neoliberal feminism has rested on the fantasy of empowering "Third World" women and girls—predominantly Black and Brown women and girls—to work as entrepreneurs and laborers in for-profit markets. This fantasy, they argue, has obscured the realities of whose work continues to be the most appropriated, exploited, and underpaid in global labor markets that neoliberal feminism props up: that of Black and Brown women.[9]

Self-described "free-market feminist" Deirdre McCloskey has used definitions similar to Ghodsee's, even though the two inhabit different ends of the political spectrum when it comes to capitalism. In McCloskey's words, "Free-market feminism . . . acknowledges the embedded character of economic agents . . . and yet it does not conclude therefore that the capitalist bedding needs to be torn off the bed and thrown away. On the contrary, it argues that the market has been the chief road for the liberation of women (as of poor men)." Building on the work of Joan Taylor Kennedy, McCloskey argues it is not "the power of government" that will spell women's liberation, nor is it "a musty version of socialism." Instead, she claims, for-profit "deals, not laws" will secure "women's liberation" from structures of oppression.[10] At the core of such definitions of free-market and neoliberal feminism is the idea that the nation-state—particularly robust welfare state programs in areas such as health care, education, labor protections, and food and housing security—and international action on issues such as state-level debt forgiveness and equitable terms of trade are unnecessary or even counterproductive to the dismantling of patriarchy and intersecting forms of oppression, such as race and class.

Many have critiqued the concept of neoliberalism from various political standpoints. Some have argued that the term has become so capacious as to lose meaning and should be refined if not downright abandoned.[11] Scholars such as Chandra Talpade Mohanty have also long questioned the coherence of the label *feminism* given the many competing stances and political movements attached to it. The divergences between Ghodsee and McCloskey, both self-described feminists, are merely the tip of the iceberg.[12] Keeping in mind these critiques and their calls for more linguistic precision, I use both *free-market feminism* and *neoliberal feminism* as shorthand for the alignment of efforts to empower girls and women, especially in the Global South, with shrinking welfare states, the rise of for-profit humanitarianism, and declining calls for international action to address growing global inequalities in wealth.

The adoption of a special section on the girl child in Beijing represented a moment of the hegemonic solidification of free-market feminism within core spaces of international policymaking through the vehicle of girl-focused development, which scholars such as Heather Switzer, Karishma Desai, and Emily Bent have called "Girls in Development."[13] At the heart of this hegemonic emergence of Girls in Development was the perceived capacity of girls, especially in developing countries or the Global South, to drive economic growth for themselves, their communities, and the world by unleashing girl power through for-profit work in labor markets. One outcome of the focus on girls in the Beijing conference outputs was the codification of free-market feminism into global policymaking at the expense of alternative frameworks for economic and gender-based justice. Central to this process was the erasure of calls for top-down structural changes to international and national policymaking. Through the codification of Girls in Development into global norms in Beijing, the focal point for change shifted from high-level action—sometimes combined with individual action from girls and their families or communities—to bottom-up action alone.

This book provides a history of the FEMNET-UNICEF lobbying campaign in order to understand how feminism and neoliberal capitalism merged through the vehicle of Girls in Development. By narratively following UNICEF and

FEMNET's work together, the book shows how multiple contested visions of economic programming and gender justice focused on girls became whittled, contorted, and selectively erased into an increasingly singular, neoliberal framework that came to guide international policymaking. It argues that the growth and spread of free-market feminism was neither automatic with the collapse of the Cold War, as Ghodsee argues, nor an unwitting or accidental process, as Fraser suggests. It did not initially stem from the direct action of people at multinational corporations or the usual suspects in histories of neoliberal capitalism: the International Monetary Fund and World Bank. Rather, free-market feminism grew through the repeated creation, erasure, and circulation of particular ideas concerning girls, poverty, the state, racism, and colonialism among members of a Pan-African women's NGO and employees of a child-focused humanitarian agency at the United Nations.

In the generation of girl-focused knowledge within and between FEMNET and UNICEF, not all ideas about girls made it into the literature produced for the campaign to make Girls in Development into a set of international norms. Certain sets of knowledge and arguments were expanded while others were marginalized or erased completely. Carefully tracing which ideas were kept, which were amplified, and which were silenced demonstrates both the intentionality and the high levels of bureaucratic labor required to stitch together particular strands of feminism with particular strands of capitalism at the expense of alternative visions—socialist, decolonial, antiracist, and more—within institutions and spaces connected to the United Nations.

As becomes clear through a careful accounting of the history of these campaigns, girl-focused development programs have not only or always been neoliberal and supported free-market ideologies. Initially, many strands of thought existed about the relationships among girls, poverty, patriarchy, and the state. In the 1980s and early 1990s, everyone from Marxist feminists in East Africa to development experts at the World Bank's headquarters in Washington, DC, and a range of people in between evoked girls to support, oppose, call for a refinement of, or otherwise engage with discussions of shrinking welfare states, an inequitable international order, and the growth of for-profit humanitarianism. A singular vision of girl-focused thought did not exist. What was common across conversations was that people discussed girls in order to both justify and critique particular forms of capitalism. The real and imagined status of girls, and of African girls in particular, became a battleground for far-reaching debates about a perceived crisis in capitalism, decolonization, and the declining welfare state.

In exploring how multiple visions of girl-focused programming morphed into a singular strand that became dominant within the United Nations and among a broad swath of globally dispersed actors, this book makes an intervention into how knowledge—in this case, neoliberal feminist knowledge—has been created and spread into a set of international norms. Building on scholarship within global intellectual history, postcolonial studies, feminist theory, and connected histories of knowledge and science, I emphasize not only which ideas about girls and the economy have circulated and become common sense but also which ones have not widely circulated and why. Accounts of the erasure of knowledge often center *agnotology*, or the study of the production of ignorance theorized by historians of science such as Londa Schiebinger and Robert Proctor and critically built upon by scholars like Manuela Fernández Pinto.[14] Jean Allman and Joel Cabrita have used agnotological frameworks to problematize the erasure of African women as historical actors from public and academic memory.[15] Within the growing field of global intellectual history, Samuel Moyn has discussed the historical importance of the non-globalization of ideas—those ideas that did not circulate, at the expense of conceptions that would become widespread norms.[16] These works build, whether implicitly or explicitly, on the foundational thought of Michel-Rolph Trouillot on silencing and the processes through which some ideas—and some histories—have become canonical while others have been suppressed or forgotten.[17] Crucial here, too, is Saidiya Hartman's critical interrogation of "the expected and usual course of invisibility" of certain kinds of actors—in Hartman's case, enslaved African girls—within archives and written histories.[18] These discussions of agnotology, forgetting, and silencing highlight the fraught and deeply political processes through which some knowledge has spread and become widely adopted while other knowledge has been covered up, erased, or rendered obsolete.

These erasures, which are a central component of many global intellectual and political histories, serve as an invitation and a provocation to think through how to historicize not only forgotten systems of thought but also the actors who created them. Women from Africa and the diaspora have long been marginalized from intellectual and political histories, whether of individual nation-states, of particular regions, of Africa as a continent, or in international and global histories.[19] Dominant tropes often guide these scripts of erasure and selective inclusion. Sometimes, erasures of African women as political and intellectual actors within scholarly and popular histories occur because of a perceived lack of sources. Common assumptions are either that African women have not played major roles in the creation of international policymaking or that the primary sources do not exist to show when, how, and under what conditions they have done so. Another script in existing public and scholarly histories—particularly but not only in histories produced within academic spaces in the North Atlantic—has been to fixate on the capacity of women from Africa to contest power structures from below, often through one-dimensional discussions of individual agency.[20] In the former, African women are erased from global intellectual and political histories. Their absences are treated as natural, obvious, and so commonsense as to need no explanation or reflection. In the latter, they often exist as flat caricatures, perpetually resisting global structures from a fixed position of disempowerment. Kalpana Wilson has critiqued the notion that "poor women in developing countries" have a "limitless capacity to 'cope.'"[21] It is precisely this idea that serves as the subtext of the script that treats African women as if they exist in a perpetual state of one-dimensional and often romanticized resistance—a fetishization of resistance from below in ways that mirror and reproduce parts of the neoliberal logic of Girls in Development.

A third script exists in scholarship on people of various genders from Africa and the broader Global South: that of the collaborator and sellout. These tropes have been commonly applied to African men working with colonial officials in the first half of the twentieth century and to those who have headed African nation-states in the second half. They have been invoked to refer to woman actors in more recent decades—particularly regarding the roles that Global South–based women's NGOs such as FEMNET may have played, intentionally or not, in facilitating the institutionalization of neoliberal capitalism and the replacement of welfare states with private actors at various levels of governance.[22] As in the first two cases, these tropes construct one-dimensional understandings of the actions and desires of people from Africa who have operated in national and international intellectual and political spaces—spaces laden with structural hierarchies of power that further complicate overly simplistic understandings of how people have historically interacted with them.[23] None of these existing scripts are sufficient to understand the centrality of FEMNET's members to the creation of girl-focused international norms through the United Nations or the forms of selective silencing and amplification of their ideas and identities that occurred as Girls in Development internationalized.

Women whose identities have been constructed, in part, around Pan-African forms of belonging have long been central to the history of Girls in Development and to many other global intellectual and international histories, from abolitionism to nationalism and decolonization.[24] Yet they have often had to navigate rocky terrain between being tokenized, fetishized, marginalized, and co-opted in the process, all while finding avenues to continue funding and publicizing their work in spaces of international policymaking. Moreover, the category of African women is neither monolithic nor stable.

While the concept is partially rooted in Pan-Africanist women's movements, it also stems from colonial and Eurocentric tropes treating the continent and its inhabitants as a monolith, as thinkers such as Ama Ata Aidoo and Filomina Steady have long shown.[25] FEMNET alone has consisted of women with various life experiences and conflicting political stances. In its early years, and in histories this book tells, it was dominated by Kenyan women. Solidarities, ambivalences, and outright ruptures have characterized their interactions with one another, just as they have characterized the broader lobbying campaign at both UNICEF and FEMNET.

Women from Africa, such as Eddah Gachukia and Njoki Wainaina, played central roles in the creation and spread of girl-focused policymaking into a global set of norms. Yet this book is not a romantic tale of their full inclusion and unchallenged acceptance in the United Nations or broader international policymaking. It traces how women like Gachukia and Wainaina helped to define, research, and disseminate girl-focused thought into commonsense ideas, even as their identities, their labor, and some of their core arguments and political commitments were selectively erased while others were amplified in the process.

Anna Lowenhaupt Tsing and Antoinette Burton have used the term *friction* to describe the uneasy relationships that have often existed within global encounters and transnational alliances—they have been simultaneously destructive and productive of new affinities, ways of knowing, and forms of action.[26] The creation of free-market feminism through a particular focus on girls and poverty emerged from a lobbying campaign between FEMNET and UNICEF that was structured as much by frictions, vertical hierarchies, and fraught alliances as it was by horizontal cooperation and easy agreements.[27] Financial and political realities within the campaign partially determined which ideas came out of it in the end, even as the generation of these ideas depended on the intellectual labor and collective political organizing of a self-described group of Pan-African women working within FEMNET. The published research and international norms that resulted often stripped out socialist, decolonial, antiracist, and other frameworks that invoked girls in order to call for a restructuring of the global economic system. Whereas these calls helped underpin the rise of proto forms of Girls in Development in the late 1980s, by the time of the Beijing Conference on Women in 1995, neoliberal frameworks of girl power dominated the conversation.

Making visible the erasures in the history of the girl-focused lobbying campaign that drives the narrative arc of this book is possible because this story is told with sources from, and in dialogue with, FEMNET's archive. FEMNET

INTRODUCTION 11

has its own documentation center in Nairobi, part of the NGO's efforts since the late 1980s to preserve and share knowledge about women's organizing on the continent and globally. The archive has had various paid employees in charge of its curation.[28]

Stored in FEMNET's archive are the NGO's founding documents, meeting minutes, administrative records, and documentation surrounding major projects as well as a trove of unpublished and published advocacy materials about girls and women and development in Africa and globally. For the purposes of this book on the history of the internationalization of Girls in Development, reports surrounding FEMNET's girl-focused work and records about its relationship with UNICEF were especially informative.

FEMNET has also published two newsletters at various points in time since its inception: *FEMNET News*, which began circulating in 1989, and *Our Rights*, founded in 1993 to share information specific to the upcoming Fourth World Conference on Women in Beijing in 1995 and the African Regional Conference on Women in Dakar that would precede it. Most editions of both publications have been cataloged in FEMNET's archive. These newsletters, sent to a range of readers at NGOs and (inter)national organizations, provide crucial information on the trajectory of FEMNET's girl-focused advocacy and the various forms of thought and politics that the NGO's members attached to this work. Advocacy materials produced explicitly for the girl-focused lobbying campaign were also particularly instructive. These ranged from dry reports to poetry, cartoons, and stories written by schoolgirls about the relationships among girls, poverty, the state, and patriarchy. Finally, an internally published history of FEMNET, which includes interviews with many of the NGO's heads and members from the late 1980s and 1990s, provides crucial information about FEMNET's fraught relationships with UNICEF and the government of Kenya that were so central to the internationalization of Girls in Development.

By contrast, central UNICEF Archives in New York City have been closed to outside researchers for well over a decade. In July 2012, a UNICEF employee informed me in writing, "The UNICEF archives are currently closed due to UN reconstruction." As of the time of this book's publication, the UNICEF Archives website contains the message (nestled in between other paragraphs) "*The UNICEF Archives is closed to the general public due to ongoing enhancements to materials and facilities.*"[29]

Initially, I thought I would be able to sidestep the lack of access to UNICEF's main archives in New York City by seeking records from its Nairobi compound, which houses the Eastern and Southern Africa Regional Office, UNICEF's Kenya Country Office, and the headquarters for UNICEF Somalia.

However, UNICEF employees in Nairobi told me that the office had lost its local records. UNICEF's staff reportedly turned over their archive from the period before 1995 to the government of Kenya, and it is unclear where those records are now or if they remain intact. UNICEF's Nairobi staff suggested that the records' turnover may have been connected to investigations of corruption in the offices in the 1990s. News outlets such as the *New York Times* reported a US$10 million corruption scandal emanating from UNICEF's Kenya Country Office between 1993 and 1995, at the height of the girl-focused lobbying campaign.[30] The opacity surrounding UNICEF's archives, whether in New York City or in Nairobi, meant that I had to write a history involving the United Nations institution by cobbling together sources from alternative archives.

Fleshing out UNICEF's side of this history are unpublished and published reports—many of them written by UNICEF staff—that are preserved in the archives of institutions that worked alongside the organization, such as FEMNET, UNESCO, the World Health Organization, the World Bank, and various national governments. Published and unpublished materials from UNICEF's website, which contains internally created histories, published annual reports and studies, press releases, and selectively curated agency records, inform this book. Many UNICEF reports to the United Nations General Assembly are available through the UN's documentation system, which is separate from the UNICEF Archives and follows norms of open archival access that guide most of the UN recordkeeping system. Informal conversations and published interviews with current and former staff from various UNICEF offices also proved useful.

Following the UNICEF-FEMNET lobbying campaign's archival traces outward led to additional sources from the US Department of State, various ministries of the government of Kenya, the former colonial offices of the United Kingdom, the United Nations Commission on the Status of Women, the UN General Assembly, the UN Development Program, the World Bank, UNESCO, and the World Health Organization. Research took place in physical archives in Nairobi; Washington, DC; New York City; London; and Hamburg, and in a mixture of online repositories. Augmenting these are copies of emails sent to listservs of attendees of the Fourth UN World Conference on Women in Beijing. Press releases, newspaper articles from journals on various continents, and published books written by girl- and woman-focused activists also inform this book.

The records of the Girl Child Network in Nairobi provided invaluable information about the aftermath of the Fourth UN World Conference on Women and its institutionalization of Girls in Development into international norms. An NGO founded in the wake of the Beijing conference, the Girl Child Network coordinates girl-focused development programming across Kenya and works with a mix of donors, governmental officials, and fellow activists around the world. Documentation related to the Girl Child Network's founding, fundraising, meetings, key campaigns, and correspondence with donors shows essential information about what kinds of girl-focused frameworks spread and did not spread in the wake of Beijing, as mutual processes of silencing and amplification continued to characterize the history of Girls in Development.

Finally, in Nairobi, I conducted semi-structured oral histories and informal conversations with people from girl-focused governmental and nongovernmental organizations who were involved in the lobbying campaign, who were inspired by the impacts of the campaign after the Beijing Conference on Women in 1995, or who have worked in the broader world of girl-focused economic programming.[31] These organizations include FEMNET, UNICEF, the Girl Child Network, the Kenya offices of Plan International, the Federation of Women Lawyers (FIDA) in Kenya, the Child Welfare Society of Kenya, Childline Kenya, and the Gender Violence Recovery Center at the Nairobi Women's Hospital. I conducted additional interviews with people who experienced particular girl-focused interventions when they were themselves girls. Placed in conversation with documentary sources, the interviews were instrumental in helping me understand the contexts in which people acted, pointing me to more physical evidence to learn about the lobbying campaign and its aftermath, and providing fruitful directions for new research. The interviews showed how fraught this history continues to be—most people did not want to be named or identified when discussing UNICEF's girl-focused work for fear of retaliation.

I conducted research for this book in a mixture of Kiswahili, French, and English, the latter being the most common language in sources connected to FEMNET and UNICEF's girl-focused lobbying campaign. The realities of colonialism, globalization, and the Cold War and its aftermath have all made English the most common language of communication for international development work within much of Africa, followed by French. This has been true not only among people at FEMNET and UNICEF but also among members of FEMNET stationed all over Africa who have sought to speak with one another across thousands of miles and thousands of languages spoken on the continent. FEMNET's staff have long published the organization's newsletters in English, French, and occasionally Portuguese. However, English has dominated the organization's work, internally produced documents and records, and external communications with people at UNICEF and beyond.

UNICEF's work has similarly occurred in several languages, but English has been most common in and outside the lobbying campaign. Rather than turning to my Kiswahili language references, I found myself more often reaching for my French dictionaries while writing this book—a stark reminder of the painful and fraught politics of language that continue to reverberate in the international political work this book historicizes and in the writing of history itself.[32]

This book is not meant to be a social history of girlhood in Africa. It does not seek to exhaustively discuss African girls' experiences with girlhood (although this is part of the focus of chap. 1). There is an ever-growing abundance of scholarship detailing the rich inner lives of girls in Africa and the diaspora and the ways they have performed and negotiated their girlhoods.[33] The primary actors in this book are adults who cited African girls to make claims about capitalism, colonialism, and growing inequalities in wealth and health.

This book, then, is intended for readers who wish to understand how various actors have invoked girls, particularly—but not exclusively—African girls. These actors have placed girls at the center of wide-ranging debates that, at first glance, might seem to have little to do with girls. Capitalism, economic austerity, state-owned debt, poverty, a partial turn away from the welfare state, colonialism, and, above all, development have all been negotiated, defined, and critiqued through discussions of African girls, Third World girls, girls in the Global South, and women and girls in developing countries. A core aim of this book is to understand how girls became the terrain for fights over capitalism and decolonization and how they later became central to the spread of free-market feminism.

Development, Third World, Global South, and *African women and girls* are not my own terms. I use these phrases because the actors in this history used them. None of these concepts is normative, ahistorical, or apolitical; they arose out of specific contexts and have contentious sets of debates attached to them.[34] Certain parts of this book interrogate these terms, as discussions over the meanings of development and its relationship to girls and women in Africa, the Global South, and the Third World will show. In other parts of the book, and as Girls in Development solidified into an increasingly neoliberal narrative, these concepts are less contested. In all cases, readers should understand that these words are actors' categories: they appear in this book because people at FEMNET, UNICEF, and a variety of other institutions regularly employed and used them in this fraught history of the 1980s and 1990s.

INTRODUCTION 15

Most scholarship on Girls in Development to date has focused either on the first decades of the twenty-first century or on the early to mid-twentieth century. The first camp, dominated by an interdisciplinary mix of scholars in the booming field of girlhood studies, tends to critically interrogate the neoliberal politics of girl-focused development programming, especially since the 2008 financial crash that rocked much of the world. They have investigated the ways in which multinational corporations and their philanthropic arms, such as the Nike Foundation, have worked in partnership with international humanitarian organizations to promote Girls in Development in ways that serve corporate interests and protect them from calls for more regulatory oversight. Studies in this camp note that Girls in Development programming often further appropriates the underpaid labor of girls and women in the Global South by encouraging them to perform low-paid work in globally integrated markets in the name of empowerment. Taken together, this scholarship interrogates who has most benefited from Girls in Development campaigns—the girls that these campaigns target or executives and shareholders at multinational corporations.[35]

The second set of dominant scholarship consists of historians and interdisciplinary scholars who write about girls, women, and children in development during formal European colonialism in Africa. Robust literature details the growth of gendered, racialized, and generationally inflected forms of humanitarianism, welfare, and development through abolitionist and feminist calls to save presumedly powerless girls and women from sexual and other suffering at the hands of African and Asian men in the late nineteenth and early twentieth centuries.[36] Precursors to late twentieth-century and early twenty-first-century forms of Girls in Development can similarly be found in literature on social welfare reformers in imperial spaces focusing on the health, hygiene, and nutrition of mothers and children after World War I;[37] the adoption of child labor laws in response to the global expansion of capitalism at the turn of the twentieth century;[38] the codification of customary and civil laws within colonial Africa and Asia on the legal age of sexual consent and marriage, child delinquency, and custody;[39] family planning and population control that grew from the 1930s onward;[40] efforts to regulate female circumcision in Africa;[41] and the expansion of formal education.[42]

The temporal focus of this book is on the 1980s and 1990s, bridging the gap between the two aforementioned sets of scholarship. One of the imperatives driving this narrative is to historicize how the early twenty-first-century forms of girl-focused developmentalism emerged. Rather than telling a simple history of linearity and continuity in which Girls in Development was only or always neoliberal, this book explores how a much more robust set of political and economic politics were projected onto discussions about girls and the economy in the late 1980s and early 1990s. It took work to whittle down these capacious conversations into the neoliberal visions of Girls in Development that predominated in the early twenty-first century. It is at the level of bureaucratic practices of selective erasure and circulation that we see how neoliberal frameworks of Girls in Development emerged in ways that artificially appeared, from the outside, to be uncontested or inevitable.

Mapping the relationships between colonial policies focused on women, children, and girls and late twentieth-century forms of Girls in Development could fill many books. In lieu of this, it is important to note that the relationships between girl-focused development of the 1980s and 1990s and those during formal colonization were not linear. Nor were they characterized by complete rupture. The FEMNET-UNICEF campaign that would write Girls in Development into a set of international norms both grew from and stood in tension with earlier iterations of developmentalism and social welfare, ones that grew through the intertwined, global expansions of colonialism and capitalism since at least the nineteenth century.

Two individuals from UNICEF and FEMNET serve as particularly instructive examples. Richard Jolly, born in the United Kingdom, was the deputy executive director (the second-highest role) at UNICEF between 1982 and 1995, precisely when people at the organization helped craft Girls in Development as a mechanism to fight poverty.[43] In the 1950s, a young Jolly, who was then fresh out of Cambridge, worked for two years as a community development officer in British colonial Kenya. It was the height of the Mau Mau Emergency, an anti-imperial revolt and civil war.[44] In the 1950s, the colonial administration increasingly embraced woman-focused programming as essential to the linked movements for social and economic development and as key to the suppression of the rebellion.[45] It was in this capacity that Jolly worked to promote adult women's literacy, maternal-infant hygiene and child-rearing, handicrafts, and other domesticity-focused programs.[46]

A couple of years later and a few hundred kilometers away from Jolly's post in the Rift Valley, Eddah Gachukia worked as a young teacher in late colonial Kenya's network of church- and government-run schools. In the early 1960s, Gachukia, herself a graduate of colonial East Africa's education system, was stationed at the Thika Secondary School—an experience she would remember half a century later for the racism that she and her husband, Daniel Gachukia, a fellow educator, endured vis-à-vis white European teaching staff.[47] Gachukia would go on to become a champion of both girls' education and antiracist work within the United Nations women's movement. She became a member of Parliament in Kenya in the 1970s and 1980s, focusing on women's interests, and played various roles at the four United Nations World Conferences on Women between 1975 and 1995. Nestled in the midst of Gachukia's work with the UN women's movement, she cofounded FEMNET and became its first chairperson in 1988. The NGO grew directly out of her and her peers' efforts to decolonize the United Nations and give African women a greater role in directing the programming impacting their lives, particularly regarding development.[48]

The girl- and woman-focused FEMNET-UNICEF network that Gachukia and Jolly helped build in the 1980s and 1990s grew both through and in reaction to their early work in gender- and education-centered development programming in late colonial Kenya. The expansion of woman-focused developmentalism in the midst of a war that gained the British government notoriety for the brutality of its response; the coming of age of future national and international leaders in racially segregated colonial school systems—these were the sorts of frictions and uneasy alliances that characterized the early growth of girl- and woman-focused developmentalism in Kenya and beyond. In the last decades of the twentieth century, people like Gachukia and Jolly would variously draw from, respond to, and work to dismantle many of the same structures and systems of thought as they crafted Girls in Development, debated its meanings, and then internationalized it.

How did multiple contested strands of thought concerning girls and economic development grow and internationalize into a neoliberal set of frameworks? Chapter 1 provides an in-depth case study of how knowledge suppression and amplification emerged hand in hand as particular logics of feminism and capitalism became intertwined. Through a case study of the Girl Child Project in the early 1990s, the chapter shows how conflicting forms of knowledge about girls were selectively suppressed, erased, and narrowed into a singular narrative. Quotidian bureaucratic practices of knowledge creation, deletion, revision, and dissemination were critical to this coproduction of ignorance and knowledge as FEMNET and UNICEF worked together to generate knowledge about the status of the girl child in Africa.

Chapter 2 then goes back in time to the beginning of the story. It charts the emergence of the African Women's Task Force, the organization that would become FEMNET, surrounding the Third UN World Conference on Women in the mid-1980s. Doing so illustrates how contestations of the international system played out within and through the UN women's movement and its discussions of women, girls, and development. Unlike in the previous chapter, when selective erasures and silences characterized much of FEMNET's work with UNICEF, this chapter outlines a different set of political outcomes and possibilities for the future. The very creation of FEMNET's precursor, the African Women's Task Force, represented a moment of publicly challenging both UNICEF and the leadership of the UN women's movement. This history asserts the need to problematize the erasures and selective amplifications that would characterize FEMNET's girl-focused work with UNICEF in the future. At the same time, it foreshadows some of the dynamics that would enable these erasures to take place, including a need for donor funding and fraught political relationships between the state of Kenya and NGOs like FEMNET.

Chapter 3 shows that Girls in Development as a school of thought and set of policy frameworks arose in direct response to the global economic crash of the 1970s, the debt crises, and economic austerity and shrinking welfare states mandated by structural adjustment programs in the 1980s and beyond. Rather than springing up as a fully formed ideology within the World Bank and the United States Agency for International Development (USAID) in the 1990s, as existing scholarship tends to suggest, girl-focused development grew within UNICEF in the 1980s. It emerged largely in response to the deleterious effects of a perceived crisis in capitalism and the shift to austerity commonly associated with Margaret Thatcher and Ronald Reagan. The United Nations women's movement and the work of a critical mass of actors in South Asia also played pivotal roles. One result of this shift to Girls in Development within UNICEF was the devolution of calls for a new international economic order and more robust welfare state planning to calls for development interventions focused on girls, their families, and cultures within the Global South.

Instead of automatically expanding within the United Nations and on a global scale, early visions of Girls in Development at UNICEF existed within a broader web of talk about the girl child in the 1980s and early 1990s, as chapter 4 foregrounds in its analysis of FEMNET's girl-focused advocacy. Particular strands of feminism and capitalism and their relationships with one another were hotly contested; they did not couple seamlessly. Within FEMNET, conversations varyingly called for top-down changes to the global economic system in the name of girls, promoted development through the bottom-up utilization of girls' human capital, or advocated some mix of the two. Other strands of advocacy at the NGO critiqued the colonial and capitalist assumptions underpinning Girls in Development frameworks altogether. Consistent across conversations was that people at FEMNET, like UNICEF, worked out concerns over capitalism and poverty by invoking girls and their real and imagined education, status, capacity to work, and state of emotional empowerment.

The channeling of multiple ideas about girls, poverty, and the state into one cohesive logic is not merely a history of the spread of knowledge; it is also a history of its erasure. Through the lobbying campaign that wrote a special section on the girl child into the formal outputs of the Fourth UN World Conference on Women, detailed in chapter 5, neoliberal frameworks for Girls in Development internationalized. Denunciations of austerity capitalism and calls for its end were decoupled from the logics of girl power; they were often erased from the conference outputs altogether. Mundane and administrative practices of knowledge deletion and the power of particular nation-states—especially the United States after the end of the Cold War—further molded Girls in Development into a free-market system of thought that became common sense through its adoption in the UN-based women's movement. A major outcome of this process was making global economic inequalities and poverty seem like the result of universal yet culturally rooted patriarchy rather than tangible economic policymaking at the international and national levels. Sensationalizing the sexual and psychological suffering of girls in Africa and the broader Global South went hand in hand with the internationalization of Girls in Development before and at the Beijing conference.

Chapter 6 explores the impacts of the final United Nations World Conference on Women in Beijing. Through a focus on the Girl Child Network, a Nairobi-based NGO, it shows how the adoption of a special section on the girl child in Beijing led to the creation of new institutions and various forms of girl-focused programming. As organizations like the Girl Child Network struggled to stay afloat, multinational corporations became some of their largest and most reliable donors. In the process of meeting these donors' needs, the work of Girls in Development continued to morph and narrow in ways that have promoted free-market feminism. These initiatives have portrayed the causes of the suffering of girls and women in the Global South as biological or ahistorical. They have posited multinational corporations and the consumer goods they sell, such as sanitary pads, as primary sources of girls' empowerment. Rather than driving these programs wholesale, actors at multinational corporations seized on a preexisting movement to promote Girls in Development—a movement that partially traces back to the lobbying campaign to write girl-focused economic development into international norms through the culmination of the UN women's movement in Beijing.

Within this interwoven history of feminism, capitalism, (de)colonization, and knowledge production, attention to what did not become dominant is as important as attention to what did. So, too, are the contexts in which certain people acted and particular forms of knowledge moved or did not move within a transnational network laden with hierarchies. A perceived crisis in capitalism, a turn to economic austerity that shrank social welfare programs, repression from the Kenyan state toward NGOs like FEMNET, and the dominance of the United States as the main funder of UNICEF—which was, in turn, a core donor to FEMNET—all provided conditions through which the particular history of girl-focused economic development emerged. While such circumstances are vital to this story, their impacts often became visible on individual and collective action through bureaucratic practices of knowledge negotiation. It is at this joint level of broad contexts and quotidian knowledge creation and erasure that a fuller history of the origins and spread of free-market feminism through the vehicle of Girls in Development can be found.

1

Making Girl Power Neoliberal

Erasing Alternative Visions of African Girlhood

How did conflicting political frameworks for girl-focused economic programming become streamlined into an increasingly singular logic that would be internationalized? The growth of a hegemonic set of norms concerning Girls in Development not only involved the spread of certain ideas and forms of knowledge; it also involved the silencing, erasure, and noncirculation of others. This chapter focuses on one episode of knowledge suppression and manipulation—the creation and then altering of a set of UNICEF-commissioned and FEMNET-organized reports on the educational status of girls in Eastern and Southern Africa. Analyzing how the reports were generated shows the mundane, bureaucratic ways in which the gathering, revising, and publishing of social scientific data about the girl child led to knowledge deletions. Socialist, decolonial, antiracist, and anticapitalist knowledge frameworks—and the information supporting them—were selectively revised, marginalized, and sometimes outright erased in the process.

These deletions took place alongside the selective amplification of knowledge frameworks and supporting data that favored neoliberal capitalism. They often laid primary blame for the intertwined structures of poverty and patriarchy at the feet of allegedly corrupt, shortsighted, and oppressive men, boys, parents, cultures, and traditions in Africa, rather than on the interplay between high-level economic policymaking and gendered labor roles within families. They explicitly reworked language about the impacts of austerity-mandating structural adjustment programs on women and girls within Africa. This chapter ends with a discussion of how members of the institutions involved in the creation of the studies, especially FEMNET, responded to these erasures after UNICEF published the altered report. It concludes with a discussion of "silencing" as a bureaucratic and political strategy as girl-focused economic programming grew from a complex, contradictory, and far-reaching set of political critiques and policy stances at the dawn of the 1990s into an increasingly hegemonic, neoliberal narrative that would spread outward and become institutionalized as the decade wore on.

Creating the Girl Child Project

In 1990, officials at UNICEF's Nairobi-based Eastern and Southern Africa Regional Office (ESARO) commissioned a set of studies on the lived experiences of girls in Eastern and Southern Africa. This was part of UNICEF's broader trend to work with local and regional NGOs, as well as national governments, to produce gender-disaggregated data that would guide their advocacy and policymaking. A common strategy within UNICEF in the 1980s and early 1990s was to commission situational reports—studies on the general status of women and children in a region, usually within a given nation-state—in order to collect information, raise awareness, and guide policy frameworks.[1] The reports on Eastern and Southern Africa, conducted between 1990 and 1992, represented one of UNICEF's first widespread efforts to generate knowledge on the status of *girls* and their educational access, rather than on women and children, as part of the organization's ongoing shift toward the girl child as a locus of development planning. They were also unique in scope, as many situational reports focused on a single country rather than a broad swath of a continent.

The studies collectively came to be known as the Girl Child Project. They were intended to focus on girls' access, retention, and performance in formal schooling, stemming from UNICEF's claims that solving poverty relied on educating girls to become productive and empowered future laborers and mothers. Buttressing this claim at the dawn of the 1990s was the widespread belief within UNICEF that girls lagged far behind boys in access to formal education and faced widespread discrimination, especially in the Global South.[2]

To carry out the Girl Child Project, staff at UNICEF ESARO hired FEMNET and another organization, the Educational Research Network in Eastern and Southern Africa (ERNESA). ERNESA was created in 1985 with funding from Canada's International Development Research Centre, the Rockefeller Foundation, and, eventually, the German Agency for Technical Cooperation. The research network was founded in part to decolonize knowledge production about Africa so that researchers from across the continent would be involved in collecting less biased and more locally generated data for use in policymaking.[3] At least a dozen researchers from Eastern and Southern Africa worked to create the Girl Child Project. Many possessed doctorates and master's degrees from African, European, and North American universities, and a number were current or former educators, administrators, and policymakers.

ERNESA's members undertook research for the project in eight countries. In three of them—Madagascar, Botswana, and Kenya—they produced in-depth case studies that both presented original research and collated existing evidence. Researchers from five other countries—Burundi, Ethiopia, Mozambique, Rwanda, and Somalia—compiled existing data on girls' education.[4] FEMNET's staff were responsible for organizing the project and combining the individual country studies into a draft synthesis report. FEMNET hired Anna Obura, a Nairobi-based consultant on gender and education, to pen the final report. Obura possessed a doctorate degree and had already published extensive studies on gender and education in East Africa.[5]

Partially contradicting the narrative emanating from UNICEF's New York City headquarters—that girls lagged far behind boys in formal education because of parents' patriarchal attitudes and poor decision-making—the eight country studies found that girls' access to primary education varied by location but was roughly on par with that of boys across much of the region. In Botswana, the study's coauthors found that *more* girls than boys were enrolled in all levels of primary school: 51.5 percent of nationally registered students were girls in 1989, compared with 48.5 percent boys. By the final year of primary education the gap had widened, as 56 percent of registered students were girls compared to 44 percent boys.[6] In Rwanda, Madagascar, and Kenya, just under half (between 48.81 and 49.8 percent) of primary school students were reportedly girls compared with boys (between 50.4 and 51.2 of documented students) in 1990.[7] In Burundi, Mozambique, and Ethiopia, girls made up between 40 and 45 percent of documented primary school students. Girls fared the worst in Somalia, where girls constituted roughly 34 percent of elementary school pupils, according to available national data.[8]

Results for school performance and retention were similarly mixed. Girls reportedly outperformed and outlasted boys under certain metrics and in some locales, and boys outperformed girls and stayed in school longer in others, particularly as they progressed through secondary education and onto universities and technical schools. In Rwanda, for example, girls tended to advance to the next grade in higher proportions in the first four years of primary school while boys advanced in slightly higher numbers in the last three years.[9] In neighboring Burundi, boys dropped out at higher rates than girls, leading Obura to conclude in the draft summary report that certain aspects of Burundi's education "face a male problem, but a slight one, as regards retention rates."[10] In Mozambique, boys dropped out of school at slightly higher rates than girls, and girls scored higher on standardized tests than boys in secondary school.[11] In Botswana, boys reportedly had higher dropout rates than girls at every level of primary school until the final year. In secondary school, dropout levels for girls slightly increased vis-à-vis boys. School performance of girls and boys was roughly equal in Botswana at the primary level while boys attained slightly higher average test scores in secondary school.[12] In Madagascar, more girls reportedly passed their end-of-school exams than boys at every level of primary school except the fifth and final year, when 2 percent more boys than girls passed. Boys were documented to have dropped out and repeated grades in primary and secondary school in higher proportions than girls.[13]

The above figures reflect some of the most distilled findings of the reports, which generated more than five hundred printed pages of statistics, original qualitative research, literature reviews, and analysis. One of the most striking findings of the Girl Child Project is that the individual studies do not present a simple, cohesive narrative of girls' lived experiences or educational access across Eastern and Southern Africa. ERNESA's researchers found that a matrix of factors impacted girls' presence and performance in schools, including but not limited to familial wealth, relationships to capitalism, urban and rural divides, gendered labor roles, colonial legacies, religion, sexual violence, and a number of other factors. Reading the reports, one would be hard-pressed to find a singular, unifying experience of "African girlhood" beyond the fact that a significant proportion of girls in the region did indeed attend school—many of the countries studied had reached near-universal enrollment of children in primary education, regardless of gender, by the end of the 1980s. Among other things, the studies suggested that the countries that had the strongest national policies to fund and otherwise support public education for all children were the countries with the highest rates of girls in school; strong welfare state spending on public education correlated with lower gender-based gaps in formal education.

The studies' authors did mention a few driving causes when explaining the variances in gender-based educational access and performance where they existed. They found that "civil strife" had recently occurred in every country examined except for Botswana, with protracted wars having particularly strong impacts on the three countries with the lowest documented rates of female enrollment in schools.[14] The violence in Somalia, Mozambique, and Ethiopia was a result of imperial–turned–Cold War struggles, with a long list of countries from various political factions around the globe funneling weapons, money, and support to the warring parties. The consequence of these internationally inflected conflicts, the study authors found, was that children's previously increasing access to schools in the three countries stagnated or outright declined in the late 1970s and 1980s. This reportedly undercut trends in the other countries through which the rapid expansion of nationalist education policies since the 1960s overcame preexisting colonial-era educational disparities that favored boys' access to school over that of girls.[15]

Structural adjustment and cuts to governmental spending on education took center stage in some of the studies' findings. In the 1980s, for example, the International Monetary Fund (IMF) adjusted Somalia's debt through a series of structural adjustment programs that required decreased funding for public education, among other things. The country study and synthesis report found that girls' levels of educational access in Somalia coincided more closely with the level of state expenditure on education than they did with the actual violence of war.[16] Similarly, in Kenya, report authors Sheila Wamahiu, Fred Opondo, and Grace Nyagah discussed the government's introduction of neoliberal cost-sharing measures in the mid-1980s that levied fees for students to access public schools, which had previously been tuition-free (in theory, if not always in practice). The Kenyan government undertook these measures as part of a broader series of reforms in the face of the ongoing financial crisis and pressure from international economists at institutions such as the World Bank to slash state spending. By the late 1980s, financing for public education made up roughly 20 percent of the Kenyan government's annual expenditures and nearly 6 percent of its GDP. The same spending that the reports found had allowed Kenya to reach near-universal primary school enrollment, and therefore near parity in girls' participation in schooling, was under pressure for being too expensive.[17]

The authors of the Kenya country study for the Girl Child Project found that the neoliberal cost-sharing measures the national government had introduced—passing on some of the costs of public schooling to parents and families—depressed the proportion of students continuing from primary to secondary school, most notably for girls. They also reportedly pushed down the percentage of female students enrolled in universities vis-à-vis boys. The coauthors concluded that when parents had to choose to educate some of their children over others in the face of the introduction of school tuition, they tended to prefer sons because of their higher perceived earning potential in gendered labor markets. Rather than attributing this decision to economic irrationality and inherent patriarchy, as UNICEF's New York City leadership often argued in the organization's publications, the Kenya study authors found that cash-strapped parents made economically rational—if emotionally fraught—choices dictated by existing gendered market logic that had been introduced, in large part, through capitalism and colonialism.[18] Neoliberalism in the form of retracting state support for public education reintroduced this market logic to family decision-making, "leading to a vicious circle of low opportunities, poverty, and hopelessness" and a disproportionate "impact of the economic hardships on the girl-child," according to the Kenya study coauthors.[19]

The Country Case Studies

Discussions of the in-depth country reports that ERNESA's researchers produced for Madagascar, Kenya, and Botswana are particularly illustrative. These three country reports in particular demonstrate the variances in girls' lived experiences across the region, unifying themes found across the reports, and some fundamental differences of analytical interpretation and political stances among the researchers when explaining the relationships between gender, education, and the economy in Eastern and Southern Africa. The first in-depth country study completed through the Girl Child Project was of Madagascar in 1991. The author of the study, Suzy Ramamonjisoa, earned a doctorate in social psychology from Université Descartes, or Paris V, in 1972. She conducted research for the study in Malagasy and French and penned the report in the latter language. The Madagascar girl child study included a discussion of a 1987 survey jointly conducted by Madagascar's Ministry of Education, UNICEF, and UNESCO. In it, parents, educators, students, and community members cited economic factors such as the cost of school fees, participation in family work, and a lack of textbooks and school supplies as the top factors causing children of both genders to quit school.[20]

In addition to these causes, the biggest named factors hampering girls' educational access were the legacies of French colonialism on the island. Ramamonjisoa engaged in a lengthy discussion of how damaging French colonialism was to gender equality in Madagascar. She pointed out that the island had a number of women rulers before colonialism and that it was common for women to hold positions of political, social, and economic power. Inequalities did exist, Ramamonjisoa noted, especially with the growth of British influence in the early 1800s. After France declared Madagascar as a protectorate and then a colony in the late 1800s, colonial authorities aggressively supplanted the existing formal education system with a colonial educational regime, according to the study. Ramamonjisoa wrote that boys were taught subjects such as reading, writing, math, and how to count money while girls were taught sewing, lacemaking, cooking, and other courses in domesticity. She was particularly critical of the influence of Christian missionaries who ran many of precolonial and colonial Madagascar's schools. They focused formal education primarily on boys and institutionalized a gendered, capitalistic division of labor by emphasizing girls' and women's unremunerated work in the home and boys' and men's paid labor outside of it.[21]

After Madagascar gained independence in 1960, and especially after the socialist revolution of 1975, the young country's government explicitly committed itself to ensuring gender equality in its schools, according to the report. Ramamonjisoa noted that the percentage of girls enrolled in schools dramatically rose, and the state reformed gender-biased curricula in the 1970s to include the same subjects of study for both girls and boys. Yet the textbooks schools used continued to be produced mostly in France and followed French curricular norms. The Madagascar girl child study disseminated the results of original research that Ramamonjisoa carried out analyzing these school textbooks. It found lingering gender biases by subject: girls and women were depicted doing unpaid domestic tasks while boys were portrayed as doctors, hardware store workers, preachers, and gainfully employed public leaders. Critiques of gendered labor divides in the workforce, capitalism, neocolonialism, the damaging influences of French and British patriarchy in Madagascar, and urban/rural divides underpinned much of Ramamonjisoa's analysis.

The in-depth second country study published through the Girl Child Project was from Botswana. It contained two volumes. The first volume, finished in February 1992, included a review of existing data while the second, from July 1992, analyzed the results of original research in a case study and made policy recommendations. The Botswana studies discussed a number of factors to explain the evidence that more girls than boys were enrolled in primary school and the first years of secondary school in the country. The five coauthors noted that it was common for families to send boys to faraway cattle posts to mind livestock while daughters went to school. This had long been true in Botswana and the surrounding region, much to the chagrin of former British colonial officers, who were, according to the study, upset that Botswana parents preferred to educate their daughters over their sons in the early twentieth century.[22] Botswana had been a British protectorate—then called the Bechuanaland Protectorate—between 1885 and 1966.

The first volume of the study found that the preponderance of boys at the senior secondary level was due to the fact that secondary school was a relatively new introduction to Botswana: the British embarked on a massive campaign to expand secondary education in the 1940s. Determined not to repeat their same "mistake" of setting up schools that parents would use primarily for their daughters, many colonial secondary schools would not accept female students, and some were established near remote cattle herding posts. After British rule formally ended in 1966, the proportion of girls in secondary schools rose, and by the late 1980s, girls' documented enrollment grew to outnumber boys' in the first three years of postprimary education, according to the report.²³

The second volume of the Botswana Girl Child Project presented original research that fleshed out many of the factors impacting educational access in the country. Experts connected to the Botswana Educational Research Association carried out case studies in Mankgodi, a rural village, and areas of the capital city, Gaborone.²⁴ Based on the responses of parents, children, and teachers, they found that the cost of schooling, wealth inequalities, a general lack of secondary schools, and urban/rural disparities presented large obstacles to both boys' and girls' educational access. Girls, the study reported, were negatively impacted by harmful depictions of women in textbooks, which were usually produced in apartheid-governed South Africa or the United Kingdom. Like Ramamonjisoa in Madagascar, the authors of the second volume of the Botswana report condemned foreign-produced textbooks' depictions of women performing unpaid or poorly remunerated labor and low-status social roles compared to men.²⁵ The report also cited pregnancy as a reason many girls stopped attending school—most in the study were in their late teens and reportedly chose to leave school in order to get pregnant and/or marry.²⁶

While both volumes of the Botswana report condemned girls' lack of access to higher education and exclusion from certain forms of highly remunerated labor and legal rights, the authors also expressed concern for the boy child. Despite an ongoing narrowing of gender-based disparities in educational access as Botswana approached universal levels of school enrollment, boys continued to suffer from family preferences to use the labor of male children for livestock herding rather than formal education.²⁷ Both sections of the report also contained harsh condemnations of corporal punishment and incarceration of boys. The first volume explicitly linked this violence to the history of British colonial imprisonment of boy "criminals" and the public stripping and caning of boys and men. Girls and women were reportedly legally exempt from such public displays of state-sanctioned corporal violence. Despite the advent of legal frameworks protecting children from capital punishment and certain forms of incarceration toward the end of British rule and after independence, the study authors noted with alarm that Botswana continued to institutionalize boy juvenile offenders in the same facility the British had set up as a boys' prison.²⁸

Both volumes of the Botswana report ultimately recommended that the national government work to decolonize gender-based disparities disadvantaging boys through the reformation of incarceration, which reportedly prevented boys from receiving the educational, social, and health-related support the report authors argued children needed.[29] The authors of both volumes also discussed cultural factors impacting gendered disparities in education, but the researchers did not reach a consensus on the issue. The authors put forth different interpretations of the extent to which precolonial traditions supported or harmed women and the roles of colonial and postcolonial history, economic factors, and biology in explaining various gender roles in Botswana in the early 1990s.

The third and final in-depth country study completed through the Girl Child Project was for Kenya in March 1992. The aforementioned coauthors—Wamahiu, Opondo, and Nyagah, who possessed advanced degrees in education—found that Kenya enjoyed near-universal levels of enrollment by 1990: almost every child, girl and boy, attended primary school full-time when the report was written.[30] Kenya was a British protectorate and then colony from 1895 to 1963. When Kenya gained independence, the report stated, girls composed only 34 percent of primary school students.[31] The authors found that in the nearly three decades since, the number of both girls and boys enrolled in primary schools, and the number of schools themselves, skyrocketed, with the government and communities investing considerable resources to educate all children.

At the secondary level, girls constituted a recorded 43 percent of students in 1990.[32] More significant than this basic comparison, the authors argued, was the fact that the proportion of students continuing from primary to secondary education steadily *decreased* in the second half of the 1980s. Whereas nearly half of both boys and girls advanced from primary to secondary school in 1986, those figures had fallen to a 43 percent promotion rate for boys and a 39 percent promotion rate for girls. This was due to declining funding for education and widespread changes to formal schooling in the wake of neoliberal economic restructuring of the kind discussed previously in this chapter; Kenya had introduced cost-sharing measures that required parents to pay fees to send their children to public schools, which had been nominally tuition-free since independence. Nevertheless, between 1986 and 1990, the authors pointed out, the raw number of girls enrolled at the secondary level grew by more than that for boys, continuing what they depicted as Kenya's successful, three-decade march toward gender parity at the primary and secondary levels in the face of the painful, gendered colonial legacies and the effects of economic austerity.[33]

The biggest discrepancies in gender-based access to education in Kenya occurred at the tertiary level in universities and vocational schools. The Kenya country study reported that only 28 percent of university-level students were female as of 1990. This figure was slightly *down* from 29.6 percent in 1987.[34]

Similarly, in Kenya's three listed polytechnic institutes, girls accounted for roughly a quarter of all students in 1990. As briefly discussed in the Botswana and Madagascar reports, the subjects who studied in Kenya's tertiary education system were deeply divided by gender: at the University of Nairobi, a reported 43 percent of students studying design were female, compared with only 5.1 percent of engineering students and 5 percent of architecture students. At the postgraduate level, just over half of students pursuing graduate degrees in journalism were female, compared with only 6 percent of students in computer science and 1 percent in engineering.[35]

Wamahiu, Opondo, and Nyagah primarily attributed girls' lower levels of access to and performance in primary and secondary education to economic factors. They argued that the need for children to contribute to families' livelihoods, the cost of school fees and supplies, a lack of resources and trained teachers, and the poor financial situation of many Kenyan families worked together to prevent girls and boys from fully accessing and succeeding in schools. The authors noted that these economic factors of the 1980s and early 1990s were partially due to the effects of the global economic downturn and subsequent neoliberal economic reforms.[36] As in Madagascar and Botswana, the Kenya report also noted that the use of textbooks produced in the country that formerly colonized Kenya continued to promote gender inequalities. The coauthors argued that such depictions in textbooks harmed girls by portraying a gendered division of labor in which boys and men made money and served in public leadership roles while girls and women stayed home and performed unpaid domestic duties.[37]

Wamahiu, Opondo, and Nyagah also largely attributed the low proportion of girls in tertiary education and their marginalization from STEM subjects to colonial legacies. In the mid-1980s, fewer girls' secondary schools than boys' schools reportedly taught the hard sciences: secondary education in the country had long been dominated by single-sex boarding schools that followed British colonial educational models. Instead, girls' schools tended to focus on arts and humanities subjects such as history, geography, and religious studies. The study reported that the number of science classes available for boys outnumbered those offered to girls at a rate of five to one. As a result, girls had historically lower test scores in science and math than boys, faced limited options for degree programs in universities and polytechnic institutes, and had far fewer future career opportunities.[38]

Educational reforms in the 1980s and 1990s de-emphasizing the arts and promoting STEM subjects compounded these historical gender imbalances and further hurt girls' performance in secondary school and access to tertiary education, according to the study. Many of the educational reforms that occurred in the 1980s and early 1990s, such as the limiting of arts and humanities courses and the expansion of engineering and hard sciences at Kenya's universities and vocational schools, were implemented as part of neoliberal economic reforms—often at the behest of the World Bank and/or IMF—that were designed to encourage students to earn marketable degrees. The authors of the Kenya country study claimed that this further marginalized girls and women from formal schooling and undermined their profitable participation in the future workforce by blocking their access to higher education and the university subjects that had historically drawn them.[39] Hence the recorded decrease in the percentage of female versus male students at the University of Nairobi between 1987 and 1990, during the thick of neoliberal restructuring of Kenya's university system.

As in the Botswana study, the authors of the Kenya report blamed cultural factors for gender-based discrepancies in education and in society more broadly. The Kenya Girl Child Project identified violence against girls and women as one cause that interfered with girls' education. The report went into particular detail about an attack at the St. Kizito Mixed Secondary School in the Meru District, where seventy-one girls were reportedly raped and nineteen were killed after a series of bunk beds collapsed as many girls tried to flee the violence. The perpetrators of the attack were secondary schoolboys. According to the study coauthors, the boys were angry about a school kiosk having been given to a former student as a bribe. She had become pregnant after an implied episode of harassment and assault by a male staff member and was given the kiosk to stay quiet. It is worth noting here that the St. Kizito rapes and murders were sensationally dissected in the Kenyan national media for years. Varying reports circulated as to what motivated the boys to attack the girls en masse. Most relevant, in the Kenya study for the Girl Child Project, authors Wamahiu, Opondo, and Nyagah depicted the violence as one set of incidences in which schoolboys would "rampage," rape female students, and "destroy . . . school property." They portrayed these events as evidence of boys' and male teachers' lack of "moral discipline."[40] Worse, the authors argued, this "violence in the Kenyan society at large" reflected a "dehumanizing attitude of the dominant society towards women and girls." They provided visceral examples of men in a variety of social and legal positions, from husbands to police officers, who had recently perpetuated acts of sexual "brutaliz[ation]" against girls and women.[41]

Wamahiu, Opondo, and Nyagah blamed this sexual violence on the moral failings of boys, men, and culture more broadly. However, they theorized about the roots of such behaviors, cultural practices, and gendered oppression rather than depicting them as inherent, unchanging monoliths with wholly local causes. Girls in Kenya, the authors argued, performed more housework than boys in the early 1990s, allowing the latter more time for leisure and homework. But they argued gendered labor divisions were diverse in precolonial societies and varied widely according to region, with precolonial Maasai women building houses and women doctors and religious leaders practicing across the continent. Wamahiu, Opondo, and Nyagah therefore concluded that many of the gendered labor divisions children and adults performed in the 1990s, and gender-based discrepancies as a whole in the country, must "be traced back to Kenya's colonial legacy."[42] They ultimately condemned the intertwined forces of colonialism, capitalism, and Christianity for creating these gender-based disparities: "In Kenya, though variations existed between ethnic groups, the colonial experience coupled with penetration of the capitalist economy and evangelization were instrumental in widening the power gap between genders within particular societies." They continued to note that "the colonial brand of patriarchal ideology, by emphasizing female reproductive and nurturance roles, denigrated the African woman's productive/economic roles within the indigenous economy. Instead it promoted the image of the male patriarch: head of household, defender of the family and provider of all their needs."[43]

The Kenya country study did not solely blame what the authors called the "three C's" of colonialism, capitalism, and Christianity for the existence of patriarchy in the country. The authors analyzed a range of factors, both exogenous and endogenous, for contributing to the marginalization of girls and women from higher education and the profitable world of work, and for creating gender-based violence. Yet Wamahiu, Opondo, and Nyagah were also clear: many, but not all, of the barriers to girls' education and women's gender-based equality stemmed from a colonial legacy and grew through capitalist initiatives, including neoliberal structural adjustment programs and cost-sharing measures. They argued that any policymaking to meaningfully address girls' access to education would need to address these issues, along with a broader lack of resources for education and the deeply intertwined economic, historical, and cultural factors at work.

The Unpublished Synthesis Report

At FEMNET's behest, Anna Obura collated these three in-depth country studies, along with the five other reports, into one document that provided data and analysis for girls' educational access across the region. She completed the report in 1992. The draft synthesis report reached a number of conclusions. First, it found that girls' and boys' educational access and experiences varied across Eastern and Southern Africa, with war and the effects of neoliberal economic restructuring having particularly deleterious effects on school access in some regions. Second, Obura argued that the histories of colonialism and international interventions in the region must foreground any contemporary analysis of gender in education. Finally, and most importantly, the report concluded that the achievement of gender-based parity, both in education and in broader society, depended on a fundamental reworking of existing gendered labor divides. These divisions often made the work of girls and women more time-consuming, less visible, and less remunerated than that of men.

Obura paid particularly close attention to the impacts of Cold War–stoked violence in the three countries in the region with the lowest rates of female school enrollment.[44] As a result of the conflicts, children's increasing access to schools stagnated or outright declined in the late 1970s and throughout the 1980s. Mozambique saw a slight decline in its total number of pupils in the 1980s. While girls' proportional representation remained roughly constant, the conflict widened urban versus rural disparities in educational access for both genders.[45] In Ethiopia, rapidly increasing educational access plateaued in the mid- to late 1980s, and the total number of enrolled students decreased at the end of the decade.[46] Meanwhile, in Somalia, recorded primary enrollments fell to less than 10 percent in the late 1980s, down from a high of 44 percent in 1975. One-quarter of primary and secondary schools outright closed during that period, and the proportion of recorded female students versus male students declined.[47] Obura argued that the wars bred sexual violence against girls and women, especially in Somalia and Ethiopia, and prompted many parents to remove daughters from school as a matter of safety.[48]

It was not only war that hampered girls' proportional representation in school and net enrollment rates, according to the synthesis report. As in the individual country studies, structural adjustment and reductions to state spending on public education received particular condemnation—Obura recounted much of the evidence and analysis on these topics from the individual studies. She also argued that in Somalia, where girls fared the worst in terms of educational access, the twin forces of neoliberal capitalism and war worked together to disrupt education and broader life in the country.[49] The synthesis report found that the joint devastation of global economic collapse, economic austerity, and state violence uniquely impacted the girl child. These changes also reportedly promoted the "feminization of poverty" and further marginalized women from the world of remunerated work—a set of intertwined factors that, to Obura's reading of the evidence in the eight country studies, compounded one another.[50]

The FEMNET-commissioned synthesis report wove this analysis into a broader narrative about the codependent relationships between colonialism and capitalism in the region. Drawing on the country case studies, Obura noted that seven of the eight countries had gained independence from a Western European colonizer within the last thirty years. As the Madagascar, Botswana, and Kenya reports found—and Obura noted—colonial education systems focused on educating boys for paid labor and centered girls' instruction on domesticity and noncompensated labor in the home. Compounding this "heavy historical burden" was the fact that colonial education systems were neither democratic nor designed to promote social justice and did not meet the basic needs of most colonial subjects.[51] As a result, Obura argued, newly independent nations in the region had to commit themselves to the monumental task of addressing inherited colonial-era disparities in education, gendered and otherwise.

After focusing on the postcolonial handover of power and nationalization of the civil service in the 1960s, Obura claimed that many of the countries in the region made great progress in promoting high net enrollment in schools and increasing girls' representation in the 1970s, especially through efforts to restructure, nationalize, and democratize formal schooling.[52] Yet the global economic crash and ensuing turn to neoliberal capitalism interrupted this progress and in some cases reversed it in the 1980s and at the start of the 1990s, according to the synthesis report.[53] Obura expressed frustration with the slow pace of reforms to nationalize formerly colonial education systems, which she argued were "inappropriate and maladjusted for the task of national development." However, she claimed that decolonization efforts had been undertaken "with courage and fortitude" and urged the reader to view shortcomings in national policymaking in Eastern and Southern Africa "with sympathy and an appreciation of the historical context, and to recognize the successes."[54]

The unpublished synthesis report for the Girl Child Project, as many of the eight country studies, centers the unequal remuneration and recognition of girls' and women's labor as driving educational inequalities and broader gender disparities. Colonialism, capitalism, warfare, and a range of local factors combined to promote gender roles in which girls and women worked inside the home and in subsistence agriculture for little pay while men earned cash and prestige in the formal economy. For Obura, the collective findings of the eight country studies were clear: the governments and educators of Eastern and Southern Africa had worked admirably to address inherited imbalances in gender and education, particularly at the primary level. But until education was more fully decolonized, until austerity in public education spending encouraged by structural adjustment programs ended, and until women's labor was "recognized, quantified, and remunerated" at the same level as that of men, gender-based inequalities in education and the "feminization of poverty" would continue.⁵⁵

Doctoring the Data

Before UNICEF ESARO published the 1992 synthesis report that FEMNET commissioned Obura to write, the document was edited. Someone—the publication and other publicly available records do not indicate their name(s)—removed or reworked multiple portions of the study. One section explicitly naming the global economic collapse, structural adjustment programs, and economic austerity for harming girls' educational prospects and increasing feminized poverty across Africa was deleted. Instead, the revised report blamed the failures of education-focused structural adjustment programs on African "leaders" who made "politically expedient" decisions without thinking through their impacts. The altered report that UNICEF published added language blaming gender-based educational disparities on the fact that structural adjustment programs were incomplete—that rather than being harmful, they were ineffective because they did not go far enough in reducing state spending on public education. This section again placed the problem on the shoulders of allegedly incompetent and shortsighted African leaders.⁵⁶

The revised report that UNICEF ESARO published similarly erased and altered sections on gendered divisions of labor and the complexity of girls' and women's lives in Africa. One section of Obura's unedited synthesis report reprinted a quotation from the Kenya case study, which mirrored language in a UNICEF publication from 1990 describing the institution's widescale embrace of girl-focused economic programming.⁵⁷ The Kenya report read, "Women and girls in particular continue to suffer subordinate status vis-à-vis men and boys in all societies."⁵⁸ After reprinting this quotation and agreeing in the synthesis report that patriarchy was universal in Eastern and Southern Africa due to girls' disadvantages in "finding an occupation and a cash income," Obura argued that the eight country studies showed how the influences of "Western ideology" were ultimately to blame. "In traditional society," Obura wrote, African women built houses, acted as "doctors and healers," and occupied positions of religious authority. She cited the country studies to argue that it was the influence of constraining Western attitudes toward women that curtailed African girls' and women's economic power. Nevertheless, Obura argued, the "modern African woman" continued to perform a variety of roles that gave her more power and flexibility than the Western woman. The prevalence of Eurocentric scholarship, particularly through colonial anthropology, had distorted understandings of African traditions and erased knowledge of the power many African women had and continued to wield, even if it was not properly compensated, according to her original, unpublished analysis.[59]

The version of the study that UNICEF ESARO published reworked that section. It reprinted excerpts of the report discussing the universality of patriarchy. However, it erased the segments of the study partially locating the roots of this universality in Eastern and Southern Africa on gendered labor divides under capitalism and colonialism. The document that UNICEF published erased Obura's lengthy discussion of how diverse African girls' and women's experiences were, particularly compared to Western women. Instead, the altered published study discussed factors influencing girls' discrimination "at the level of the family," blaming parents for preventing girls from going to school.[60] The altered report then added another sentence condemning the "traditional status of women" for diminishing girls' and women's well-being regarding work, health, and legal protections.[61]

Other sections of the final study that UNICEF ESARO published continued this trend, deleting discussions of harmful colonial, capitalistic, and austerity-driven influences on the African girl child and her education; centering local culture and tradition as the main culprits of gender-based discrimination; and pushing to the background the focus on unequally remunerated gendered labor divides under capitalism as a key force behind gender-based inequities in school access to the extent that they existed. The revised synthesis report also obfuscated the sections of Obura's synthesis report that showed girls were not universally oppressed in Eastern and Southern Africa and that painted a more complex picture. The findings that girls attended primary schools at higher rates than boys in Botswana and at nearly the same rate in many of the other countries surveyed were systemically downplayed; the revised synthesis report removed dozens of pages of qualitative and quantitative data specifying how varied girls' realities were across the region and detailing their outperformance of boys in various areas of school access, retention, and achievement.[62] It also removed much of Obura's country-by-country analysis, making the region seem more like a monolith in which girls lacked access to schooling and basic rights across the board in sweeping, one-dimensional ways. Finally, the revised report inserted sections praising UNICEF ESARO's work in children's education and health care and added the UNICEF logo to every page.[63]

Included in the same publication with the revised report was a summary of a workshop that UNICEF ESARO staff convened to discuss the findings of the Girl Child Project. Held over three days in Gaborone, Botswana, in 1992, "The Girl Child: Opportunities and Disparities in Education" was nominally organized around the findings of the eight country studies and the draft synthesis report Obura wrote.[64] In Gaborone, Obura and authors of most of the country reports presented their findings and facilitated the first day of workshop sessions.[65] Yet, in the summary of the conference that UNICEF ESARO published with the final altered synthesis report, almost none of the findings of the original country reports or the draft synthesis report were foregrounded. There was no discussion of whether and how participants engaged with the data or analyses presented in the studies. Instead, the conference summary that was published with the doctored final report repeatedly blamed "traditional gender stereotypes" and "culture" for girls' marginalization from education.[66] The individual "choices" of girls and their parents were often singled out for causing girls' low rates of participation in STEM subjects. Teachers and schools were condemned for their inherent biases against the girl child. In a discussion of the spread of HIV/AIDS, the published workshop summary printed a sensational and unsourced anecdote about "adult men seeking out very young girls as sexual partners."[67] Colonialism, capitalism, Christianity, war, gendered labor divides, and history—all central topics in the studies—either did not appear at all or were downplayed in the published description of the workshop to discuss said studies. In both the workshop proceedings and the revised synthesis report, other culprits were increasingly to blame for girls' allegedly universal oppression: parents, teachers, girls themselves, and especially African men and traditional cultures.

Where the eight country studies and Obura's draft synthesis report often analyzed structural and foreign factors impacting girls' educational access, the workshop summary—like the revised report—focused on causes seemingly inherent to Africa and the continent's individuals and communities. Like the revised synthesis report, the workshop findings also downplayed evidence of girls' educational strengths and boys' vulnerabilities. Instead, it contradicted many of the studies' findings with the declaration, "It seems that girls fall short of equal participation in all the quantitative aspects of schooling."[68]

On a policy level, the eight country studies and Obura's unaltered summary called for more state and international funding for girls' education, ongoing decolonization and de-Westernization of educational curriculum, and systemic efforts to address gendered labor divisions and their unequal compensation under capitalism. The altered synthesis report and the summary workshop proceedings, by contrast, endorsed interventions mostly at the individual level: educating men and boys about gender bias, "sensitizing" allegedly apathetic or blatantly hostile national leaders to the importance of girls' education, training teachers, and "empowering" the girl child to fully participate in education and society.[69] In the face of extensive data about gender-biased curriculum, the workshop report called for the collection of yet more data on the subject, obliquely precluding any immediate tangible action.[70] The predominantly individual-level initiatives that the workshop summary did put forth were to take place under the guidance of UNICEF ESARO and broader partnerships between international donors, NGOs, and national governments.[71]

With sleight of hand, the findings of the eight girl child studies and the original synthesis report were manipulated, skewed, selectively amplified, and erased from public consumption in the published and widely disseminated findings of *The Girl Child: Opportunities and Disparities in Education*. Yet because of the extensiveness, rigor, and academic nature of the data collection and original analysis of the studies, the revised synthesis report and written workshop summary were touted as proof that the African girl child lacked rights due to cultural factors. The purported solution was to sensitize girls, their parents, their teachers, their public leaders, and their communities.[72]

Investigating the Altered Report: Layers of Silence

Commonsense questions to ask at this point are: Who stripped and altered key parts of the published findings of the Girl Child Project? Why? How did people connected with the creation of the original reports respond to these revisions? Archival silences, gaps, and erasures characterize both the editing of the report and the responses to it. No publicly available documents from FEMNET or UNICEF or interviews that I conducted revealed who altered the report before it was published. What is left are educated guesses. Praising UNICEF's work, adding the UNICEF logo to every page, and deleting or altering such core components of the synthesis report—in some cases fundamentally altering the report's analytical frameworks and policy implications—suggest that it was someone at UNICEF, rather than Obura or a FEMNET employee, who made the changes. If Obura or someone at FEMNET had wanted to alter the document, they likely would have done so before FEMNET's staff printed, bound, and submitted the draft synthesis report to UNICEF. The Pan-African NGO's staff have kept a copy of the printed, bound, and submitted report in FEMNET's Nairobi-based reading room for over twenty years. While not impossible, the likelihood that someone or many people at FEMNET were responsible for the alterations to the published document seems highly negligible, especially given the politics of the girl-focused advocacy coming out of the NGO. Differing opinions existed at FEMNET about the causes, relationships, and solutions to patriarchy—as well as its entanglements with poverty, girls, and the state. However, the plurality of views expressed within the organization—and especially among its core leaders and staff at the Nairobi-based secretariat that hired Obura to pen the synthesis report—was much more in line with the unpublished report than with the doctored published version.

While the revisions were likely made somewhere on UNICEF's end, many questions remain. UNICEF ESARO published the doctored study in 1992. Archival gaps make it impossible to know exactly what happened in between the time when UNICEF staff received Obura's draft synthesis report in 1992, along with the eight country studies as they were completed before then; organized the Gaborone workshop to discuss the studies; and published the revised document. When I visited the UNICEF ESARO offices in Nairobi in 2014 after struggling to secure an appointment in the heavily guarded UN compound, I was told by two employees that their records from the 1990s had been turned over to the government of Kenya and then "lost" in connection with a governmental investigation that involved UNICEF. The purported turnover of records to the government may or may not have been connected to the 1993–94 embezzlement scandal that rocked UNICEF's Nairobi-based compound when it became public in 1995 and led to the firing of multiple staff members in the complex that housed various UNICEF suboffices and employed roughly 245 people at the time. International newspapers such as the *New York Times* reported on the scandal, in which more than twenty UNICEF staff members were accused of having misspent or embezzled over 25 percent of the Nairobi offices' annual budget of $37 million over a two-year period. In response, UNICEF's New York City leadership reportedly "pared back" the Nairobi office staff to 138 people by the middle of 1995 with plans to implement further staff cuts.[73] Neither of the employees I spoke with in 2014 had worked in the UNICEF ESARO offices in the 1990s. After I asked about the Girl Child Project and UNICEF's broader girl-focused advocacy, one of the employees explicitly warned me to be careful about anything I wrote that mentions UNICEF because "UNICEF is very protective of its image."[74]

These archival erasures and silences—and, as I interpreted the warning from the employee, an encouragement to silence and censor my own research into the topic—add extra layers of complexity to reconstructing this story and figuring out who carried out the erasures in the study and why. My best educated guess at this point is that the unpublished synthesis report was seen as too challenging of the central narratives underpinning UNICEF's embrace of girl-focused economic policymaking in the 1980s and early 1990s. When confronted with publishing a document that fundamentally questioned and sometimes contradicted the programming that had been developed by staff at the international institution's global headquarters in New York City for the last decade, it is conceivable that staff within the organization decided it would be better—perhaps easier, perhaps less threatening to their own careers; perhaps they simply did not believe much of the data from the unedited Girl Child Project—to alter the findings in order to make them fit more in line with UNICEF's dominant preexisting narrative.

Regardless of who carried out the alterations, the outcome is that the published report rearticulated, doubled down on, and expanded the assumptions, political commitments, and policy proposals that were so central to the girl-focused programming that had been coming out of the institution's New York City headquarters under the leadership of James Grant and Richard Jolly. This framework is exemplified in the following quotation, printed in the version of the girl child study that UNICEF published:

> The concept of "the girl child" derives from the appreciation that educating a girl is a sure way to improve the lives of women and to break the cycle of poverty and underdevelopment. Attention given to the girl child, focus on her development, is a mechanism to transform the lives of adult women. . . . Higher productivity [and] lower fertility of women [occurs] when girls are educated.[75]

To accept this premise that educating girls was a key to breaking the cycle of poverty in Africa, one had to first assume that girls were largely uneducated. Otherwise, how could one explain the fact that, in the early 1990s, as the Girl Child Project findings pointed out until some of this information was scrubbed from the UNICEF ESARO publication, most girls in the region were already attending school, yet the feminized "cycle of poverty and underdevelopment" continued? It could be argued that girls' education was seen as a long-term solution to an immediate crisis. However, the findings of the unpublished synthesis report and country studies made clear that the relationships between girls' education and poverty were not nearly so one-directional or simplistic, even if the goal was a long-term one. How could educating girls break the cycle of poverty if an overwhelming consensus emerging from the studies was that poverty itself, compounded by economic austerity, was a leading cause for girls' lack of access to education? The unedited synthesis report and country case studies had been clear: education alone was not enough to solve the economic crisis and entrenched poverty, and in some cases—whether through sexist stereotypes in school textbooks or in discussions of the lower earning potential of girl and women graduates—the unedited synthesis report depicted formal education not as a site of the alleviation of poverty and gender-based disparities but as a mechanism of their reproduction and exacerbation through the "feminization of poverty."

In the process of doubling down on UNICEF's institutional vision for poverty alleviation through educated and empowered girls, the study that UNICEF ESARO published erased knowledge of a much more complex reality in which girls in Eastern and Southern Africa lived. In political terms, this inverted the causality of the arguments put forth in the eight country studies and initial synthesis report. Some of the political implications of the unaltered synthesis report would have been to rework international economic and political structures, particularly by ending economic austerity measures and decreasing coercive, neocolonial policymaking and cultural influences. By contrast, the political implications of the doctored study were very different: the only way to develop Africa, eradicate poverty, and secure the rights of the girl child was to promote more external intervention in order to fix the "local cultures" and improve the behaviors of individual men and women who were allegedly oppressing girls. Through this revision of knowledge, many of the very things authors of the Girl Child Study argued created gender-based and economic inequalities—such as an over reliance on neocolonial norms, advisers, and interventions—were hailed as solutions to empowering girls and economically developing the Global South.

"Loud Silences" and FEMNET's Response to the Revisions

Further silence characterizes FEMNET's response to these revisions. I found no record of a direct response to the revisions within FEMNET's archive or public-facing advocacy from the time. Interviews proved that no one was willing to be publicly quoted speaking about UNICEF in ways that could be perceived as negative, for fear of reprisal or other forms of negative impacts in the fraught world of NGO politics.

Financial dependencies may partially explain this silence. FEMNET's staff were highly reliant on UNICEF for funding to keep their organization alive. Multiple records from FEMNET's archive that date to the late 1980s and 1990s refer to the fact that the young NGO struggled to get off the ground and nearly did not survive after its founding in 1988 because of a lack of funding.[76] Various documents also repeatedly state that accepting UNICEF money to work on the Girl Child Project is in large part what stabilized FEMNET as an organization, helped earn it international legitimacy, and ensured its survival.[77] One edition of *FEMNET News* from 1992 described UNICEF funding from 1990, at the start of the Girl Child Project, as a "lease on life" that helped immensely because FEMNET was "struggling and striving to survive."[78] Nearly all of the early editions of *FEMNET News*, which began circulation in 1989, thanked UNICEF for funding the publication. FEMNET's physical headquarters were located inside of UNICEF's Nairobi office complex throughout the late 1980s and early 1990s. This was reportedly due to budgetary constraints and problems registering the NGO with the Kenyan government.[79] The lack of a strong, public response from FEMNET's members to the altering of the final report for the Girl Child Project should be viewed in the context of the organization's heavy reliance on UNICEF for survival in the Pan-African NGO's first years of existence.

Despite these official silences, FEMNET's public advocacy of the time did contain carefully worded denunciations of neocolonial or otherwise unequal relationships between international donors and Africa-based NGOs. It often situated these critiques within a broader context in which FEMNET's leaders felt caught in the middle between donors like UNICEF and state governments, particularly that of Kenya. For example, a printed conversation between Njoki Wainaina and FEMNET staff member Esther Kamweru appeared in an issue of *FEMNET News* from 1994, a year after UNICEF ESARO published the altered Girl Child Project findings. In the conversation, Kamweru brought up the disproportionate impact of structural adjustment programs on "women and especially on the education of girls." In response, Wainaina reportedly said, "It is real. So real that it is indeed painful. . . . I am afraid that NGOs have been known to go along with what governments and donors want." She insinuated that alliances between local NGOs and national governments in Africa could make the former more effective advocates in relation to foreign donors, the United Nations, and the international system. When Kamweru asked a follow-up question about potential alliances between NGOs like FEMNET and the government of Kenya, Wainaina responded, "I cannot comment." She utilized the passive voice—"what I can say is that Kenya is not mentioned as a country that will support NGOs." Wainaina's careful wording criticized the state while attributing this criticism to an unnamed external source.[80]

At the time, the administration of Kenyan president Daniel arap Moi, under increasing local and international pressure to democratize and introduce multiparty elections, was known for imprisoning, torturing, and disappearing activists who criticized its politics. In 1992, police besieged and then broke into the home of Wangari Maathai, a prominent women's rights advocate, environmentalist, and NGO founder who would go on to win the Nobel Peace Prize. In widely publicized proceedings, she was jailed and then charged with "spreading malicious rumors," sedition, and treason. For Maathai, the backing of international institutions and individuals based in the North Atlantic proved essential to the eventual dropping of the charges the state brought against her.[81]

Moi's government made it difficult for FEMNET's founders to register as an NGO with the government of Kenya, a legal requirement for operation that would pave the way for the organization to receive donor funding more easily. FEMNET records from the late 1980s and early 1990s reference these registration struggles, although they do so using cautious and oblique language exemplified by Wainaina's interview with Kamweru. An internally produced FEMNET history published in 2012, which includes printed interviews with the NGO's founders and draws from many of the organization's early records, recounts this period from the relative safety provided by decades of elapsed time and changes in Kenya's political leadership. Describing the environment in which FEMNET was founded after the end of the Third UN World Conference on Women in Nairobi in 1985, the internal history states, "The women of the world took away with them the *Spirit of Nairobi*. The women of Kenya, however, got the backlash that deliberately and decisively fractured, destroyed and quenched the women's movement—an onslaught from which Kenyan women have never fully recovered." The history continues:

> The backlash was so swift and unexpected that it left Kenya women wondering what had hit them. The political forces set some women up against others and scattered the NGO Steering Committee [of the Third UN World Conference on Women, headed by Eddah Gachukia] soon after the Conference ended. . . . Government agents were used to frustrate every effort of the women to regroup. Meetings were cancelled and the war on the NGOs and individuals who led them was waged from invisible sources. It was in this volatile environment that the registration of FEMNET was being pursued, and it became an uphill task, since there was hostility, suspicion and under-currents that suggested that women's activities were subversive.[82]

This battle to register FEMNET with the Kenyan government reportedly lasted for years, dragging on from the late 1980s and into the early 1990s. During this time—when the Girl Child Project was being carried out—the internally produced history recalled that "the political environment in Kenya had by then become highly repressive, characterized by detentions and intimidation of anybody suspected of involvement in rights-based activities and movements. Individuals were intimidated and threatened and those working with Government were afraid of losing their jobs or even worse consequences."[83]

The takeover of the largest women's group in Kenya by the Moi Regime in 1987 also likely loomed large in the minds of FEMNET's staff. Many of FEMNET's Kenyan members had belonged to the organization, named Maendeleo ya Wanawake (Progress of Women). The group had been founded in colonial Kenya in the 1950s.[84] Writing about the forced governmental seizure of Maendeleo ya Wanawake, Marilyn Muthoni Kamuru has referenced long-standing tensions around "silence as the preferred political language" in Kenya. She has noted that Moi's one-party state led a forced takeover of the multimillion-member women's group and contorted it into "an appendage of the state" and "a voice for the ruling party KANU." Kamuru has noted the "loud silence" that Maendeleo ya Wanawake members employed as a political tactic in the face of the takeover and maintain in the country's still-fraught present. While trying to avoid the same fate as Maendeleo ya Wanawake and navigating necessary yet dangerous relationships between UNICEF and the government of Kenya, FEMNET's members used what could arguably be called "loud silence" in response to the erasures, strategic amplifications, and distortions of various strands of advocacy in the Girl Child Project that the NGO coordinated and in their broader girl-focused advocacy with UNICEF.[85]

It was within these overlapping political contexts of the early 1990s that Njoki Wainaina obliquely criticized donors who pushed particular narratives about girls' education and declining state funding while referencing her mistrust of the governments of said states, particularly of Kenya. These fears and frustrations indicate the precariousness of the positions FEMNET and its members occupied—partnerships with national governments like that of Moi's Kenya and international agencies such as UNICEF were essential for FEMNET's institutional survival. On the flip side, angering people at these institutions carried real threats to survival. These threats were organizational in the case of FEMNET's reliance on UNICEF for funding and its need for the government of Kenya to legally allow FEMNET to operate in the country without subverting it. The threats were also physical for individual members who were based in Kenya or who traveled to the country, as in the case of fellow NGO workers and women's rights activists like Wangari Maathai whose lives were threatened and other activists who were disappeared. It was precisely this dilemma that, as Wainaina articulated, often led NGOs and their staff to "to go along with what governments and donors want." It is similarly against this backdrop that we can begin to interpret FEMNET's ostensible silence in response to the distortion of the findings of the Girl Child Project.

This incidence is one of many cases of calculated speech, insinuations, and strategic silences from FEMNET's advocacy related to its girl-focused work with UNICEF in the early to mid-1990s. The fact that such veiled criticisms in *FEMNET News* were printed in the capital city of Kenya and in the same newsletters that UNICEF and other donors funded—as acknowledgments sections in most journal issues reminded readers—speaks to the tightrope FEMNET's members walked. Multiple forms of silences and disappearing, alongside tactical forms of communication and circulation, characterize this transnational history of knowledge and the birth of Girls in Development.

Conclusion

Not all aspects of the noncirculation of knowledge about girls were so blatantly suppressive as the Girl Child Project. FEMNET's work with UNICEF surrounding the girl-focused studies represents one of multiple episodes on a spectrum of collaboration and erasure, of alliances and frictions in a world in which FEMNET relied on UNICEF for financial survival and international access, just as UNICEF relied on the US government. Similar frictions and a range of forms of cooperation, ambivalent codependencies, and outright hostilities characterized the relationships between FEMNET and the government of Kenya over time. Relevant here is that the history of Girls in Development is a story of the intentional *noncirculation* and silencing of particular forms of knowledge that did not become dominant—that at times were not even publicly utterable—alongside the circulation of ideas that did. While the variety of girls' lived experiences in Africa and the reportedly detrimental and gendered impacts of colonialism, capitalism, warfare, structural adjustment, Christianity, and other factors were erased from view, the supposed universality of patriarchy due to local cultures, traditions, and discrimination enacted within families took center stage in narratives about girl-focused economic planning within the Nairobi–New York City network out of which proto visions of girl-focused economic programming had earlier emerged. What followed was the internationalization of this increasingly singular, neoliberal strand of girl-focused economic thought into a set of norms that would guide UN and global policymaking well into the present.

2

Pan-African Organizing and the UN World Conference on Women in Nairobi

How did the episode detailed in the previous chapter, of the erasure of certain forms of knowledge about girls, come about? Was the eventual dominance of neoliberal feminism through the vehicle of Girls in Development inevitable, predictable even? In order to make legible the selective exclusions and contingencies that are so central to this history, we must broaden the story beyond the single incident of the eight country studies for the Girl Child Project.

This chapter traces the emergence of the African Women's Task Force, the organization that transformed into FEMNET, surrounding the United Nations' Third World Conference on Women in 1985. The conference marked the end of the UN Women's Decade. It served as a crowning achievement of the United Nations' women's movement—until the final World Conference on Women took place in Beijing ten years later. Whereas the formal outputs in Beijing cemented neoliberal feminism within international norms, the outputs from Nairobi a decade before were markedly different. It is easy to look back from the vantage point of the present and view the end of the story—the dominance of neoliberal feminism through the vehicle of Girls in Development and the marginalization of competing policy frameworks and systems of thought—as inevitable. But doing so overlooks the contestations and frictions that were essential to this history and how it unfolded. Such a linear retrospective view reproduces many of the erasures that were characterized the fraught history of how Girls in Development emerged and internationalized.

Tracing the growth of the African Women's Task Force shows how contestations of the international system played out within and through the UN women's movement and its focus on women, girls, and development. Various groups called for a fundamental restructuring and decolonization of the global economy to distribute resources more equitably, whether through the New International Economic Order or otherwise. Connected calls existed to decolonize the political leadership of the UN women's movement and to move the presence and needs of women from the Global South, including Africa, from the periphery to the center of the then-upcoming UN Third World Conference on Women.

Unlike in the previous chapter, which detailed how selective erasures and silences characterized much of FEMNET's work with UNICEF, this chapter shows a different set of political outcomes and possibilities for the future. The very creation of FEMNET's precursor, the African Women's Task Force, represented a moment of publicly challenging both UNICEF and the leadership of the UN women's movement; it was a visible political victory for Pan-African women's organizing and the women who would go on to found FEMNET. The proceedings of the UN World Conference on Women in Nairobi and their embrace of development as essential to women's status similarly represented public-facing political victories for the African Women's Task Force and the individuals leading it. African women as a political collective were not only highly visible at the Nairobi conference. The women organizing them, such as Eddah Gachukia and Njoki Wainaina, successfully internationalized many of their ideas and policy frameworks. At the end of the Third UN World Conference on Women in Nairobi in 1985, potential futures looked possible that were very different from what would come to pass.

Historicizing erasure and marginalization necessarily involves finding what was there before it was cast aside. It is important to know how this story turned out by the turn of the new millennium. But it is also important to know that this ending was not a foregone conclusion; that different possibilities and imaginings existed before and during, both in the dealings of the African Women's Task Force–turned–FEMNET with UNICEF and in the broader course of the UN women's movement and the World Conferences on Women attached to it.

The UN Women's Movement and the New International Economic Order

The United Nations hosted four World Conferences on Women: in Mexico City in 1975, Copenhagen in 1980, Nairobi in 1985, and Beijing in 1995. The first three conferences punctuated the UN-proclaimed International Women's Year (1975) and Decade for Women (1976–85). The African Women's Task Force emerged and then morphed into FEMNET surrounding the Third UN World Conference on Women, which was held in Nairobi at the end of the

Women's Decade in 1985. The girl-focused lobbying campaign that members of FEMNET and UNICEF carried out would, in turn, profoundly shape the outputs of the Fourth (and final, to date) UN World Conference on Women in Beijing.

Tensions over the intertwined processes of decolonization and the Cold War—and between and within Global North and South—characterized the UN World Conferences on Women from the start.[1] The New International Economic Order (NIEO) was one of many flashpoints. Formally endorsed by the UN General Assembly in 1974, a year before the United Nations' First World Conference on Women took place in Mexico City, the NIEO called for an end to "the widening gap between the developed and the developing countries" in the world. It condemned the existing international order for having been built through "colonial domination, foreign occupation, racial discrimination, *apartheid* and neo-colonialism." To fix these fundamental imbalances, the NIEO put forth a series of policy proposals: more regulatory oversight of "transnational corporations," new terms of trade concerning raw materials and manufactured goods that were more "just and equitable" for developing countries, and the sharing of technological breakthroughs, to name a few. The NIEO also affirmed the right of independent states to nationalize their "natural resources and all economic activities." On a higher level, the NIEO called for "prevailing disparities in the world" to be "banished" through "the adoption of special measures in favour of the least developed."[2]

The UN General Assembly's adoption of the NIEO was aspirational. Like all General Assembly resolutions, it was not legally binding. No enforcement mechanism accompanied it, despite the General Assembly's passage of the Charter on Economic Rights and Duties of States a few months later in an effort to promote concrete policy changes and future legal frameworks in support of the NIEO. The NIEO was, instead, a push to create new norms. It served as a call to action, an attempt to shift the Overton window of what was viewed as politically possible, to fundamentally restructure an economic system that, its authors argued, had been forged and maintained through colonial and imperial violence.

The formally adopted outputs of the first three UN World Conferences on Women all endorsed the creation of the NIEO. However, this adoption belied tensions that surrounded the NIEO and the broader topics of colonialism, imperialism, and the global economy during the UN Women's Decade. Ruth Bacon, a former foreign service office director for the United States Department of State, was a US delegate to the First UN World Conference on Women in Mexico City in 1975. She also served on the UN Commission on the Status of Women—the body that organized all of the UN World Conferences on Women—and directed the US Center for the International Women's Year. In a newsletter organizing the US delegation going to Mexico City, Bacon pointed to conflicts over the NIEO that had marred conference organizing: "The NIEO is strongly supported by the developing countries which now form a large majority of UN members." However, "the subject is a complicated one," she wrote. Bacon noted the "sympathy among UN members, developed as well as developing" toward the call for a new international economic order. "Where serious questions arise are as to whether and how, in practical terms, a redistribution could equitably be made; and also whether the real remedy rests not in redistribution, but rather in an expansion of productive capacity and of the world economy embracing developing as well as developed nations."[3]

Beyond her insinuation that a more effective solution to the NIEO lay with economic growth and better integration of developing countries into the world economy—standard talking points of US foreign policy during and after the Cold War—Bacon questioned the relevance of the NIEO to a UN conference dedicated to discussing the status of women. She referenced a fight that had broken out at a planning meeting of the Commission on the Status of Women in March 1975. While some members claimed that the NIEO's calls for "a redistribution of the world's wealth and know-how" were prerequisites for improving the status of women, others argued that discussing the NIEO in Mexico City would shift attention away from the fundamental purposes of the conference. Bacon shared this concern when she concluded, "It is to be hoped that the issue will not be allowed to deflect the Conference from its main objectives."[4] To Bacon and a number of other attendees—mostly delegates from the Global North—the NIEO and broader calls to remake the global economy were incidental to women's issues, a distraction. Some even questioned if the delegates putting forth these proposals and others were dupes, mere pawns of the men running their governments who wanted to hijack the UN women's movement to talk about peripheral issues.[5]

If Ruth Bacon used diplomatic language to share talking points about the NIEO with the US delegation ahead of the Mexico City World Conference on Women, private correspondences within the US government were less reserved. Sheila Rabb Weidenfeld, the press secretary to US First Lady Betty Ford, jotted down notes of a conversation that she'd had with General Brent Skowcroft, the national security adviser to President Gerald Ford, ahead of the Mexico City conference. "U.S. going to get clobbered" by the "3rd World," she wrote and then emphasized by drawing a box around it. The United States would be the "whipping boy." These fears over how developing countries would use the platform of the Mexico City conference to condemn the

United States' role in propping up existing global economic and political systems led to concern that Betty Ford might be publicly "embarrassed" if she were to attend.[6] In the end, she did not go to the First UN World Conference on Women in Mexico City. An early draft of Betty Ford's remarks to the conference, delivered in her absence, used the age-old excuse of "conflicts in my schedule."[7] This line was deleted from the speech that was actually delivered, and she gave no reason for her absence.

Some of the fears of the US delegation did indeed come to fruition. Many attendees used the first three UN World Conferences on Women as platforms to denounce the US government, whether for its invasion of Vietnam, its neocolonial policymaking in Latin America and elsewhere, its racism, or its ongoing support of Israel's armed annexation of UN-designated Palestinian territories.[8] Relevant here is that tensions over the global economy, imperialism, decolonization, and more were interwoven with the fabric of the UN Women's Decade. And, unlike the outputs of the final UN World Conference on Women in Beijing in 1995, all three of the formal conference outputs between 1975 and 1985 called for a fundamental restructuring of the global economic system from above, in part through formal endorsement of the NIEO.

The Road to the African Women's Task Force through the United Nations' Women's Movement

The African Women's Task Force emerged from these tensions in the lead-up to the Third UN World Conference on Women in Nairobi in 1985. It particularly grew from a fight over who should represent African women on the international stage of the United Nations. The conflict arose during the regional preparatory process ahead of the main event in Nairobi. Before each of the UN World Conferences on Women, various United Nations bodies hosted preparatory conferences for different parts of the world. Attendees at the preparatory meetings devised regional plans of action and lobbying strategies that would shape the proceedings of the global conferences. To plan for the 1985 UN World Conference on Women in Nairobi, the African regional conference took place in Arusha, Tanzania, from October 8 to 12, 1984.

Within this bureaucratic world of conference organizing, two distinct events played foundational roles. Both took place as part of the UN World Conferences on Women and at the regional preparatory conferences like the one held in Arusha. One event was the formal conference held for delegates from national governments that belonged to the United Nations. The other event, which ran parallel to the official conference, was the NGO Forum. The latter drew significantly larger crowds than the governmental proceedings.

At the UN Second World Conference on Women in Copenhagen in 1980, for example, the NGO Forum saw more than four times as many participants as the governmental conference: between six and seven thousand attendees versus fifteen hundred.[9] Beyond members of nongovernmental organizations, the NGO Forums attracted individual activists, researchers, members of governmental delegations, representatives of international agencies, and ad hoc groups of people who were interested in women's issues from a variety of perspectives. Less scripted and sanitized than the governmental plenaries, the NGO Forum saw some of the ugliest fights occur as well as new alliances being forged. They were, in the words of Finnish diplomat Hilkka Pietilä, where "the 'real' world conferences of participating women" took place.[10]

It was the last plenary on the last day of the NGO Forum at the African regional preparatory conference in Arusha in October of 1984. Participants had spent the previous four days hammering out the details of a draft report. Between the end of the African region's Arusha conference and the start of the World Conference on Women in Nairobi nine months later, someone needed to finalize the draft plan of action for the African Regional NGO Forum, disseminate it to relevant institutions and individuals on the continent, and organize the continent's lobbying strategy.

The fight that birthed the African Women's Task Force broke out over who had responsibility for and ownership of this draft plan to guide African advocacy at the global NGO Forum. Njoki Wainaina, one of the attendees of the NGO Forum in Arusha who would go on to become a leader of the African Women's Task Force and FEMNET, recounted this moment: "The plenary received the draft report of the Forum and then came the question of who the draft report belonged to, who would finalize it and what the next step in the process would be. Most participants thought it was obvious that it belonged to them"—to the roughly fifty "women from different parts of Africa (mostly from Kenya and Tanzania) who were in attendance" at the Arusha meeting. However, "Dame Nita Barrow and Virginia Hazzard maintained that it belonged to the NGO Forum in New York as the convenor of the Arusha NGO Forum."[11]

At stake here was who was in charge of organizing African women ahead of the World Conference to mark the end of the United Nations Women's Decade in 1985, a conference that would take place in a major African city. Should African women lead the mobilization of people on the continent going into the global NGO Forum in Nairobi? Or should the UN-appointed, New York City–based conference organizing team head the preparatory process for the African region from half a world away? On a continent that had been formally colonized by various European empires until the recent past and that still faced coercive interventions from governments and agencies based in the Global North—including the United States—this debate in Arusha was not merely about a conference document. It tapped into explosive politics surrounding decolonization and the Cold War that were inseparable from the UN women's movement.

The identities of the key women involved in the debate in Arusha add humanity to this bureaucratic history and help flesh out the thorny politics involved. They also show that the battle lines were more fraught than a quick glance might suggest. On one side of the fight over who should control the outputs of the African Regional NGO Forum going into the World Conference to end the UN Decade for Women—the side that wanted the New York City–based organizing team of the NGO Forum in control—were the two women named above, Dame Nita Barrow and Virginia Hazzard. Born in 1916, Nita Barrow was a Black diplomat who lived under British colonialism until Barbados, her home country, gained formal independence in 1966. Trained as a nurse in the Caribbean and internationally, Barrow became a university instructor and public health official in Barbados and Jamaica in the mid-twentieth century. As the British-governed Caribbean gained formal independence in the 1960s, Barrow transitioned into a career in international diplomacy. Around the same time, one of her younger brothers, Errol, became a high-profile politician. He would go on to become prime minister of Barbados, making fiery denunciations of American imperialism in the Caribbean during the Cold War.[12]

Between the 1960s and the time of the Arusha meeting in 1984, Nita Barrow held senior organizational roles with a slew of international organizations. "Her leadership of these international bodies," notes a UNESCO summary of Barrow's work, "were all the more significant because prior to her holding these posts women, and particularly Black women, were excluded from such positions of power."[13] At the same time, her political connections—familial and otherwise—and her own status within the UN apparatus marked Barrow as an elite surrounding the UN Third World Conference on Women. In Arusha in 1984, Nita Barrow presided over the African Regional NGO Forum in her role as the UN-designated chairperson of the upcoming NGO Forum at the Nairobi conference.

Joining Barrow's side of the argument that would give rise to the African Women's Task Force—the side that wanted the New York City–based planning committee of the NGO Forum to finalize the African Regional NGO Forum's outputs going into the upcoming World Conference on Women—was Virginia Hazzard. A white American woman born at the end of World War I, Hazzard held a master's degree in community development from

Columbia.[14] Her career focused on the promotion of the welfare and education of women and girls, particularly in Africa. Hazzard started working with UNICEF in 1969. During the 1970s and early 1980s, she spent a seven-year stretch in UNICEF's Nairobi compound, where she served as both a program officer for Kenya and a regional adviser on programming for women in Eastern Africa. Hazzard officially retired from UNICEF in 1983. However, she remained deeply involved with the agency's Nairobi-based offices in the mid-1980s.

While Hazzard was one of comparatively few women at the time who worked for the United Nations in a role that was not secretarial, she occupied a position of power surrounding the UN Third World Conference on Women in Nairobi and in UNICEF's East African offices. In Arusha in 1984, Virginia Hazzard held an official role as the coordinator of the NGO Forum for the upcoming World Conference on Women in Nairobi. Nita Barrow was the event's chairperson and official head; Hazzard was responsible for part of the hands-on organizing.[15] Through UNICEF, she had helped to fund the participation of many women from Africa in the preparatory activities leading up to the Nairobi World Conference. This included the regional conference in Arusha in October 1984. With Hazzard on one side of the fight over who should control the African regional preparatory process leading into Nairobi, opposing her were many of the women whom Hazzard had helped to fund—with UNICEF money—to travel to Arusha and physically be in the room. This power dynamic over money and access to key policymaking spaces vis-à-vis UNICEF and people connected to it would become familiar to the women who sat opposite Hazzard as they formed the African Women's Task Force and worked with UNICEF to globalize girl-focused development planning.

Records of the motivations driving Barrow and Hazzard's actions in Arusha are patchy. Most sources recounting this event were produced by the people on the opposite side of the argument, the women from Africa—especially Kenya—who wanted to have control over the continent's official preparatory activities for the global NGO Forum. Woven throughout their accounts are references to anxieties, held by both sides of the argument, that African women did not have the organizational apparatus in place that would be necessary to organize an effective lobbying strategy. "When African women representing NGOs met in Arusha for the African Regional Preparatory Meeting in October 1984," reminisced the first edition of FEMNET's newsletter from 1989, "the one thing that was very obvious is that they needed a mechanism for communicating and sharing information." The article, which did not list an author but was likely written by either Njoki Wainaina or Eddah Gachukia, noted that African women "were going to be the hosts of one of the most important conferences in the history of the struggle for the advancement of women. The rest of the world knew a whole lot about what was going to happen in Nairobi in July 1985 and were getting their agenda ready. The majority of African women, including their leadership, had at best only a very vague idea about the Conference, the [NGO] Forum and even the Decade for women."[16] It was fear over this lack of general awareness about the UN Women's Decade and the need for more organizational capacity that likely drove part of Barrow and Hazzard's insistence that responsibility for finalizing the draft report of the African Regional NGO Forum in Arusha belonged in New York City with the NGO Forum's central planning committee, rather than with women or institutions based in Africa.

Yet this is only part of the story. Also woven throughout accounts of the fight in Arusha over who should control the organization of African women going into the UN Third World Conference on Women in 1985 was the fact that *not* having local or regional control over this process was business as usual at the time. There was a long history of people from outside of Africa coming to the continent and deciding what was in people's best interests, both through formal colonialism and through the forms of neocolonialism that were topics of hot debate in the women's movement and the broader United Nations. FEMNET's early sources and historical context suggest that, as Nita Barrow and Virginia Hazzard walked into that room on the final day of the African Regional NGO Forum in Arusha, they likely assumed that the New York City–based NGO Forum planning committee would control the remainder of the preparatory process going into the World Conference in Nairobi. For them, it may have been expected, just as it was likely standard that they had been the ones to organize the African Regional NGO Forum in Arusha, rather than delegating this job to an Africa-based institution. Foreign experts appointed by people in metropoles like New York City having control over policy proposals for Africa was still often the norm.

What was not initially obvious to Barrow and Hazzard was clear to many of the fifty or so women from Africa in the room in Arusha in 1984: control over the bureaucratic processes that would inform both norms and policymaking concerning women in Africa needed to reside locally. Leading this side of the argument was Eddah Gachukia. Briefly discussed in this book's introduction, Gachukia (née Wacheke, also spelled Waceke) was born in colonial Kenya in 1936. After completing secondary school at the prestigious Alliance Girls' High School, Gachukia continued on to Makerere College in Uganda, the first university in British East Africa. Eddah Gachukia and her husband, Daniel, both taught in Christian missionary schools in late colonial Kenya's racially segregated education system in the early 1960s. Eddah

Gachukia has frequently remarked on the racism that she and Daniel experienced, including receiving less pay and a smaller house than their white counterparts on the teaching staff for doing the same work.[17]

Commitments to antiracism and to decolonizing education within Africa have driven much of Eddah Gachukia's career. After Kenya formally gained independence from the United Kingdom in 1963, Gachukia pursued graduate education in the United Kingdom and the University of Nairobi. She earned master's and doctorate degrees in literature from the latter before joining the university's faculty as an instructor. Eddah Gachukia was at the University of Nairobi during campus protests—part of the global student movement of 1968—and was closely involved in efforts to both decolonize and Africanize the university's curriculum. In 1974, the Gachukias purchased the first of what would become a small group of private schools in Nairobi. At the time that they bought it, the school did not allow admission of African students. The Gachukias integrated it as part of a self-described mission to broaden the availability of high-quality education to Black Africans.[18]

Dovetailing with her career as an antiracist and decolonial educator, Eddah Gachukia was both a politician and a leader in various women's movements. In 1967, she was elected as vice president of Kenya's largest women's organization, Maendeleo ya Wanawake, briefly mentioned in the previous chapter. She served as a member of Parliament from 1974 to 1984, having been appointed to the position by Kenya's first president, Jomo Kenyatta. Gachukia also served as the chairperson of the National Council of Women of Kenya from 1976 to 1979. Much of her work as a member of Parliament and a leader of Kenya's largest and most visible women's organizations involved promoting programming related to Women in Development.[19]

Eddah Gachukia played leading roles, both nationally and internationally, at the four World Conferences on Women that the United Nations hosted. In 1975, she headed the Kenyan delegation to the UN First World Conference on Women in Mexico City that marked the celebration of the International Women's Year and kicked off the Decade for Women. After occupying a similar role at the UN Second World Conference on Women in Copenhagen in 1980, Gachukia became the chairperson of the Kenya NGO Organizing Committee for the UN Third World Conference that was to be held in Nairobi. Nita Barrow was the NGO Forum's global head and Virginia Hazzard its global coordinator. Gachukia led the Kenyan team that would be in charge of much of the on-site preparation.

In Arusha, the heads of the global New York City–based team organizing the NGO Forum at the upcoming World Conference on Women in Nairobi and the head of the Kenyan team in charge of it clashed. On the line was who contained both real and symbolic leadership over the mobilization of women from Africa on the international stage of the UN women's movement. Records of what exactly Gachukia and the women in the room with her in Arusha said to justify their control over the preparatory process for the African Regional NGO Forum are sparse. A FEMNET newsletter written nearly a decade later recounted the meeting. "It is wonderful to be a dreamer, especially if you are the kind whose dreams come true. It is not so wonderful to be angry, but occasionally, it helps to get really angry. This was the case on October 8, 1984 at the Arusha Conference Center: Women did really get angry." It was, in the words of the article, "the night FEMNET was conceived out of frustration and anger." The article in FEMNET's newsletter, which did not list an author but was likely written by Njoki Wainaina, listed some of the women who were present in the room alongside Eddah Gachukia: Ivy Matsepe-Casaburri (South Africa; she would briefly become the country's acting president in 2005), Prisca Molotsi (South Africa), Nadia Haggag Youssef (Egypt), Norah Olembo (Kenya), Christina Nsekela (Tanzania), and Nana Platt.[20] It is clear that these women vehemently opposed people from outside of the continent controlling the political rallying of African women ahead of a World Conference that would be hosted in Nairobi.

Records also suggest a feeling that the voices and needs of women from Africa had not been taken into ample consideration at the previous two UN World Conferences on Women. Four years after the Arusha meeting in October 1984, Gachukia reflected, "At that time, there was a feeling that the venue" of Nairobi for the World Conference on Women and its NGO Forum "should not be taken for granted, that because the conferences were being held in an African country, the presence of African women should be felt." She continued, "Their needs and priorities should be articulated, certainly more than had happened in Mexico City and Copenhagen in 1980."[21] Njoki Wainaina put it more bluntly decades later: "When we went to Arusha, we realized that the 1976–85 UN Decade for Women was ending and most women on the African continent had not even heard about it." She continued, "By that time in October 1984, Western women were already preparing to come. They were going to come to Nairobi, talk about their issues, dominate and control the meetings, while African women would be passive observers."[22]

Gachukia and Wainaina's side of the argument won. The result was the creation of a new organizational body, the African Women's Task Force, which would rebrand itself as FEMNET four years later. Founded as an explicitly Pan-African group, the Task Force's mandate was to mobilize women on the continent for the upcoming NGO Forum at the UN World Conference on Women in Nairobi. The women assembled in Arusha, "highly animated" after their victory, elected Eddah Gachukia as chairperson.[23] Njoki Wainaina was named coordinator. She already served as a member of the Kenyan NGO Organizing Committee that Gachukia headed.[24]

Njoki Wainaina has been retrospectively described in the Kenyan press as "one of the kingpins of Kenya's women's liberation movement, especially from the point of view of the UN Decade for Women Conference held in Nairobi in 1985."[25] Wainaina's upbringing contained parallels to Gachukia's, although Wainaina was half of a generation younger and often butted up against not only the colonial government but the newly independent Kenyan state in her young adulthood. Njoki Wainaina graduated from the Alliance Girls' High School and University College, Nairobi, in the 1960s, studying art and design. She returned to higher education a decade later. Wainaina graduated from the University of Nairobi with a degree in adult education in 1974 and earned a master's degree in education from the University of Hull in the United Kingdom in 1977.[26]

Like Gachukia, Njoki Wainaina remembers her childhood during colonialism as being marked by the racism of segregation. "As a young adult, I became more aware about racial discrimination than I knew about gender discrimination because in school, the *wazungu* (white) teachers were treated differently from the black teachers. Even in buses and trains, there were separate places for Africans, Asians and Whites." She contrasts this racism with the comparative absence of sexism in her childhood. Wainaina remembers her family as a space of gender equality, where girls and boys performed the same forms of household labor and where both of her parents were staunch "campaigners for the rights of women."[27]

Some of the first impactful encounters with sexism that Wainaina remembers stemmed from the policymaking of the postcolonial Kenyan state. As a civil servant at the Ministry of Lands and Settlement from 1969 to 1972, Njoki Wainaina's governmental employer told her that, "as a married woman," she could not have a permanent job contract. She was in a role dedicated to antiracism and decolonization, helping to transfer land "from the white settlers to the blacks who had lived as squatters and worked for the white people on that land" in the former settler colony.[28] And yet she faced another form of discrimination from the new state, one based on her gender.

Over the course of the 1970s, Wainaina continued her work on redistribution and to promote adult education in order to "decolonize the mind so that [new Black landowners in Kenya] would see themselves as freed people." She combined this work with her growing interest in women's movements in Kenya and globally. Njoki Wainaina began to politically organize with women's groups—the subject of her MA thesis—to encourage them to form collectives to buy land in order to increase the number of Black African women landowners in Kenya. Looming over this work were bitter fights with the government of Kenya over women's abilities to legally own land, which partially stemmed back to colonial-era lawmaking.

The growth of Women in Development policymaking in the 1970s meant that the "government was mobilizing women groups to use them as channels for development," observed Wainaina. Kenya had its own mosaic of women's movements stemming back decades, led by "strong women" from the region.[29] These groups, combined with the increasing visibility of global feminism through the UN Decade for Women, put pressure on the Kenyan state to ramp up its woman-focused development planning. Fraught relationships with the postcolonial Kenyan government, which promoted Women in Development programming with one hand while erecting or maintaining colonial-era barriers to women's status and legal rights with the other, would continue to flare up at various points not only for Njoki Wainaina as an individual but in the broader work that the African Women's Task Force, and then FEMNET, carried out as they worked to define and then internationalize policymaking focused on girls and women.

The African Women's Task Force, Funding, and UNICEF

When Gachukia and Wainaina left Arusha, they faced practical challenges in carrying out their heavy mandate as heads of the newly formed African Women's Task Force. FEMNET's internal history, which Wainaina compiled, recounts that a large part of the reason she and Gachukia were chosen to lead the Task Force was because they were some of the only members from that fateful Arusha meeting who lived in the same place. They were now in charge of organizing women and allies to women's issues across the second largest continent on the planet, one with thousands of languages. And they had been allotted no formal budget, office space, or support staff to do it.[30]

Working with large, well-funded international organizations proved essential to the early work of the Task Force. When Njoki Wainaina was chosen as the coordinator of the African Women's Task Force, she worked for the International Planned Parenthood Federation. This employment proved auspicious. To deal with the financial and organizational difficulties of mobilizing women across the continent, she and Gachukia used Planned Parenthood's resources, technology, and networks to disseminate information. "Telephones, meetings, telexes and letters" were their modes of communication as they finalized the Arusha NGO Forum's outputs, distributed them, and tried to mobilize African women going into Nairobi.[31]

UNICEF also became an essential ally to the African Women's Task Force as they prepared for the Nairobi NGO Forum. It was at this moment that Virginia Hazzard and UNICEF more broadly crossed back over the line from opponent in Arusha to supporter of the Task Force and then FEMNET's Pan-African women's organizing—a line that would become blurry many times in the decade ahead. FEMNET's documentation since the late 1980s repeatedly thanks Virginia Hazzard and UNICEF for the essential roles that they played in funding and organizationally supporting the African Women's Task Force as it gained its proverbial feet in 1984 and then morphed into FEMNET in 1988.[32] A list of "memorable individuals" in FEMNET's internal history sums up these relationships. Out of the nine people listed, five were FEMNET's founding members (including Gachukia and Wainaina). Three were UNICEF employees, and the remaining one was both a FEMNET founder and a former UNICEF staff member, Aida Gindy from Egypt. Virginia Hazzard ranked among the UNICEF employees listed, described as someone who "supported FEMNET for many years."[33] One could read these thanks as layered speech, given UNICEF's role as one of the main financial and organizational supporters of the African Women's Task Force and FEMNET. The art of passive aggression tells us that "thank you" can be laced with ambivalence and hostility. Whether or not these layers exist, it is noteworthy how regularly UNICEF and Virginia Hazzard are mentioned in FEMNET's founding documents and internal history. Rather than pure allyship or singular hostility, a fraught alliance between the two organizations emerged from the start of their relationship.

Working with Hazzard and others at UNICEF in the mid-1980s proved essential to Gachukia and Wainaina's ability to raise funds and otherwise organize the African Women's Task Force going into the Nairobi World Conference in 1985. "They made it possible," Wainaina remembers, "for us to raise money and hold the African Women's Encounter at the UN Complex in Gigiri, Nairobi, just before the Nairobi Forum."[34] The African Women's Encounter was central to the lobbying that people from the continent carried out at the World Conference that summer. Attended by more than five hundred African women, the Encounter took place on July 6, 1985, just four days before the kickoff of the global NGO Forum. It provided a venue where participants "deliberated on the priority issues for African women" and "prepared the African women to take leadership in the NGO Forum '85."[35]

The participants at the African Women's Encounter at the UNICEF offices in Nairobi gave the African Women's Task Force a mandate to expand its work. Attendees reached a consensus that Gachukia, Wainaina, and the broader Task Force should "set up a network that would link African women and continue the discussions started in Arusha and at the Encounter" in the future, well after the Nairobi World Conference would end.[36] UNICEF's funding, event space, and organizational support—and the political legitimacy that it lent the nascent African Women's Task Force, given UNICEF's status as a UN agency with wide name recognition on and off the continent—were crucial to the work of the African Women's Task Force surrounding the UN Third World Conference on Women in Nairobi. In Arusha, members of the fateful meeting that had created the Task Force asked that Gachukia and Wainaina organize a preparatory meeting six months before the Nairobi NGO Forum. The African Women's Task Force heads were unable to meet this request; the financial and organizational burdens were too high without more time and money to prepare. Instead, they convened the African Women's Encounter immediately before the NGO Forum in Nairobi. They did so with UNICEF's support and using UNICEF's Nairobi offices as their event space.[37]

During the NGO Forum at the World Conference on Women in Nairobi, the African Women's Task Force met multiple more times. Despite the organizational difficulties, most accounts of the influence of the African Women's Task Force and its members on the Nairobi conference are jubilant. A 1989 edition of FEMNET's newsletter reflected on "the remarkable presence of African women at [the NGO] Forum '85." It noted, "The impact that this presence had in bringing to the forefront the issues and concerns of African and other third world women was a great achievement, partly the result of the Arusha meeting."[38] A deeper discussion of the Nairobi conference provides more information about these concerns and how the people connected to the African Women's Task Force and the broader world of UN conference organizing from which it sprang negotiated them.

The UN World Conference on Women in Nairobi

In July 1985, roughly seventeen thousand people from 140 countries convened in Nairobi for the Third UN World Conference on Women, ending the United Nations Decade for Women. It was the largest recorded women's event in world history until the Beijing conference a decade later. Under the UN World Conference umbrella, the NGO Forum ran from July 10 to 19, the governmental plenary from July 15 to 26. The NGO Forum alone hosted over a thousand different "workshops, roundtable discussions, practical exhibitions and displays, films and visits to rural women's development projects" in a variety of languages, many of them with simultaneous translation into still other languages.[39] In addition to these formal events, people from nearly every country on earth, most of them women, met informally. They sat together on the lawns of the University of Nairobi, the venue of the NGO Forum. They talked, shared meals, quilted, struggled to overcome language barriers, got into fights, debated the meanings of womanhood, and plotted.

Eddah Gachukia, Njoki Wainaina, Nita Barrow, Virginia Hazzard, and the hundreds of other Nairobi NGO Forum organizers from the Kenyan team that the first two sat on and from the international team that the latter two represented helped pull off a public relations coup, both within the UN women's movement and in much of its international press coverage. Public accounts of the prior two UN World Conferences on Women often focused on their acrimony. Jocelyn Olcott has written about sensationalized international media coverage of "global catfights" between women delegates at the first conference in Mexico City in 1975.[40] A decade later, public narratives had changed dramatically. They hailed the Nairobi event as a watershed moment for the new levels of comity reached between delegates from Global North and South. Newspaper, radio, and television reports referred to the "Spirit of Nairobi"—a sense of camaraderie, sisterhood, and mutual understanding. "Something that can never come across in news accounts of such meetings," claimed an article in the *Los Angeles Times*, "is the intensity of feelings, the connections made, the motivation to return home to change one's corner of the world."[41]

Eddah Gachukia, as the head of both the Kenyan organizing team for the NGO Forum and the African Women's Task Force, had a particularly large influence over the public successes of the Third UN World Conference on Women. A breakthrough in this newly depicted sense of sisterhood occurred when women from Kenya took international attendees on excursions to the countryside outside of Nairobi to watch local women travel long distances to fetch clean water, farm subsistence crops, and engage in other forms of manual labor to meet life's basic necessities.

At issue in the previous two conferences was the extent to which *women* was truly a universal category with the power to cross-cut cleavages in race, class, experiences with colonial conquest, different relationships to capitalism and communism in the Cold War, and beyond. In Nairobi, the decision from Gachukia and the Kenya-based team that she led to take international attendees on field trips to watch women labor to carry heavy jugs of water over long distances viscerally hammered home that women around the world were *not* all equal.[42] Women in Africa and in other parts of the Global South faced disparities when compared with their counterparts in the Global North over basic standards of living and broader issues of development. According to contemporaneous reports, it was in Nairobi that many women from the Global

North finally "got it," bringing a new sense of cohesion to the UN women's movement precisely because of this acknowledgment of how structural differences operated among them.

The pivotal moment of the Nairobi World Conference on Women—bringing about a public-facing consensus within the UN women's movement on the importance of development and global inequalities among women related to living standards—stands in stark contrast to the previous two World Conferences on Women in Mexico City in 1975 and Copenhagen in 1980. While development had always been an official theme of the UN World Conferences on Women that surrounded the Women's Decade, many delegates, especially from the Global North (and, to complicate this term, from the Eastern and Western bloc rivalries that characterized much of the UN Decade for Women) had failed to grasp its significance. Some delegates were derisive or hostile.

Margaret Fulton—a Canadian delegate to the NGO Forms in Mexico City, Copenhagen, and Nairobi—serves as a case in point. Writing after the Copenhagen conference of 1980, she condemned "the politicization which destroyed the consensus" at both the governmental conference and the NGO Forum. Fulton reserved particularly harsh words for "African women," especially for those connected to AAWORD, the Association of African Women for Research and Development. Based in Dakar, Senegal, since 1977, AAWORD (AFARD in French) was founded by women researchers from across Africa who wished to decolonize knowledge production, particularly related to development, on the continent.[43] Fulton pointedly wrote about AAWORD's role at the World Conference on Women in Copenhagen, denouncing it as a "politicized group" whose members "excluded all white women," went about "touting their political slogans (in the absence of any substantive contributions)" and "disrupted meetings." Vacillating in tone between incredulous and mocking, Fulton described how AAWORD's members "demanded unlimited financial support from the West for unspecified economic development, which they claim must come first—and before all women's needs. Discrimination against women, they claim, will somehow disappear with large sums provided for 'development.'"[44] After the first two UN World Conferences on Women, Fulton was highly suspicious of the importance of development and derided Black Pan-African women's organizing around it.

Five years later, after Nairobi, Fulton did an about-face. "The [Nairobi] Conference in many ways belonged to the African and Asian women," she wrote approvingly. "Women of the world had been gathered together for the third time in ten years: the greatest of all 'happenings' of this century occurred." While Fulton remained more committed to the UN Women's Decade theme of peace than she did to the other two themes of development and equality, she spoke encouragingly of efforts to increase spending on "development" and "the basic needs of women and children for clean water, adequate food and shelter." She condemned "the mega-projects of the multinationals, the banks" and called for "a new kind of world order" based on "sharing the world's resources." Her words after the Nairobi conference supported the demand for a new international economic order that AAWORD's members and so many other people, especially from the Global South, had called for since 1974. Fulton also echoed the talking points of the field trips that Gachukia's team of Kenya-based organizers had put on to take conference attendees to observe the hard physical labor of rural women—staged and curated displays that, for Fulton and in a slew of international press accounts of the conference, hit their intended mark.

This message about the necessity of development as a precondition for women's equality (with men *and* among women of the world) and as core to the international women's movement had been further highlighted in many of the thousands of workshops and official plenaries in Nairobi. Fulton was convinced: "What made the experience at Nairobi so exciting and positive was that the Conference took place in Africa." For African women, she noted, "having their land turned into cash crops—which are used in turn to buy military goods—in no way serves their needs." In Fulton's account, as in others, this acknowledgment of unequal standards of living and access to basic needs among women is a large part of what fostered the emotional unity of the conference. "As women from all parts of the world shared their problems in Nairobi, the sense of sisterhood and solidarity strengthened. The women of the world were at peace with each other."[45] Noteworthy is that in Fulton's understanding of development, and in the visions of development that Gachukia and many of the Pan-African women's organizing put forth in Nairobi, the term included economic redistribution from above. These were not the neoliberal politics that so many scholars have observed underpinned Women in Development policymaking since the 1970s; this was, among other things, a call for a form of Women in Development that entailed a redistribution of wealth and control over resources as one part of a larger strategy to give women more control over their lives.

Margaret Fulton was not the only person to get on board with the importance of development—and, at times, with a fundamental redistribution of global resources akin to what the NIEO called for—to feminism because of the Third UN World Conference in Nairobi in 1985. Descriptions of the conference repeatedly describe it as a crowning achievement of the UN women's movement, one that stitched over long-festering wounds between and within

Global North and South in politically deft ways. The formal conference summary for the European Commission, for example, claimed that the Nairobi NGO Forum created "a renewed spirit of solidarity" within the UN women's movement. "One journalist called the Forum '85 'not only the apotheosis of the Decade, but above all a powerful trampoline towards the next stage,'" crowed the report.[46] FEMNET's internal history remarked on this feat and noted its importance for national women's movements in Kenya. It called the Nairobi NGO Forum "the greatest thing that ever happened to the women of Kenya. It placed them and their programmes in the global limelight," particularly concerning "women's development projects" and their acceptance within the mainstream of UN women's organizing.[47]

Frictions Surrounding the Third UN World Conference on Women: Girls and Political Repression

Not all of the UN Third World Conference on Women in Nairobi was rosy. Two points are especially pertinent to this history of the growth of neoliberal feminism and the origins of the FEMNET-UNICEF lobbying campaign that would internationalize Girls in Development in the final UN World Conference on Women in Beijing. First, girls emerged as a flashpoint at the Nairobi conference in ways that challenged solidarity between Global North and South. Second, the very successes of the conference from a public relations perspective led to political backlash from the Kenyan state. This drove the African Women's Task Force, and then FEMNET, to rely on UNICEF even more heavily in order to shield itself as an institution and its individual members from governmental persecution. As the people behind the African Women's Task Force left Nairobi, morphed the organization into FEMNET in 1988, and began their girl-focused work with UNICEF in 1989, these two sets of political tensions would deepen.

Contentious fights over African girls broke out at the UN Third World Conference on Women in Nairobi. Multiple attendees remember tense discussions over the issue of female circumcision, female genital mutilation, or female genital modification—even the terminology involved has staked different political stances and sparked bitter debate.[48] In a summary of the Nairobi NGO Forum written in French in 1985, attendee Martine Gibert described "impassioned discussions" between "women from North and South" at the NGO Forum's workshop on "Traditional Practices Affecting Women's and Children's Health in Africa." The workshop's focus was on "genital mutilation, clitoridectomy and infibulation." On one side were "European NGOs and collectives campaigning for the abolition of these practices and, on the other, African women's organizations criticizing the former for focusing on the 'sensational' aspects of their health."⁴⁹ Shouting matches took place between women from Global North and South at the workshop and at the broader conference surrounding it—a continuation of similar fights that had broken out over the issue at the UN Second World Conference on Women in Copenhagen.⁵⁰

Decades later, Eddah Gachukia reflected on the girl-focused fights over female circumcision at the Nairobi World Conference on Women. "I remember my daughter who was in high school asking me, 'Mommy what is female circumcision?' It was a hot issue with northern feminists." Gachukia noted that these feminists came to Nairobi and "accused us of being complacent. However, African women came out strongly to say to their northern sisters that, when our children are malnourished, when many mothers die in childbirth . . . you choose to go under our skirts to identify our problems." She remembered, "We did not want little babies and girls circumcised. What we wanted was sensitization and educational campaigns in communities where this was happening." More, "we argued that banning female circumcision would force it underground. . . . The northern feminists disagreed with us. . . . They preferred militarization, an issue that continued to be divisive within the movement for many years."⁵¹

While Gachukia and Gibert described fights over female circumcision in Nairobi as divided along battle lines of Global North and South, the realities of the conflict were often more complex.⁵² Like Gachukia, many of the African delegates who were criticized by their peers from Western Europe and North America opposed the practice or felt ambivalent about it. Some people situated within the Global North argued for the need to place female circumcision within a wider context and/or to see how sensationalized the issue had been under European colonial and, later, North American hegemony on the continent. Multiple and sometimes divisive perspectives on female circumcision similarly existed within Black feminist and women of color movements.⁵³

Clear in discussions at the UN Third World Conference on Women in Nairobi was that the real and perceived status of the genitalia of African girls were vehicles through which racism, imperialism, and broader power dynamics within the transnational women's movement were contested. If the importance of development as a theme helped to bridge long-simmering tensions between women from Global North and South and evoked warm feelings of sisterhood and solidarity in Nairobi, discussions surrounding African girls' and women's genitalia were a space where these tensions boiled over. According to the dominant version of development that the UN Third World

Conference on Women in Nairobi put forth, the improvement of women's status in the Global South partially rested on a structural redistribution of global wealth. In this formulation, macroeconomic factors were intimately connected to women's labor roles within the family and within their local communities. Fights over girls in Nairobi served to point the finger back at the local level while divorcing the status of women and girls from the global economic system: in the discussions about female circumcision, local patriarchy, culture, and custom were largely to blame for women's inequalities in Africa while discussions of structural economic causes disappeared from the conversation. This tension over the necessary location of political change, and of patriarchy's causes and effects, would increasingly play out in and through discussions of African and Third World girls between the end of the UN Third World Conference on Women in Nairobi in 1985 and the start of the UN Fourth World Conference on Women in Beijing a decade later.

The second set of tensions surrounding the end of the UN Third World Conference on Women in Nairobi that is essential to this backstory of the FEMNET-UNICEF campaign that would internationalize Girls in Development concerns the Kenyan state. The Nairobi conference was a resounding success for Kenyan and Pan-African women's movements on many levels, including in the press. These successes alarmed the government of President Daniel arap Moi, which was then under mounting pressure to open multiparty elections in the single-party state. Moi had become president in 1978, the year that Jomo Kenyatta died, after serving as Kenyatta's vice president since 1967. In a bid to marginalize the role of rival political blocs in his new government and consolidate power, Moi overhauled the country's police and security services in the late 1970s, increased surveillance of political groups, and amended the constitution in 1982 to officially make Kenya a one-party state.[54]

This control and surveillance extended beyond the scope of high-level rivalries within and outside of the ruling party, the Kenya African National Union (KANU). Social welfare associations, human rights groups, student movements, and journalists were among those that the Moi government targeted for surveillance and, at times, torture, imprisonment, death, and disappearance during his time in office, which ended in 2002. State-sanctioned detainment, violence, and killings of political dissidents had long characterized governance in Kenya. This was true during Kenyatta's time in office (Tom Mboya's killing in 1969 is one of the most well-known cases) and, before that, in British practices of colonial governance (which included the mass detention, imprisonment, torture, and killings of suspected Mau Mau supporters). Moi's government continued to use both judicial and extrajudicial forms of political repression. These practices escalated in the face of growing human rights movements, the NGO boom of the 1980s, and increased calls for democratization at the end of the Cold War.[55]

The women who led the African Women's Task Force and the broader UN World Conference on Women from which it sprang were not exempt from state surveillance. Njoki Wainaina recalled years later that "when Kenya agreed to host the End of the Decade Conference in Nairobi, they did not know what they were agreeing to." The government "threatened to cancel the event" on multiple occasions. Political leaders "summoned" Nita Barrow "frequently" to Nairobi to discuss the World Conference. Wainaina recalls angrily pushing back against this repression in the lead-up to the conference: "We once wrote a bitter letter at midnight to the Government from Eddah's house, reminding them that they were the ones who committed Kenya to host the Forum and actually convened the NGO Organizing Committee" that Gachukia headed and Wainaina sat on.[56]

The public political successes of the 1985 World Conference on Women in Nairobi served only to escalate the backlash. Wainaina describes the government of Kenya becoming "frightened" by the NGO Forum "because it showed the political class the power of the woman."[57] FEMNET's internal history did not mince words when describing this blowback. "The women of the world took away with them the *Spirit of Nairobi*. The women of Kenya, however, got the backlash that deliberately and decisively fractured, destroyed, and quelched the women's movement—an onslaught from which Kenyan women have never fully recovered." This governmental repression—which "was so swift and unexpected that it left Kenya women wondering what had hit them"—prevented the NGO Steering Committee, the organizing team from the NGO Forum in Nairobi, from ever meeting again after the conference ended to discuss the outcomes and future steps.[58] Wainaina remembered, "Wrap-up meetings were cancelled at the last minute with no explanation. There was persecution of individual women leaders and great suspicion among different women's organizations. The women's movement was targeted for destruction."[59]

In practical terms, this destruction accompanied the governmental takeover of Maendeleo ya Wanawake, the largest women's organization in Kenya, in 1987 by presidential decree.[60] Maureen Ajiambo Muleka and Pontian Godfrey Okoth have written about how Moi forced Maendeleo ya Wanawake into becoming the "women's wing" of the ruling party, KANU, "using it to mobilize women to vote for him at the time when he stayed at the helm of the country's leadership for 23 years."[61] This included the 1988 elections in which Moi ran uncontested but used Maendeleo ya Wanawake to drum up voter turnout for him and KANU. The hostile takeover of the organization, in which Gachukia had previously served a leadership role, led to a "loss of donors" from Maendeleo ya Wanawake members and transformed its operations.[62] Rosemary Wanjiku Mbugua notes that "national leadership ruled the organization with an iron fist and the objectives for which it was established were shelved as it submerged itself in party activities and campaigns. . . . Corruption spread and pervaded the organization. . . . The net effect is that MYWO [Maendeleo ya Wanawake Organization] has never recovered from this era. Its image as a KANU appendage has proved difficult to erase."[63]

It was in this existentially threatening context that members of the African Women's Task Force struggled to continue operations after the UN Third World Conference on Women in 1985. Registering as a formal organization with the government of Kenya was a necessity for the Task Force to survive. Doing so would allow the African Women's Task Force to legally receive donations and would increase its legitimacy, among other things. However, Wainaina recounts that members of the government "opposed" the registration "with claims that we [the Task Force's founders] had not consulted them." She continues, "One time, our personal bank accounts were analysed after claims that we were getting a lot of money" in donations.[64]

In the years immediately after the end of the Nairobi conference, most of the Task Force's organizing took place informally. It focused on establishing bureaucratic, legal, and financial legitimacy. Eddah Gachukia remembers regularly hosting Njoki Wainaina and Norah Khadzini Olembo on the veranda of her home. There, they would "write proposals" for funding, drafted a "constitution to register" the organization "in order to have an office space," and strategized.[65]

Olembo was essential to this process. Born in 1941 to Quaker parents in colonial Kenya, Norah Khadzini Olembo has been celebrated as one of Kenya's "most brilliant scientific minds."[66] After pursuing a doctoral degree in biochemistry at the University of Nairobi and postdoctoral training in molecular biology in London, Olembo became the first professor of biochemistry in all of Africa, joining the faculty of the University of Nairobi.[67]

Olembo was deeply involved in the UN women's movement and the creation of the African Women's Task Force. In FEMNET's internal history, she described herself as an informal "secretary to Dr. Eddah Gachukia during the preparation for the Third World Conference on Women in NGO Forum in 1985 held in Nairobi." Olembo attended the fateful Arusha meeting that created the African Women's Task Force and was a founding member alongside Gachukia and Wainaina. Tongue in cheek, she recalled the headiness that surrounded the UN Third World Conference on Women: "there was extreme excitement from the women. . . . We felt effective and we even terrorized our men."[68] As the exhilaration of the conference wore off in the face of governmental backlash, Olembo continued to work with Gachukia and Wainaina behind the scenes on the bureaucratic humdrum of growing the Task Force. This work was essential to the public and formal establishment of the African Women's Task Force as a Pan-African organization focused on women in development. It led to the meeting in 1988 at which the African Women's Task Force would publicly establish itself and rebrand as the African Women's Communication and Development Network, or FEMNET.

The meeting that transformed the African Women's Task Force into FEMNET took place in Nairobi from April 11 to 15 of 1988. It brought together thirty-nine women from sixteen African countries to assess the progress made since the conclusion of the 1985 Nairobi World Conference. Attendees formally adopted a constitution for FEMNET and elected officers. They also discussed two papers presented at the conference on the importance of "networking for women's rights, and for increasing women's empowerment."[69]

In the face of ongoing opposition to FEMNET's formal registration with the government of Kenya, UNICEF's support continued to be essential for FEMNET's survival. In her opening section of the report that summarized the 1988 meeting that turned the African Women's Task Force into FEMNET, Eddah Gachukia thanked the many organizations that had donated money or services to the African Women's Task Force. She wrote, "UNICEF deserves special mention for hosting the Task Force Secretariat, a facility they have extended beyond the Task Force Meeting, until the formal registration of the Network."[70] FEMNET would continue to base their offices in UNICEF's Nairobi compound until it was finally able to register as an NGO in 1992, the same year that Kenya held its first multiparty elections—which Moi and his party won, despite widespread allegations of ballot stuffing and state-sanctioned electoral violence.

Conclusion

Was the hegemony of neoliberal feminism by the start of the twenty-first century, partially spread through the vehicle of Girls in Development, inevitable? Were the events of the previous chapter—the silencing of certain forms of knowledge and the circulation of neoliberal understandings of Girls in Development in their place as FEMNET and UNICEF worked together—the most likely outcomes of this history, predictable even? Asking these questions took us back to this story's beginning (or one of its beginnings): the emergence of the African Women's Task Force surrounding the UN Third World Conference on Women in Nairobi in 1985. Controversies over decolonizing the international system, including the United Nations' women's movement, provided the crucible from which the African Women's Task Force emerged. Members of the African Women's Task Force and the conference's Kenya-based organizing team successfully cemented development as a central concern of the UN women's movement. This was a form of development that went hand in hand with calls to redistribute global resources in order to alleviate the burdensome forms of labor that many women performed within their families and communities.

How did this moment—of the triumph of the organizing power of women from Africa, especially Kenya, to influence the outputs of the UN Women's Decade and the norms that it cemented regarding the need for structural change—morph into the forms of erasure that transpired in the previous chapter, which took place less than a decade later? And how did girls become the battleground for this fight and for a women's movement that would increasingly become neoliberal through its adoption of girl-focused development programming? African girls were a topic of heated disagreement at the UN Third World Conference on Women in Nairobi. The real and imagined sexual suffering of girls, and of African girls in particular, served as a space where various people fought over the causes of girls' and women's oppression and the necessary locus of change to address it—through high-level action to remake global economic and political systems or through a focus on the sexual and intimate lives of girls in Africa.

Also surrounding the 1985 World Conference on Women in Nairobi, repression from the government of Kenya and FEMNET's financial and organizational reliance on UNICEF constrained the forms of advocacy, political organizing, and knowledge sharing that FEMNET's members were able to undertake. These dynamics forced the members of the African Women's Task Force, and then FEMNET, into fraught relationships with both the government and UNICEF alike—relationships that contained a range of interactions, from collaborative support to outright hostility and everything in between. While hints of how this story would end emerge, so do gestures at alternative possible outcomes. The endpoint—the rise of neoliberal feminism and the erasures of competing frameworks from being codified in high-level norms at the Fourth UN World Conference on Women in Beijing in 1995—was neither a foregone conclusion nor entirely unexpected. This chapter ended with FEMNET's creation from the African Women's Task Force in 1988. In order to institutionally survive in the face of the Kenyan government's refusal to register FEMNET as an NGO, FEMNET's members looked to UNICEF's Nairobi offices to host their secretariat until 1992. During this period, the two institutions began to work together to define and then internationalize Girls in Development before they successfully lobbied to include a special section on the girl child in the outputs of the UN Fourth World Conference on Women in Beijing. The next two chapters focus on this "girl turn"—the shift to girls as a locus of development planning within UNICEF and FEMNET.

3

Neoliberal Austerity Births Girl-Focused Economic Development at UNICEF

How did *girls* become central to development efforts, especially within the UNICEF-FEMNET lobbying campaign that would internationalize Girls in Development at the Fourth UN World Conference on Women in Beijing in 1995? This chapter shows how ideas about girls as economic investments grew within UNICEF and the global network in which the agency was situated in the 1980s. It explores how UNICEF's staff increasingly singled out girls as a locus for development planning in the context of the global economic crisis stemming back to the oil shocks of the 1970s and neoliberal cuts to the welfare state that followed. Girl power frameworks for economic development grew within the context of a perceived crisis in capitalism, the "neoliberal turn," and anxieties about widening global inequalities in wealth and health. It was against this backdrop that girls became key sites for economic development planning, initially within UNICEF and then among a broader swath of actors.

The adoption of girls as a site of development planning within UNICEF devolved calls for top-down changes to the global economic system into a discussion of the need to empower girls to serve as agents of development from below. In the process, custom, culture, and patriarchy enacted within the family became increasingly blamed for the intertwined problems of women's inequality and poverty. What started within the agency as a critique of the global economic system for its impact on children morphed, through a growing focus on girls, into a critique of local patriarchy and cultures. In policy terms, this entailed a shift from advocacy for high-level changes, such as for a new international economic order and the expansion of national welfare state programming, to individualistic solutions focused on girls and their families under the status quo of austerity capitalism. The individually focused interventions that UNICEF favored as the 1980s wore on often included free-market initiatives such as microcredit loans financed by for-profit lenders and public-private partnerships to promote girls' basic education and empowerment.

Locating UNICEF in the Shift from Women in Development to Girls in Development

In 1990, UNICEF published a book written by Agnes Akosua Aidoo declaring the "development of the girl child" to be "one of the most productive investments a country can make." In this formulation, the physical and psychological development of girls, especially in the Global South, was inseparably bound with the economic and social development of nations and "the global fight against poverty."[1] Aidoo, born in Ghana and educated internationally, was then a senior adviser for development programs for women at UNICEF's headquarters in New York City. An overriding logic of the book appeared in its title: *The Girl Child: An Investment in the Future*. Initially, UNICEF disseminated the publication as one section of a larger volume produced in advance of the World Summit for Children of 1990, a hallmark in the global children's rights movement.[2] Later that year, UNICEF published an expanded version of Aidoo's section as a stand-alone book with the same title, *The Girl Child: An Investment in the Future*.

Existing histories of Girls in Development, and of how it came to be neoliberal, frequently cite Lawrence "Larry" Summers. The chief economist of the World Bank from 1991 to 1993, Summers would go on to serve in high-level positions in the Clinton and Obama administrations in the United States. He would also become the president of Harvard University. In 1992, Summers stated, "Educating girls quite possibly yields a higher rate of return than any other investment available in the developing world."[3] Summers repeated multiple versions of this quotation, from the opening line of his essay in the journal *Scientific American* to his keynote lecture at the Pakistan Society of Development Economists in Islamabad to his foreword in the World Bank's publication *Women's Education in Developing Countries*.[4] Various versions of this statement—always emphasizing that girls' education was the best "investment available in the developing world"—have been a staple in booming literature on girlhood studies since about 2010. In critiquing the neoliberal economic underpinnings of girl power as unrealistic or disingenuous (partly illustrated by Summers's own chauvinism in a widely publicized set of remarks from 2005, when he questioned girls' and women's scientific intellect), many of these studies trace the origins of free-market, girl-focused frameworks to Larry Summers and his employer, the World Bank, in the early 1990s.

The existing tendency to center Larry Summers is part of a broader trend to locate the origins of Girls in Development with the usual suspects in broader histories of neoliberal capitalism: the Chicago school of economics, the World Bank, and the United States Agency for International Development (USAID). Collectively, scholars such as Kathryn Moeller, Michelle Murphy, and Sydney Calkin have traced the prehistory of Girls in Development to the Chicago school of economics after the end of World War II, when future Nobel Prize–winning economists Theodore Schultz and Gary Becker championed human capital theory. Claudia Goldin sums up human capital theory as "the notion that there are investments in people (e.g., education, training, health) and that these investments increase an individual's productivity."[5] Moeller and Calkin then examine the application of human capital theory to the Women in Development movement of the 1970s and beyond, via the notion that women were "untapped human capital resources" whose labor could drive development.[6] Epitomized in the Danish economist Ester Boserup's classic tome *Women's Role in Economic Development*, the guiding assumption of Women in Development was that orthodox development planning, which blossomed after World War II, failed to achieve many of its objectives because it did not properly acknowledge or incorporate women's labor.[7]

A number of scholars, including Moeller, Murphy, and Joanne Meyerowitz, note the embrace of Women in Development within the World Bank and USAID between the 1970s and 1990s, precisely when both institutions were critical to the neoliberal turn embodied in the Washington Consensus. Within these narratives, in the 1990s, leaders of USAID and the World Bank, such as Summers, vociferously argued that girls were untapped sources of human capital. This marked a pivotal shift from Women in Development to *Girls* in Development as a key framework for economic development planning. Finally, Murphy, Moeller, Calkin, and a number of other scholars follow the spread of Girls in Development out from the World Bank and USAID to a bevy of corporations, corporate foundations, NGOs, and other actors in the late 1990s and early 2000s, from Credit Suisse and the Nike Foundation to Plan International and the Clinton Global Initiative, to name just a few.[8]

While many parts of this narrative are true, it is incomplete. And it is incomplete in ways that elide a more troubled origin story, both for Girls in Development and for neoliberal capitalism more broadly. There are a variety of ways to complicate this narrative—including through a history of the growth of woman-focused development frameworks and human resource theories (different from but linked to human capital theory) in socialist and communist development planning in various parts of the Eastern Bloc and

Global South.[9] For the purposes of this history, we will focus on how, where, and when the shift from Women in Development to Girls in Development took place. Summers's statements from 1992 about girls' education providing a "higher rate of return than any other investment available in the developing world" are eerily similar to the arguments of UNICEF employee Agnes Akosua Aidoo in 1990, when she declared the "development of the girl child" to be "one of the most productive investments a country can make." Her comments, in turn, built on advocacy within UNICEF and a connected set of actors from as early as 1983. UNICEF's flagship publication was the annual *State of the World's Children*, a set of assessments and policy recommendations that guided programming both within the agency and among a broader network of child-focused organizations. The 1983 version of the publication, authored by UNICEF's executive director, James Grant, stated that educating girls for at least four years represented "one of the most cost-effective investments in which any country can make its own future."[10] Grant's logic, in turn, drew from long-standing colonial development and nationalist frameworks, especially in Africa, Asia, and Latin America. These frameworks emphasized the importance of educating and properly socializing women and girls—usually as future mothers, wives, and care workers—to achieving progress, morality, and prosperity.

Placing UNICEF at the center of this history helps to complicate overly one-dimensional understandings of how neoliberal capitalism grew and spread internationally. It was not a conspiracy theory driven by a tiny cadre of global elites who duped or solely strong-armed others into adopting neoliberal austerity. Pressuring fiscal-crisis-laden state governments into signing loan agreements that would require them to slash state spending on social safety nets were indeed sometimes part of the World Bank and IMF's behaviors in the 1980s and 1990s, as many scholars have shown.[11] But this is not *only* a story of coercion. In the case of girl-focused economic development, the narrative that economies could develop and prosper if only girls received a basic education and gained self-esteem—and that this kind of girl-focused programming could replace calls for a new international economic order or could blunt the sharpest edges of widespread cuts to state funding, including to public education and health care—served as less of a coercive policy framework than a seductive humanitarian fantasy. People across the political spectrum and in many parts of the world embraced it.

At the same time, placing UNICEF at the center of the turn to girl-focused economic development frameworks also widens the lens so that neoliberal capitalism is not the only subject in focus. Doing so makes space for other kinds of stories about girls, their status, their education, and the economy to be told. It also problematizes how and why these other stories became eclipsed as Girls in Development started to universalize in the early 1990s. Centering UNICEF within the history of the girl turn in development planning serves as one step in a broader history of contingency that the book tells. It does not assume that neoliberal feminism was the natural, inevitable, or only outcome of the end of the Cold War or of flaws embedded in what many people still call "second wave" feminism.[12] Likewise for neoliberal development planning. Instead, it problematizes why, how, where, and under what conditions this merger of free-market capitalism and feminism took place through the vehicle of girl-focused development programs. The result is a story of how girls increasingly served as the imagined battlefield for debates over an ongoing global economic downturn, cuts to the welfare state, and the perceived crisis in capitalism and in human well-being that these events—often dubbed "the neoliberal turn"—provoked during the final years of the Cold War and in its aftermath as particular forms of feminism internationalized, often at the expense of others.

UNICEF Partially Retreats from Alma Ata and the New International Economic Order

In the spring of 1983, the head of the World Health Organization (WHO), Halfdan Mahler, publicly denounced UNICEF for undermining the principles that had been established in support of the New International Economic Order. Mahler was a Danish physician who served as WHO's director-general from 1973 to 1988. In a speech to WHO delegates in Geneva in 1983, he directed his ire at UNICEF for reneging on the agreements that had been established at the Alma Ata Conference on Primary Health Care. WHO and UNICEF had jointly hosted the conference in 1978. It was held in Alma Ata, the largest city in what was then the Kazakh Soviet Socialist Republic.

Health care journals and pundits have regularly described the Alma Ata conference as a "landmark" and "groundbreaking" for the global provision of public health care.[13] The conference was motivated by efforts to promote a new international economic order.[14] Discussed in the previous chapter, the NIEO that the UN General Assembly voted to adopt in 1974 had demanded a decolonization of the international system and a more equitable distribution of global resources. The "full and effective participation . . . of all countries in the solving of world economic problems" lay at the heart of the NIEO.[15] This vision of "participation" involved giving the neediest countries in the "developing world" more control over the high-level international policies, such as financial and trade agreements, that hampered their "economic and social development" and that undermined global "peace and justice."[16]

In support of the NIEO, the Declaration of the Alma Ata Conference of 1978 that UNICEF and WHO jointly hosted called for a global embrace of "primary health care." This vision of primary health care was based largely on encouraging "community and individual self-reliance and participation" in health. But this was not the kind of individualism that would underpin later neoliberal calls for bootstrapping self-help. The individualism of Alma Ata rested on giving people authority over the "planning, organization, [and] operation" of health care. It was about devolving "control" over health-related decisions to the lowest levels.[17]

The Alma Ata conference outputs depicted change from above as essential to meeting the needs of individuals and communities. They argued that national governments and the international community needed to listen to these bottom-up demands and "channel increased technical and financial support" to meet them. Robust, state-led social welfare programming in the provision of "food . . . education, housing," and more were essential to the forms of primary health care that the Alma Ata conference promoted.[18] China's million "barefoot doctors"—medical professionals deployed en masse to rural areas as a staple of Mao Zedong's Cultural Revolution—had a particularly strong influence on the conceptions of primary health care put forth in Alma Ata.[19]

Five years after the Alma Ata conference ended, WHO Executive Director Halfdan Mahler publicly denounced UNICEF for backing away from the commitments adopted there in his 1983 Geneva speech. Mahler condemned UNICEF and its new head, James Grant, for promoting a watered down and distorted version of primary health care, dubbed "selective primary health care." Mahler would regularly reiterate his condemnations to the WHO during his tenure as its head and after his retirement from the organization in 1988. In Mahler's view, selective primary health care—an "ominous name"— "reflected the biases of national and international donors and not the needs and demands of developing countries."[20] It was, in Mahler's eyes, a betrayal of the sweeping structural changes that Alma Ata called for in favor of piecemeal interventions that upheld the interests of those already in power.

An internally produced UNICEF history also reflected on Mahler's attacks on the children's agency embrace of "selective primary health care," rather than full primary health care, in the wake of Alma Ata. It claimed that "on Unicef's side, there was a feeling of both betrayal and misunderstanding at this unnecessarily public castigation."[21] James P. Grant was UNICEF's executive director from 1980 to 1995. An American born to a medical missionary family in Beijing in 1922, Grant held an economics degree from UC Berkeley and a Harvard law degree. Before joining UNICEF, Grant worked for USAID. He then helped to found the Overseas Development Council in 1969. A brainchild of the Ford and Rockefeller Foundations, the Overseas Development Council arose in the United States during the Cold War. Its aim was to funnel corporate philanthropic aid to development projects in parts of the world threatened by what Grant called the "anarchy and subversion" created by "the revolution of rising expectations" for the quality of life.[22] Grant was, in other words, a humanitarian and public health advocate whose own career had long been entangled with efforts of the US government and US-based corporate philanthropies to counter communist and leftist revolutionary influences via development planning. He took over as UNICEF's head two years after his predecessor, Henry R. Labouisse, had led the agency in co-hosting the Alma Ata conference in support of the NIEO.

Under the leadership of James Grant, UNICEF's embrace of selective primary health care served as a way to shift the location of change to promote health and development away from the international system and robust, state-led social welfare programming and onto individuals, families, and communities. Using some of the same language as the Alma Ata Declaration about "participation," "cost-effectiveness," and "efficiency," UNICEF divorced these terms from their accompanying prescriptions for changes at the macroeconomic level and the creation or beefing up of nationally run universal health care systems. By calling for a "children's revolution" that relied largely on mothers, and then girls, for its implementation, UNICEF's leadership did an end run around the NIEO. They promoted versions of health care and development that could be achieved from below, without large-scale changes to the international system or redistributions in global resources.

Economic Crisis and Cuts to the Welfare State Birth a Children's Revolution

In 1982, UNICEF's flagship publication, *The State of the World's Children*, began with a stark statistic: roughly 40,000 children around the world were dying every day, totaling nearly 14.5 million child deaths per year.[23] The vast majority of these deaths resulted from preventable causes such as malnutrition and disease, which affected roughly one-quarter of children in the "developing world," according to the multihundred-page document.[24] Such high child death rates marked a departure from UNICEF's previously documented trends in child health and mortality. "Between the end of World War II and the beginning of the 1970s," *The State of the World's Children* argued, "child death rates in the low-income countries were reduced by half. Yet in recent years that progress has not been maintained." In some cases, children's quality of life and physical well-being were now worse off. This was true "for many of the children in the developing countries, particularly in Africa and in the poorest urban neighborhoods of Asia and Latin America," where "the quality of life has actually begun to fall as the foothold of their parents begins to crumble."[25]

UNICEF's official institutional stance—under the leadership of Grant, alongside British Deputy Director Richard Jolly (introduced in this book's introduction) and Italian Chief Economist Giovanni Andrea Cornia—attributed these negative changes in rates of mortality, poverty, illness, and living standards to a few interwoven causes. The first was the global recession. Punctuated by the oil shocks of the 1970s, changes in US monetary policy in 1979, and the debt crises of the early 1980s, the recession impacted locales differently but lasted longer and hit harder in Africa, Latin America, and deindustrializing regions of the North Atlantic. A series of UNICEF studies detailed the devastation the economic downturn wreaked: plummeting prices for raw commodities and spikes in inflation and unemployment translated into declining incomes in industries from coffee growing in Latin America and Africa to steel working in the North American Rust Belt. As people across the globe saw their standards of living drop or felt economic instability, UNICEF's staff noted that children often suffered disproportionately.[26]

The second set of causes that UNICEF's public-facing advocacy identified in the early 1980s, when the agency's staff depicted a crisis in human survival, were the economic measures nominally adopted to stem the carnage of the global recession: cuts to welfare state spending, often implemented through structural adjustment programs.[27] The World Bank and IMF offered structural adjustment programs to national governments around the world from the early 1980s onward. The programs were particularly widespread across Latin America, Africa, and Asia. Structural adjustment provided loans to national governments that were unable to pay the interest rates on their existing debt because of inflation and the global economic downturn. In exchange, these governments agreed to reduce public spending on education, health care, and housing; privatize or deregulate state-managed industries; open up countries to foreign investors; and implement hiring freezes, layoffs, or salary cuts to civil servants. While neoliberal capitalism is commonly associated with Margaret Thatcher and Ronald Reagan in the Global North, structural adjustment was a vehicle for the spread of neoliberal cuts to the welfare state and the further integration of countries into global capitalist markets across much of the Global South.[28]

In the early to mid-1980s, UNICEF regularly criticized economic austerity measures for their impacts on child welfare.[29] As one example, in 1984, UNICEF published a volume of studies, edited by Deputy Director Jolly and Chief Economist Cornia, titled *The Impact of World Recession on Children*. In their introduction to the book, Jolly and Cornia denounced structural adjustment programs for leading to a reduction in state spending on "child-focused" programs. They also condemned broader forms of "international influence" that led governments to cut social welfare beyond the confines of structural adjustment.[30] In the volume's conclusion, Cornia blamed these neoliberal reforms for increasing children's rates of "poverty" and "death."[31]

One of the case studies in *The Impact of World Recession on Children* focused on Tanzania. It noted that the country's government, led by Julius Nyerere—a titan of Pan-Africanism and a particular brand of socialist internationalism—"succumbed to pressure from the IMF and World Bank to liberalize imports" beginning in 1977.[32] This, combined with the impacts of the global recession, caused a debt crisis in the country in the early 1980s that followed a similar pattern to many countries around the world. The government of Tanzania adopted a series of structural adjustment programs in the years that followed. As a result, the state's annual expenditures on basic needs fell by almost one-third between 1977 and 1982. Because of these cuts and the "debilitating economic crisis" that Tanzania continued to face in the early 1980s, children's immunization levels, "after rising" during the 1970s, had "fallen back to perhaps one-third its peak level. . . . A comparable situation exists in education."[33] The amount of food that children received diminished to levels insufficient for survival. The result, the publication argued, was that child mortality levels were increasing and life expectancy decreasing.[34]

UNICEF's publications from the early to mid-1980s contained many case studies like the one for Tanzania. Most followed a similar pattern: an external (global) economic crisis precipitated cuts to welfare state spending on the provision of health care, education, housing allocation, food production, and/or wage protections, often at the behest of the IMF and World Bank. Analysis about how all of this led to more children and youth dying, being sick, or otherwise suffering followed. Through this and a number of other studies, UNICEF's publications from the early to mid-1980s—especially those to which Jolly and Cornia were attached—argued that slashing welfare state spending in many countries during the recession increased child death and illness.

Beyond the recession and the welfare-state-cutting economic austerity measures widely implemented in their wake, UNICEF's staff and the network of scholars and policymakers they collaborated with in the 1980s argued that 14.5 million children were now dying each year from largely preventable causes because of a fundamentally inequitable global balance of power. *The State of the World's Children 1984* contained one of many instances in which the agency's leaders denounced the skewed geopolitical system: "The industrialized nations, containing a quarter of the world's people, still control more than three quarters of the world's wealth." This, according to Executive Director Grant, "gives them the power to lay down the rules of world trade, regulate the workings of the international monetary system," and design global economic systems to serve "their own interests." The outcome of such an unbalanced geopolitical order was that "the majority of developing countries have correspondingly little control over" the economic conditions in which the people in them build their lives. Grant, speaking for UNICEF as an institution, argued that such an international system had a "direct effect" on child survival.[35] A number of UNICEF advocacy materials, including *The Impact of World Recession on Children*, attributed the origins of these "structural" causes of poverty to imperialism and colonialism—or, as Cornia put it, to "colonial inheritance" and "the overall dependence of many developing countries on the industrialized nations."[36]

UNICEF's leadership and staff were far from alone in making these kinds of arguments. They were staples of dependency theory since the 1940s, which rose in challenge to orthodox models of development planning that had boomed after World War II.[37] Hans Singer, one of the architects of dependency theory, was one of two authors of the Tanzanian case study mentioned above that UNICEF published; the United Nations Children's Fund regularly collaborated with well-known development economists and other scholars who challenged orthodox development planning to show the connections between different kinds of development planning and children's well-being. Where UNICEF began to differ from some of its individual collaborators, and certainly from the WHO's leadership, lay in how to fix the problem.

James Grant argued that the money and political headwinds involved in achieving high-level policy changes prevented their implementation. In the same document in which he stated the need for macro-level "fundamental changes" to fix the root causes of "malnutrition and life-denying poverty," Grant claimed they were too "slow and painful" to expect to occur in the near future.[38] "As the half-way point in the 1980s approaches," he wrote, this "high road to economic development remains almost impassable. . . . Progress towards a more just and workable international economic order remains becalmed."[39]

In the face of what UNICEF's leadership interpreted as an immutable political reality and the unlikelihood of the NIEO coming to fruition, they called for what they saw as a more achievable set of solutions to the upswing in the number of sick and dying children around the world. This included the utilization of "low-cost opportunities," increasing the efficiency of existing resources, and "making more of what you have," particularly through the development of the human capital of women and children.[40] In the end, UNICEF's short-term answer to a crisis in child survival was not to work to change the geopolitical system from above—it was to foment change from below via a children's revolution.

UNICEF outlined its children's revolution in *The State of the World's Children 1982–83*, one of the same documents that began with the ominous information that over fourteen million children around the world were dying each year due to the "dark times" ushered in by the global economic downturn, austerity, and widening gaps in wealth stemming from macroeconomic causes.[41] In the publication, Grant called for a "children's revolution"— interchangeably called a "child revolution"—that promised to cut the rates of child mortality and malnutrition in half by the start of the new millennium and decrease population growth. The mechanisms for this revolution consisted of four interventions in basic health care under the widely used acronym of GOBI: *growth* charts to monitor children's height and weight percentiles, *oral* rehydration therapy to combat diarrhea, an increase in maternal *breastfeeding* of infants, and universal *immunization* of children against preventable diseases.[42]

The GOBI initiatives built on proposals put forth at a Rockefeller Foundation–sponsored conference in 1979. Afterward, they were fleshed out in a yearlong study that UNICEF's staff conducted. This study, in turn, built on existing work from the World Bank, WHO, and United Nations Development Program.[43] UNICEF's leadership voted to formally adopt GOBI at a two-day meeting of the agency's New York City headquarters in September 1982.[44]

By implementing the GOBI-driven children's revolution, Grant argued, fewer children would die. At the same time, there would not be a short-term need for "the economic and political changes which are necessary in the longer term if poverty itself is to be eradicated."[45] Grant was repeatedly clear from 1982 onward that the institution's measures were intended to be cost-effective, immediate solutions to child mortality and malnutrition and would not require structural changes to the global political and economic order from above.

UNICEF's calls for a children's revolution gained widespread praise from many of the international leaders who were championing the implementation of neoliberal economic reforms in the early 1980s. The UNICEF annual report covering 1983 recounts a conversation between Grant and Margaret Thatcher. The Iron Lady reportedly called UNICEF's children's revolution "very exciting." Yet it was not only the Thatcherites who supported the children's revolution. Leading figures who occupied different spaces in an international environment structured by the contentious economic politics of the Cold War and decolonization also embraced it. Indian Prime Minister Indira Gandhi (a populist socialist), Swedish Prime Minister Olof Palme (head of the country's Social Democratic Party), and French Prime Minister Pierre Mauroy (a Socialist Party leader who served alongside President Mitterand) were just a few of the world leaders who endorsed the children's revolution.[46]

But not everyone was enamored. As head of the WHO, Halfdan Mahler repeatedly criticized GOBI as a retreat from the aspirational principles of Alma Ata and as catering to the wishes of international donors at the expense of the promotion of health care norms and policymaking connected to the NIEO. Many of GOBI's other critics were health care professionals, practitioners, and researchers. One was Ben Wisner, a professor at Hampshire College in Massachusetts, whose criticism of GOBI appeared in the journal *Social Science and Medicine*. "UNICEF is dangerously mistaken in believing that its present emphasis on selective primary health care is a precursor or 'leading edge' of comprehensive primary health care," he wrote. Wisner condemned GOBI for undercutting the needs of local communities and re-entrenching foreign control over health in ways that fundamentally worked against the community empowerment principles of Alma Ata. He also criticized GOBI's economic politics. "UNICEF's so-called revolution has in common with other selective approaches an ideology accepting as inevitable the health effects of economic crisis in the 1980s, further undermining the confidence of local groups and health workers who might otherwise conceive of their desire to control health conditions as a right." He determined that GOBI "should either be abandoned or integrated into comprehensive primary health care programs that put parents and local workers in control."[47] Wisner was not alone in his criticisms; for him, Mahler, and others, the agency had been too hasty to abandon the principles of the NIEO and the various primary health care schemes that attempted to support it.

Integrating Women and Girls into GOBI

How did girls become an increasing focus of the children's revolution and of UNICEF's embrace of selective primary health care, which was interwoven with the neoliberal turn of the late 1970s and 1980s? Soon after UNICEF launched the GOBI-driven revolution, the organization continued to grapple with mounting evidence about the devastation wrought by the economic collapse, structural adjustment, and an imbalanced world order. It was in this context that UNICEF's leadership added three critical components to the children's revolution in 1983. All three of the additions revolved around women and girls.

Through the "three F's"—(1) "food supplements" to pregnant women, (2) "family planning" targeting potential mothers, and (3) "female education"— James Grant and UNICEF's public advocacy argued that child health and the development of the Global South could be promoted without a radical expansion of state-run "official health services," "modern" health care, or large-scale economic and political change.[48] In *The State of the World's Children 1984*, Grant defined women as "the mother of change." He claimed the three F's would foster efficiency in the delivery of health care by "empowering women" to ensure the health and survival of their children as frontline health care providers within the unit of the nuclear family.[49]

The first of the three F's advocated for the provision of food and vitamin supplements to pregnant women. The crux of the argument was that increasing pregnant women's daily food intake by a small number of calories and nutrients would combat the birth of premature infants and babies with too low of a birth weight. More, Grant argued, the first F was "cost-effective."[50] Rather than directly providing pregnant women with food and vitamin supplements, Grant advocated for an increase in food production by giving farmers access to microcredit from banks. These kinds of for-profit, market-based solutions that relied on increasing individual indebtedness looked markedly different from the proposals put forth in Alma Ata. Here, the locus of imagined action—and of who should hold the debt of the future—shifted from the state to individuals and local communities. It was in this vein that UNICEF's advocacy further called for increased farm labor on the part of "poor people" to produce the food and nutrients necessary to supplement pregnant women's diets in order to meet the first F. Through an increase in agricultural labor that produced more food for pregnant women, Grant argued, newborn death rates and malnutrition would decrease, and mothers would have an "energy bank" from which to draw for future breastfeeding. More well-fed children would, in turn, create more "energy," "productivity," "income," and "investment in community development in the future."[51] The language of women, children, and girls as financial investments, often couched through the language of banking and economic growth, featured prominently in GOBI-FFF.

Family planning was the second of the three F's that UNICEF added to its embrace of selective primary health care. Arguing for the importance of child spacing and for women to bear children at specific points in their own lives, *The State of the World's Children 1984* used the mantra "too close, too many, too old or too young" to explain the risks posed to both mother and child in certain forms of pregnancy. "Too close" meant having too many children close together, "too many" meant having too many children at all, "too old" referred to mothers who had children later in life, and "too young" referred to mothers who had children too early, according to UNICEF's calculus. While the agency's advocacy materials cited a number of studies showing that women around the world generally knew that too many children born too close together was bad for their own health, they framed the issue as a problem of women not having sufficient comprehension or "control over their own fertility." The solution, Grant argued, was "empowering mothers with the knowledge and means" to use family planning measures. Family planning was also a staple of the proposals put forth in Alma Ata. However, rather than relying primarily on expanded state programming to provide family planning services, UNICEF emphasized the increasing importance of private and nongovernmental organizations in connecting individuals with the knowledge and technology necessary to further child spacing as part of the second F of the GOBI-FFF child revolution.[52]

More, according to UNICEF's internal historian and former employee Maggie Black, Grant refused to explicitly endorse the use of contraceptives as part of UNICEF's call for more family planning through the second F because he wished to sidestep contentious politics over "contraception and abortion." Instead, "Grant ducked the issue entirely. He wanted UNICEF to have no part in promoting contraception either on grounds of women's reproductive rights or for the sake of population control. At the same time, he wanted to avoid criticism." Black writes that Grant maneuvered around this "apparent contradiction" by arguing that mothers who used GOBI to have fewer children die would naturally have less children once they knew more would survive into adulthood. The approach, Black notes, "was popular neither with the international health and planning community nor with those active on behalf of women's rights." UNICEF's stance on contraception and abortion differed from the approaches of the WHO, the UN Population Fund, and the World Bank. There were, Black writes, "donors Grant was naturally anxious not to offend" by explicitly promoting women's access to contraception or abortions.[53]

The third and final F that UNICEF's leadership added to the core components of the children's revolution was "female education." Partly underpinning this call to action was the belief that "the mother" is the most important provider of children's health care. The 1983 *State of the World's Children* cited a handful of studies to argue that educated mothers had fewer children, healthier children, and more children survive into adulthood.[54]

According to Grant and UNICEF's high-level advocacy from 1983 onward, the world could foment a "social breakthrough" in which educated girls gained the information and "confidence" necessary to embrace the new technologies and knowledge that would stem the rising tide of child mortality and poor health. Building on their earlier advocacy for the utilization of "human capital" rather than more financial capital—money—in order to address the crisis in health and mortality brought about by the recession and shift to austerity, Grant argued that educated and confident girls would be inclined toward more "participation" to ensure the health and well-being of their future children and societies. "Empowering women" by "investing in a minimum of four years at school for every girl is one of the most cost-effective investments which any country can make in its own future," wrote Grant.[55] For UNICEF, the dividends that girls' education would pay in health care could occur even with "low levels of economic development," ongoing structural adjustment programs, and the existing geopolitical order.[56]

It is important to note here that, as with the second F, UNICEF's actual programming related to the third F sometimes undermined its rhetoric. Despite UNICEF's insistence on the importance of female education, Maggie Black—whom James Grant personally invited to write the two internal histories of UNICEF that she produced in 1986 and 1996—notes that UNICEF's expenditures on "formal and non-formal education" actually fell by more than US$4 million between 1983 and 1987, from $40.4 million to $36 million—a reduction of roughly 10 percent.[57] To put this in context, UNICEF's budget grew by about two-thirds during this same period, increasing from $342 million in 1983 to $576 million in 1987.[58] Black wrote that "the presentation of GOBI as a formula for women's empowerment caused some anguish among senior women in UNICEF" who viewed the agency's claims to empowering women via GOBI as disingenuous.[59] Maggie Black's book from 1996, from which the aforementioned quotations originate, is publicly available on UNICEF's website. It is curious that the full book is posted there, minus Black's thirty-one-page chapter on "The Gender Dimension," which contains her critiques of the three F's attached to GOBI and UNICEF's broader policymaking focused on girls and women.[60]

Despite Black's criticism that UNICEF did not always put its money where its mouth was, GOBI-FFF was influential as a rhetorical device. It proposed a set of norms that moved the location of action to address interconnected problems of development and health care away from macroeconomic policymaking and welfare state programming to individuals and parents within the imagined unit of the nuclear heterosexual family in the Global South. Lenses of individualism and parental responsibility guided much of UNICEF's expanded girl- and woman-oriented children's revolution. The language of "empowerment" figured prominently in this line of argumentation. "Parents must be empowered" to ensure their children's well-being, Grant claimed, not only by directly combating child mortality and malnutrition but by taking familial action in favor of "economic justice" and against the "poverty" and "inequality" driving them.[61] To fight poverty stemming from the global economic level, UNICEF publicly promoted a new ethos of "self-reliance" and enhanced parental "participation in health." In turn, the agency's official line claimed that individuals and families could seize technological advances in health care to save their own children.[62] This was, again, a stark departure from the Alma Ata conference, which used the terms *participation* and *self-reliance* as part of a larger process through which the needs and desires of individuals, families, and communities would drive changes in policymaking at the international and national levels.

If educated and empowered girls, as investments and future mothers, were a proposed mechanism of implementing the GOBI-FFF children's revolution, UNICEF's leadership often depicted patriarchy as the stumbling block. Grant claimed that educating girls to become proper mothers was too often stymied by "resistance" to girls' education and the patriarchal "fear that it might lead to the emancipation" of women in much of the world. This claim partially contradicted data that the agency presented on the rapid growth of girls' school enrollment around the world. *The State of the World's Children* claimed that 34 percent of six-year-old girls were enrolled in school "in the poorest half of the world" in 1960. By 1980, that figure reportedly jumped to 80 percent. Yet girls' formal education in "low-income countries" still lagged behind that of boys, with nine out of ten boys of all ages and only six out of ten girls reportedly enrolled in formal education in 1980. UNICEF publicly blamed this continued gender-based educational disparity on "society" and the poor decision-making of parents living in "poverty." Grant argued that poor parents often used girls' labor as "help with household tasks and childcare" and did not view the benefits of girls' education as worth the "expense." As a result, UNICEF's public communications argued that poor parents— often guided by patriarchal fear—failed to make "an investment which could improve life tomorrow [but] is withdrawn to help cope with life today."[63]

The agency's logic directly built on that used in the 1980 *World Bank Development Report*. It approached girls' school attendance through the analytical framework of rational choice theory, a hallmark of neoclassical, and then neoliberal, economics that was resuscitated during the Cold War and has since underpinned many studies in economics and other social science fields.[64] UNICEF's logic on the barriers to girls' school access made gender-based disparities in education and broader society appear to be the results of "cultural" factors, behavior, and bad parental decision-making rather than the result of complex historical factors stemming in part from the fact that colonial education systems initially did not accept female students and/or focused heavily on educating boys for paid work outside of the home and girls for unremunerated work inside of it.[65] It also dismissed the data that UNICEF had previously presented, which showed that disparities in girls' access to education had rapidly declined since many countries in the Global South gained formal independence from the Western European empires that had overseen the creation or expansion of formal educational systems in which boys far outnumbered girls. Instead, UNICEF publicly portrayed the failure of "developing" countries to embrace a critical step in the economic and physical development of children and of the nation—the education of girls—as the results of cultural patriarchy and bad microeconomic decision-making at the level of the family. Through discussions of girls and the discrimination they faced, the stated causes of and solutions to poverty shifted away from economic crisis, structural adjustment programs, geopolitical factors, and history and toward dissections of familial behavior, individual attitudes, and local cultures.

In a step that would mark a turning point in the dominant logic of children's welfare and development economics, UNICEF's leadership inverted the direction of causality between wealth inequality, poverty, and children in the 1980s. After showing data that pointed to the global economic recession, shrinking welfare states, and an uneven balance of power between the Global North and South as root causes of worsening child survival rates and poverty, and after lamenting the lack of action to fix these core issues, the agency's official stance concluded that improving children's health held the power to address "some of the fundamental problems of world poverty."[66] Through the "cost-effective investment" of girls' education, Grant argued, rising rates of poverty and mortality could be mitigated.[67] Enabling individuals to use new scientific innovations driving the GOBI-FFF children's revolution promised to "build a sense of self-respect and self-determination" and contribute to "greater justice." The children's revolution would, in turn, foment a process of "'inner development' in the growing minds and bodies of young children." It claimed to help break the structural "cycle of poverty and injustice" by making families, and especially girls-turned-mothers, more self-sufficient and less reliant on the state and outside resources in the future.[68]

Ben Wisner summed up UNICEF's inversion of causality between poverty and children through GOBI-FFF in his aforementioned article from 1988. Primary health care "was crystallized as an approach at a time when there was wide agreement that the causes of poverty were nonnatural and that social justice was a requisite for health," he wrote. "By naturalizing poverty once again by its emphasis on external, uncontrollable economic forces, population growth, and female ignorance, UNICEF locates health action wholly outside the realm of socio-economic rights and responsibilities."[69] Whereas the NIEO, the Alma Ata conference, and previous high-level consensus held that poverty and underdevelopment originated at the level of geopolitics, UNICEF now portrayed poverty as stemming largely from local causes at the level of the individual, family, and community. Patriarchy, divorced from its macroeconomic dimensions and depicted as part of a state of nature in a supposedly culturally unevolved Global South, became a primary culprit driving poverty. "Putting the blame on culture, apathy and illiteracy," wrote WHO's head Halfdan Mahler in the WHO's magazine in 1983, merely served as "another escape mechanism" and "a handy excuse for non-action."[70]

Many aspects of GOBI-FFF drew from long-standing tropes and policies in colonial-turned-national development programming. These preexisting programs placed educated mothers within the nuclear family at the center of efforts to control fertility (whether to grow or diminish it) and to create healthy, morally upright, and prosperous families, colonies, and nations.[71] UNICEF Deputy Director Richard Jolly's own experiences promoting woman-focused development in colonial Kenya in the 1950s likely proved pivotal; there, his work as a colonial officer focused largely on women as agents of development.[72] Similarly consistent with colonial-era development programs, a preoccupation with the perceived failures and irrationalities of local cultures and families accompanied UNICEF's embrace of GOBI-FFF. Where UNICEF diverged from many existing development frameworks was in its increasing focus on girls as a way to shift development programming away from robust state action and away from the international-level action envisioned in the NIEO. Individually driven and, increasingly, free-market solutions replaced them.

It is difficult to fully historicize why UNICEF made this pivot, especially in the face of the ongoing closure of UNICEF's physical archives to outside researchers. Clear from available documents is that the shift partially stemmed from the United States government's influence over UNICEF as an institution during the late Cold War. The United States was the single largest donor to UNICEF throughout the 1980s. It was the top donor to the agency's general funds during every individual year in the decade. The US government was a particularly important donor to UNICEF between 1981 and 1986; during those years, the United States donated between 12 and 20 percent of UNICEF's total annual budget. The rest of the agency's budget originated from a mix of annual donations from more than a hundred other national governments and NGOs, with Western Bloc countries dominating the list of top donors. These included Italy, Sweden (officially neutral, but with strong ties to the Western Bloc), Norway, Denmark, Canada, Finland (also officially neutral and with a complicated relationship to the USSR due to shared history and proximity), and Japan. Governments from the Eastern Bloc donated comparatively negligible sums to UNICEF throughout the decade. The USSR, for example, generally gave about fifty times less money than the United States in a given year throughout the 1980s. Most countries in Africa, Asia, and Latin America were large-scale recipients of UNICEF programming, rather than large-scale donors.[73]

The influence of the United States over UNICEF can be seen in the agency's economic politics. Both the Carter and Reagan administrations supported structural adjustment. Describing the US government's hostility to ongoing calls for a new international economic order and a remaking of the global economy, scholars like Courtney Hercus have argued that the Carter administration undermined "welfare state principles" around the world and instead promoted a "'basic needs' approach" to economic development.[74] A similar logic focused on the provision of basic needs and then poverty alleviation, rather than robust state programming or changes in international economic policies, drove UNICEF's children's revolution. Women and, as the 1980s wore on, girls were a key vehicle through which this devolution took place. As Grant's own professional history attests, the economics politics of the Cold War were the backdrop against which this shift within UNICEF took place.

Girls and Women as Economic Providers and the UN Third World Conference on Women in Nairobi

UNICEF continued to single out girls—increasingly treated as distinct from women—in its connected advocacy for health care and development as the 1980s wore on. The agency did so as part of a broader ongoing turn away from calls for high-level structural change to the geopolitical system. It also did so in the face of ongoing structural adjustment programs and cuts to welfare state programming in areas such as health care, public education, and housing. During the second half of the 1980s, UNICEF increasingly depicted the training of girls to be good mothers *and* to labor in for-profit economies as essential to the attainment of economic development.

A pivotal moment occurred in 1985, in anticipation of the United Nations' Third World Conference on Women in Nairobi and the end of the UN Decade for Women. From April 16 to 18, 1985, two months before the Nairobi conference, members of UNICEF's executive board and NGO Committee convened a three-day forum titled "The Female Child Today: Problems and Strategies."[75] Representatives from Christian and secular NGOs and staff from UNICEF country offices from across Africa, Europe, and North America attended. The forum was intended to discuss the ways that UNICEF's staff could further incorporate Women in Development into the agency's work.

Women in Development had been pioneered in part by the Economic Commission for Africa during the late 1960s and early 1970s. The Danish economist Esther Boserup's now-classic tome from 1970, *Women's Role in Economic Development*, helped to spread it beyond the continent.[76] One of the main tenets of Women in Development was that top-down, state-led development initiatives of the 1940s–1960s had not been effective because of their failure to fully recognize the importance of women's labor outside of the home, in areas such as farming, to economic growth.[77]

Three linked notions drove UNICEF's 1985 Forum on the Female Child that aimed to better integrate Women in Development into the institution's work. First, it held that girls in the Global South were the victims of systematic "discriminatory treatments . . . in the fields of health and education," "in the home," "in paid work," in the sex "trafficking" industry, and through "harmful traditional" practices such as "female circumcision." Second, UNICEF's Forum on the Female Child furthered the premise that discrimination against girls hindered their ability to grow into women who could productively participate in economic development. Third, it argued that oppressed and uneducated girls could not become proper future mothers who were "essential for carrying out the 'child survival and development revolution'" at the heart of UNICEF's organizational mission.[78]

Here was a partial continuation of the logic laid out in GOBI-FFF. This logic blamed local cultures and patriarchy within the family for leading to failures in development by preventing girls from growing into properly socialized mothers who could keep their children alive as the providers of selective primary health care. However, the Forum on the Female Child also represented an important shift in UNICEF's girl-focused logic: girls were increasingly viewed as agents of development not only as future mothers but as future economic providers in their own right.

It is striking that UNICEF's Forum on the Female Child did not occur only as part of the agency's preparation for the UN Third World Conference on Women to mark the end of the UN Women's Decade; it also took place as many UNICEF board members were calling on the agency and the broader UN to open their doors more fully to hiring and promoting women to senior levels of their staff. The 1985 report of the UNICEF executive board to the UN Economic and Social Council, for example, commented on the apparent boys' club within UNICEF. The report stressed the need both for the agency to hire more women and for its leadership to be held more fully "accountable" for following through on its stated commitment to women's issues: "The Board noted the intention of the Executive Director to achieve the goal of 33 per cent of women professional staff by 1990 and encouraged movement in this direction."[79]

This growing push to hire more women at UNICEF mirrored the change within the agency to view girls' future labor in for-profit markets as essential to economic development. The 1985 report of UNICEF's executive board tapped into long-standing debates, particularly between the delegates who made up the executive board and UNICEF's leadership team, headed by Grant. The minutes from a 1980 session of the UNICEF executive board, for example, noted that after "debate," the executive board "agreed" that "UNICEF should . . . advocate a broad perception of women in society and in the development process, taking the view that women were not limited to motherhood or domestic roles but should be seen in the totality of women's roles—as mothers, wives, as economic providers, as citizens and leaders at all levels, and as individuals in their own right."[80] Another set of executive board meeting minutes, these from May 1983, similarly noted, "UNICEF has long emphasized the crucial role of women in the delivery of children's services; however, the concept of women as economic providers received special attention." The minutes noted that the executive board "commended the move towards that concept as more accurately reflecting the multiplicity of women's potential as key partners in development. . . . It was pointed out that income-generating activities for women, especially in urban areas, were in many cases a prerequisite for improving conditions for children."[81]

It was in 1985, in preparation for the UN World Conference on Women in Nairobi and in response to the Forum on the Female Child, that James Grant and UNICEF's other top staff members began to institutionalize these repeated calls from the board for the agency to take a more capacious view of women's roles in development. According to UNICEF employee Virginia Hazzard, introduced in the previous chapter, the upcoming "World Conference on the Decade for Women" in Nairobi led to "a major policy review" of UNICEF's work on women. The result was "considerable change in UNICEF's outlook" through "an increasing focus on programs for women other than mothers only." Hazzard writes that one month before the Nairobi women's conference, James Grant sent a report to UNICEF's executive board explaining how the agency was institutionalizing the view that "women's roles go well beyond that of mother and nurturer."[82] The board responded to Grant's report by affirming that "women-centered activities should be development-oriented rather than welfare based and made integral to all UNICEF-assisted projects and programmes."[83]

This language of "development-oriented rather than welfare based" is crucial. It reflected a larger shift within the agency during the 1980s away from social-welfare-based programming at the level of the state, aided by international organizations, to promote women's status and development. Instead, it embraced the view that "development" and gender justice were inherently achieved from the bottom up—through action from individuals, local communities, and especially girls and women. This change in language meant, in policy terms, an increasing shift to market-based solutions to the joined problems of development and patriarchy: "This entails," Hazzard wrote, "commitment to an entrepreneurial orientation" achieved through increasing women's access to "credit" via for-profit lending schemes and training them in "production, marketing, and management" techniques. It also went hand in hand with efforts to teach girls and women "occupational skills" to help them with "attaining jobs and cash earnings."[84] Here was the partial birth of the fantasy that would become widespread by the turn of the twenty-first century: that girls trained to be confident entrepreneurs could pull the Global South up out of poverty as future women working in for-profit markets under capitalism.

The same 1985 report of the executive board favorably responding to James Grant's commitment to view women as economic providers within UNICEF's work urged the agency to make "the female child" a "priority," in line with the Forum on the Female Child. The driving logic behind the board's report was that "female education," particularly for girls, was "essential for ensuring that women achieved their greatest potential not only as informed mothers and household providers but also as active participants in the development process."[85] The promotion of women's labor as employees of UNICEF and of their labor beyond the household in UNICEF's development programming went hand in hand. They were, in turn, both reflections and proponents of efforts—often contentious—to encourage, recognize, and properly pay for the labor of women outside of the home that were part of Women in Development as a school of thought and that were promoted and contested through the UN women's movement and the broader internationalization of feminism in the 1970s and 1980s. These efforts became entangled with UNICEF's shift from welfare-based to market-based approaches to development in the 1980s, with girls—envisioned as future mothers and, now, as future workers in for-profit markets—becoming a locus for development planning that promised to address poverty from the bottom up.

From the "Female Child" to the "Girl Child," 1985–90

A series of published reports, speeches, conferences, and policy shifts continued to reflect UNICEF's embrace of Girls in Development—increasingly separated from Women in Development—in the context of a devolution of action from the macro to the micro level during the late 1980s and early 1990s. One was the work of UNICEF employees and a broader network of actors in South Asia to popularize the term *girl child* and connect it with development planning. An increasing focus on the status of girls within local cultures and the growing children's rights movements accompanied this shift.

As Ashwini Tambe has noted, the term *girl child* conceptually became linked with notions of economic and social development, first within South Asia in the 1980s and then within the United Nations.[86] UNICEF played an active role in this history from the start. In 1985, the National Media Center of the government of India partnered with UNICEF to host a workshop on the "Girl Child" in New Delhi over three days in October. Attendees—researchers, policymakers, and advocates who were largely from India—presented papers on topics from "Sex Bias in Child Nutrition" to the media's lack of attention to the "Girl Child" and the over reliance on girl children to perform household labor such as gathering firewood and water.[87] The workshop drew attention to the ways in which girls' gender-based discrimination in childhood hampered the country's development process.

Two years later, in 1987, the government of India under Prime Minister Rajiv Gandhi again hosted a workshop, this time without UNICEF's cosponsorship and held under the auspices of the government's Women Development Division of the National Institute of Public Cooperation and Child Development.[88] Titled The National Workshop on the Girl Child, the event featured themes similar to the joint workshop from two years before. In addition to presentations on girls' access to nutrition—such as Capoor Indu's paper on "Nutrition and Health Discrimination against Girls from 0–20 Years of Age"—the conference saw a large focus on girls and child labor.[89] Neera Burra, for example, presented at the 1987 conference on the "female working child."[90] A sociologist with a doctorate from the Delhi School of Economics, Burra would go on to work with the International Labour Organization women's program and for various United Nations agencies in the late 1980s and 1990s. A prolific researcher who was, in the mid-1980s, early in her career, Burra began to work on the girl child as part of her broader research on child labor; in the second half of the 1980s alone, she published more than ten articles on the topic. At least two were reports that Burra prepared for UNICEF's

New Delhi Office in 1987, in the same year as the government of India workshop on "the girl child."[91]

In 1988, the focus on the girl child spread outward from India to the broader region, as the South Asian Association for Regional Cooperation (SAARC) hosted a workshop on the girl in New Delhi.[92] The leaders of the South Asian Association for Regional Cooperation declared 1990 as the SAARC Year of the Girl Child and then proclaimed 1991–2000 as the SAARC Decade of the Girl Child. An increasing stream of published works, events, and public advocacy focused on the girl child—primarily concerning labor protections and access to adequate nutrition—continued to emerge from scholars in South Asia. Many of the authors of these pieces had been participants at one or more of the aforementioned workshops that the government of India and/or UNICEF cohosted—such as a piece from Neera Burra for the *International Labour Review* in 1989 and renowned feminist economist and UN adviser Devaki Jain's work on "Girl Child" laborers for *Kurukshetra* in November of 1990.[93]

The term *girl child* spread outward from the South Asian subcontinent, particularly to East Africa, in part through international cooperation between governmental officials in both locations. Within South Asia, it also spread outward from spaces like New Delhi to Madras and Islamabad. In 1990, the government of Kenya released a country report on the status of girls in honor of the SAARC Year of the Girl Child. The term similarly spread from regional action within South Asia to UNICEF's headquarters in New York City and through the organization's global network of offices, the largest branch of which was located in Kenya's capital city of Nairobi by 1990. It is in this context of the popularization of the term within India and then its outward circulation that UNICEF's embrace of the term can be understood.

What does knowing that the term *girl child* emerged as a development-related concept from South Asian networks in which UNICEF was enmeshed have to do with the larger history that this chapter and book tells? On a basic level, it challenges existing histories of Girls in Development that too often focus only on the World Bank, USAID, and the application of human capital theory to notions of Women in Development among known institutions that championed neoliberal reforms from the late 1970s onward. In this chapter, and as Tambe's book fleshes out, a group of people in India and then broader South Asia were integral to defining and popularizing the concept of the girl child and its relationships to human rights and development.

Second and at least as importantly, the growing focus on the girl child within South Asia was sometimes connected to the larger shift in development planning away from support for a new international economic order, the expansion of social welfare state programming, and a redistribution of resources from above toward action by individuals and local communities—the latter depicted as inherently patriarchal in the Global South. The work of renowned economist Amartya Sen serves as a case in point. In 1990, Amartya Sen wrote a now-iconic essay in the *New York Review of Books* claiming that one hundred million women were "missing" from the existing global population due to sex-based discrimination.[94] As a baseline against which to compare the rest of the world, Sen argued that "women outnumber men substantially in Europe, the US and Japan."

This was a fascinating argument for a number of reasons, fore among them that women significantly outnumbered men in Europe and Japan after World War II because of gendered divides in who was expected to fight in the two world wars (generally men, despite the importance of women fighters in spaces such as Eastern Europe and the Soviet Union) and who, therefore, died in these wars (also more often men, despite high civilian casualty rates, again in Eastern Europe). In Germany in 1950, for example, there were a recorded 86 men for every 100 women. In the Soviet Union the ratio was 79 men to 100 women, in France and the United Kingdom, 93:100. In Japan it was 96:100.[95]

Sen argued that women outnumbered men in Europe, the United States, and Japan because they faced "little discrimination" in access to health care and nutrition in those areas. This, for Sen, reflected a supposedly natural, biological reality in which women outnumber men in the general population if given access to the same resources. By contrast, Sen argued that "the fate of women is quite different in most of Asia and North Africa." He attributed this to "the failure to give women medical care similar to what men get and to provide them with comparable food and social services." The outcome was, according to Sen, more women dying.

To prove his point, Sen cited mortality rates for girls and women versus boys and men in India. He concluded that "the death rate is higher for women than for men" and that this was true "fairly consistently in all age groups until the late thirties." While Sen used the term *women*, he largely referred to biases in nutrition and health care that began and were often the most pronounced in childhood. Sen then extrapolated the argument beyond India, arguing that a similar neglect of girls and women vis-à-vis boys and men could be seen in many other parts of the world—particularly in "Asia and North Africa, and to a lesser extent Latin America." The result of sex biases in girls' and women's access to nutrition and medical care was, as the title of the article notes, that "More Than 100 Million Women Are Missing" from the global population as of 1990 due to premature death.[96]

Sen's highly visible article in the *New York Review of Books* from 1990 built on years of research he had been conducting that focused on girls and women and that connected to the shift in focus on the girl child within India. In 1983, Amartya Sen and Sunil Sengupta, both researchers connected to the Agro-Economic Research Centre at Santiniketan (Sen was also a professor of political economy at Oxford at the time), published a paper exposing what they termed a "sex bias" in the nutrition of "rural children." Appearing in the journal *Economic and Political Weekly*, the studies compared the nutrition of children under the age of five in two villages in West Bengal, India. Their study found that a "systemic sex bias" existed against girls in both villages, causing a "greater prevalence of undernourishment of various degrees among girls than among boys." The paper was published in the context of vociferous debates over ongoing land reform in India. The authors concluded that "the economic benefits accruing to the children of Kuchli [one of the villages studied] through land reform, etc., seem to have primarily benefitted boys vis-à-vis girls."[97] Crucially, the argument from Sen and Sengupta was that, even in the face of structural reforms from above intended to promote more just and equitable visions of development—such as state-led efforts to redistribute land ownership to people living in rural areas—girls and women would face ongoing discrimination. This, in turn, would hamper India's development process.[98]

The 1983 study was one point in a long line of research for Sen in an internationally high-profile career that would see him go on to win a Nobel Prize in economics in 1998, among other things. But in his work on what he termed "sex biases" on child nutrition in India in the 1980s, Sen was hardly unique. Between the early 1980s and early 1990s, there was a spate of research about sex-based biases in child and adult survival within the context of larger discussions about why orthodox development planning had failed to achieve many of its stated aims. It was this research on sex biases in child nutrition, coupled with growing concern about the gendered dimensions of child labor, that underpinned the proceedings of the aforementioned 1985 workshop on the girl child in New Delhi cohosted by the government of India and UNICEF. Similar concerns drove the spread of the term *girl child* within South Asia and then globally.

An important aspect of Sen's work—and the global spread of the term *girl child*—was identifying a problem in a specific place and time and then universalizing it. Claiming that the problem of gendered discrimination within the family existed everywhere (especially in the Global South) and removing it from temporal and historical context was central to this process of universalization. Under these frameworks, local patriarchy appeared timeless. It was the apparent result of a state of nature because communities within the Global South had not yet socially developed from the default of patriarchy toward the more gender egalitarian Global North (a claim that can be challenged on many levels, as the prevalence of sexism and various forms of violence against women and girls within "developed" countries in the 1980s and beyond attests).

Other studies from the 1980s onward complicated these universalizing narratives. They showed that, in some locales, girls in South Asia received more calories per day than their brothers. For example, in a 1988 article published in *Food and Nutrition Bulletin*, author Rafiqul Huda Chaudhury found that girls in Muyiarchar, Bangladesh, were more likely than boys to receive the number of calories needed to survive in three out of four age groups during childhood.[99] Like Chaudhury, Alaka Malwade Basu nuanced understandings of "sex differences in child mortality" in South Asia in a 1989 article in *Population Studies*.[100] Looking at communities from two different parts of India, she found that girls were healthier than boys according to some metrics—such as "severe malnutrition"—while boys were healthier than girls in others. She similarly found that one community, from Uttar Pradesh, had higher rates of child mortality for girls than boys while in Tamil Nadu, girls "often fared better" than boys.[101] Crucially, Basu's research supported then-existing studies showing that "the sex differential in infant and child mortality is greater among the higher castes and the more propertied classes." She found that in some higher-caste and wealthier communities, significantly higher rates of child death existed than in lower caste communities and that girls tended to fare worse in the former than in the latter. Basu attributed these findings to the "frequently noted inverse association between socioeconomic status and the status of women"; in other words, in parts of India, the wealthier and more high status a community, the more girls and women faced oppression within the household, even when women had been formally educated.[102] This was, to Basu, connected to both gendered labor divides and to the ways in which certain higher castes and wealth impacted the enactment of culture within the family to the detriment of girls and women. The overall trend that Basu found, both in her own work and in a literature review of existing evidence, was that "in India, at least . . . a clear regional pattern of sex differences in childhood mortality" exists. This trend was not universal and did not apply equally across the country: "girls in the northern and northwestern parts of the country far[e] much worse relatively to boys than in the south."[103]

Beyond nuancing data on child health and survival, these studies challenged universalizing narratives about the girl child by reinforcing the importance of the state provision of robust social welfare programs, such as health care, to child survival. Both Basu and Chaudhury argued that a lack of access to health care outside of the home was a primary cause of death among children.[104] Basu found that, in Karala, lower levels of child mortality existed, despite lower levels of "economic development" than in areas in the North such as West Bengal. The existence of "a radical political tradition" and "a politically aware population has made sure that the state's health facilities are evenly distributed, and a highly literate female population has been more disposed to use these facilities once they became available" in Kerala, she argued.[105]

This was not UNICEF's formulation of educated mothers providing health care for their own children in the home; this was closer to part of what the Alma Ata conference and the WHO envisioned, of local populations making demands for the provision of adequate health care from the state. At least as import as women's education, Basu cited existing research to argue that "medical factors—specifically the availability of medical facilities and the percentage of births attended by trained medical practitioners—explained about 52 per cent of the regional variation in infant mortality. In fact, most of the effect of women's literacy . . . also operated through its association with the above medical factors." The state's provision of "health-care services" to people living in rural areas was, for Basu, an essential element in preventing sex-based disparities in the survival of children and adults where they existed.[106]

As shown in chapter 1 with the Girl Child Study that FEMNET compiled and UNICEF published, the selective amplification of particular narratives—about the universality of patriarchy in the Global South, decoupled from macroeconomic causes, location, context, and history—accompanied the marginalization of narratives that contradicted or added nuance to the story. Despite the existence of published research from scholars like Chaudhury and Basu—who were not alone in their findings—the claim that girls were oppressed throughout South Asia and the Global South, and that they universally faced family-inflicted discrimination in their access to food and health care, increasingly circulated in the late 1980s and early 1990s as a focus on the girl child spread. Sen's 1990 article about one hundred million "missing women" from the global population was a particularly visible flashpoint in this trend, as was UNICEF's continued support and use of the idea that girls in South Asia and the broader Global South were universally the victims of life-threatening patriarchy within the family. Findings that complicated the argument about educated and empowered women serving as engines of both development and gender justice—such as Basu's findings that linked wealthier and higher-caste families to *more* patriarchal treatment of daughters—were similarly marginalized, and often outright ignored, in increasingly dominant discourses of Girls in Development within UNICEF and beyond.

Cementing Girls in Development within UNICEF

UNICEF's embrace of Girls in Development came to a head with the 1990 publication of Agnes Aidoo's book *The Girl Child: An Investment in the Future*, referenced at the start of this chapter. Initially, Aidoo wrote *The Girl Child* as a section of a couple-hundred-page UNICEF advocacy book titled *Children and Development in the 1990s*—a document that UNICEF's staff produced surrounding the 1989 Convention on the Rights of the Child, the 1990 African Charter on the Rights and Welfare of the Child, and the World Summit for Children of 1990. The book explicitly served to identify UNICEF's strategy for the new decade.[107] It named the girl child as one of the core focuses of UNICEF's strategy. Also in 1990, UNICEF published a significantly expanded version of Aidoo's section as a stand-alone book. Doing so publicized the agency's work to make girl-focused programming an essential component of international campaigns for economic and social development. The front matter of the book notes that Aidoo based *The Girl Child: An Investment in the Future* on "an initial report" penned by Neera Sohoni. As Ashwini Tambe notes, Sohoni was "an Indian economist who worked for UNICEF in New Delhi and New York," further attesting to the role of South Asian actors in globalizing early forms of Girls in Development.[108]

The Girl Child: An Investment in the Future cemented much of UNICEF's logic, by then seven years old, deeming girls essential to linked notions of economic development and health. Aidoo depicted the development of the girl child as inherently connected to broader notions of economic and social development and the "global fight against poverty."[109] She portrayed patriarchy as universal "in most countries today" and remarked on the widespread "deprivation of girls and women" in "developing countries" in their access to "food, healthcare, and education."[110] Among the targets of Aidoo's ire were "prejudices rooted in culture and customs" and parents who made the "decision not to invest in the education of the girl child" or to feed her enough in comparison to her brothers.[111] Depicting girls as inherently vulnerable and in need of protection when compared with boys, Aidoo argued that "the girl child . . . is more vulnerable to sickness and disease than the boy child."[112]

A key sentence from *The Girl Child: An Investment in the Future* underlined part of the logic driving UNICEF's work at the time: "The education of girls and women also has significant effects on infant and child survival, economic productivity, reduction in fertility, and the quality of human life."[113] According to Aidoo, girls—particularly in Africa, Asia, and Latin America—served as embodied financial investments whose future (re)productive labor as mothers and as economic producers could yield high returns if they were properly educated. If parents and cultures were largely to blame for girls' lack of rights and ability to participate in development as adults, promoting girls' "self-confidence, self-worth and self-reliance" became a key solution to it.[114] Here was a variation of the line that Larry Summers would soon make famous in his work for the World Bank: "Reversing this uneven development of the girl child is . . . one of the most productive investments a country can make."[115]

Yet Aidoo's commitment to allowing girls to experience childhood with "equality" to boys at times chafed against the insistence that educating girls would serve as a savvy fiscal investment and an "economic payoff."[116] Beyond her depiction of girls in the Global South as a site of investment to drive development, Aidoo emphasized the need to allow all "children to reach their full human potential" in the name of "human dignity" and "children's rights."[117] It was at this moment—the pinnacle of the children's rights movement at the turn of the 1990s and the end of the Cold War—when a moment of creative opening took place in the logic of Girls in Development. While the public logic of UNICEF's top leadership in promoting Girls in Development appears to have followed a relatively linear progression, UNICEF staff like Aidoo and the people they worked with to define and then internationalize Girls in Development, such as FEMNET, attached different ethical and political priorities to it.

In 1990, the same year that UNICEF published Aidoo's *The Girl Child: An Investment in the Future*, UNICEF's executive board voted to formally adopt the girl child as a "priority focus" of the agency's programming.[118] The board's decision called on "all UNICEF programs and strategies in the 1990s [to] address explicitly the status of the girl child and her needs, particularly in nutrition, health and education, with a view to eliminating gender disparities."[119] At the opening session of the meeting, James Grant described support for the education of girls as an "investment" that would "empower parents and children with knowledge" and pay dividends in "health and nutrition" for many years to come.[120] His rationale, and that of the executive board in its official report, continued to revolve around the idea that educated girls would be healthy girls and, more importantly, healthy future mothers who would give birth to fewer children, engage in gainful income-generating activities, and take advantage of new technologies to lead their nations in the march toward economic growth. The UNICEF executive board based its "Focus on the Girl Child" on the notion that "many of the disadvantages facing women are rooted in the neglect of and discrimination against female children."[121]

Many historians locate the beginning of Girls in Development at this moment in 1990: "A 1990 policy decision by UNICEF to develop a specific strategy for girls marks something akin to the starting point for this trend in policy terms, which has expanded enormously in the intervening years," writes Sydney Calkin. "UNICEF's 1990 girl-focused strategy marks a starting point for the growth of girls as development agents on the global stage and also signals the central place of education on this agenda."[122] While accurate in some respects, this periodization overlooks the fact that UNICEF's adoption of a focus on the girl child in 1990 reflected the culmination of an ongoing internal process at the agency dating back to the launch of the children's revolution in 1982.

The girl-focused logic that UNICEF's New York City–based leadership outlined between 1982 and 1990 spread outward to the World Bank and US-AID in the late 1980s and early 1990s. In 1989, Karin Hyde authored groundbreaking works for the two organizations on girls' access to education, one for the World Bank on Sub-Saharan Africa and the other a USAID study of girls' educational access in developing countries around the world. Both publications reinforced the idea that educated girls were a crucial component of economic and social development, given formal schooling's ability to increase the labor of girls as mothers and as agricultural producers. The two reports concurred that impediments to girls' education in the form of "cultural" barriers, rather than economic crisis or ongoing neoliberal adjustment policies the World Bank was still implementing, were to blame for economic stagnation and the perceived failures of development, both in Africa and across the Global South.[123]

Then, in 1992, Lawrence "Larry" Summers, the chief economist of the World Bank at the time, directly borrowed from language Grant and Aidoo had recently used describing girls as an "investment" that would "empower parents and children with knowledge" and provide returns in "health and nutrition" for many years to come.[124] He wrote, "Educating girls quite possibly yields a higher rate of return than any other investment available in the developing world."[125] Summers repeatedly stated multiple versions of this quotation, from the opening line of his essay in the journal *Scientific American* to his keynote lecture at the Pakistan Society of Development Economists in Islamabad to his foreword in the World Bank's publication *Women's Education in Developing Countries*.[126] The logic underpinning this spate of lectures, publications, meetings, and broader advocacy that leaders and researchers at UNICEF, the World Bank, and USAID undertook in the late 1980s and early 1990s continued to expand what had been put forth in UNICEF's children's revolution of the mid-1980s: that women's inequality began in childhood due to oppressive "cultural norms" and sexual exploitation. The education and affective empowerment of girls, this narrative went, would produce "singular benefits" as girls grew into mothers who could properly care for children and increase their own "economic productivity."[127]

The vision of Girls in Development put forth by UNICEF's New York City–based leadership in the mid-1980s and embraced by Washington, DC– centered World Bank and USAID officials by the early 1990s is closely aligned with the form of Girls in Development that would become hegemonic by the late 1990s, in part through its adoption in the final UN World Conference in Beijing in 1995. However, this outcome was not guaranteed. Other narratives about girls, labor, education, rights, and capitalism circulated, both within UNICEF and within a broader network in the 1980s and 1990s. Fleshing out some of the contours of this network and the ideas that ran through it in the next chapter shows that the work of Girls in Development proponents within UNICEF existed within a broader global climate of "girl talk." In this milieu, people articulated and worked out anxieties over capitalism and poverty through discussions of girls and their education, status, capacity to work, and state of emotional empowerment.

Conclusion

Key elements of the "girl turn" within economic development planning occurred within UNICEF and a broader network of actors, particular in South Asia, between 1982 and 1990. At the children's agency, focusing on mothers, female children, and then the girl child served to devolve the idealized location of change away from macroeconomic policymaking at the level of the international system and the state to individuals and families within the Global South. This shift took place in the context of UNICEF's partial retreat from the principles put forth at the Alma Ata conference of 1978 and in the NIEO of 1974. It also took place against the backdrop of an ongoing economic crisis in the 1970s–1980s and the growth of neoliberal capitalism via structural adjustment programs. Through an increasing focus on girls, UNICEF's depiction of the primary causes of poverty narrowed from a skewed geopolitical system to patriarchy rooted in local cultures and enacted within the family. The corresponding solutions that the agency called for similarly shifted away from a new international economic order and robust welfare state programming toward individualized forms of empowerment, public-private partnerships, and encouraging women to labor in for-profit markets as entrepreneurs.

The UN Third World Conference on Women in Nairobi in 1985, Women in Development as a school of thought, South Asian governments and researchers, and the growth of children's rights frameworks at the end of the Cold War all inflected UNICEF's turn toward girls. What emerges from this history is an earlier periodization of Girls in Development than is currently on record. Also emergent is an insistence on placing UNICEF and the networks in which the agency was enmeshed, especially in South Asia and then East Africa, at the center of the girl turn in late twentieth-century development planning.

When viewed in light of the larger history that this book puts forth, this chapter charts a crucial step in the rise and then internationalization of neoliberal understandings of Girls in Development as competing frameworks were cast aside or erased. However, as the previous two chapters have shown, not everyone agreed with the politics that UNICEF's leadership attached to Girls in Development; the end of this story was not a fait accompli in 1990, although neither is it wholly surprising. The knowledge that UNICEF did not act alone to internationalize Girls in Development—that its staff relied on institutional partnerships with FEMNET to successfully lobby the UN women's movement through the Fourth UN World Conference on Women in Beijing in 1995—further turns our attention back to East Africa, and especially to Nairobi, where FEMNET's members worked to flesh out their own understandings of the relationships among girls, development, and notions of gendered and economic justice.

4

Girls as a Battlefield over Structural Adjustment Programs at FEMNET

The previous chapter charted the "girl turn" in development planning in the 1980s and early 1990s. Within UNICEF, a growing focus on girls devolved calls for international and welfare state action to address global inequalities in wealth and health. Interventions focused on individuals and local cultures in the Global South replaced them. The result was the rise of a model of girl-focused developmentalism that looked similar to the neoliberal forms of Girls in Development that would become dominant in the late 1990s and early 2000s, especially as multinational corporations and their foundations picked up the cause of girl power.

Instead of automatically becoming hegemonic at a global scale, however, visions of Girls in Development existed within a larger milieu of "girl talk" in the 1980s and early 1990s. Multiple understandings of the relationships among girls, capitalism, development, and the state arose within UNICEF and the network of NGOs on which its staff relied to generate knowledge, particularly FEMNET. Many people contested the versions of Girls in Development that UNICEF's headquarters promoted while others endorsed or retooled it. A consensus did not exist. Common across conversations was that girls and their perceived status were the terrain on which people worked out anxieties over capitalism and the distribution of wealth and decision-making after the global economic crash of the 1970s and the subsequent turn to austerity through structural adjustment. Pan-Africanist calls to decolonize the United Nations and broader international relations also inflected these conversations.

This chapter analyzes FEMNET's early girl-focused advocacy in the late 1980s and early 1990s. Neither FEMNET nor UNICEF worked on girls in a vacuum—their girl-focused advocacy was entangled, informing one another's work. In a few cases, individual advocates and experts who worked for UNICEF belonged to FEMNET. More commonly, the two institutions shared ideas and collaborated to generate knowledge and reports about girls, including on the Girl Child Project detailed in chapter 1. Despite these connections, and as the story of the Girl Child Project suggested, key differences existed among the girl-focused knowledge and policy frameworks that each institution put forth. It is important to trace these forms of girl-focused advocacy in order to show the processes of selective inclusion and disappearance that went hand in hand with the internationalization of girl-focused development frameworks at the UN Fourth World Conference on Women in Beijing in 1995 and more broadly.

Girls and Top-Down Changes to the International System

A consistent element of FEMNET's early advocacy used girls to call for high-level changes to the geopolitical system. According to this avenue of thought, which regularly appeared in *FEMNET News*, justice for girls and broader society could not be achieved without a fundamental restructuring of the economic and political systems that had been created through colonialism and foreign domination. Many of these arguments drew on appeals for the creation of a new international economic order, discussed in the previous chapter, which the first three UN World Conferences on Women surrounding the UN Women's Decade had endorsed. FEMNET's members built on this advocacy by envisioning a future in which the macroeconomic and structural hurdles to development, such as high levels of state indebtedness in the Global South, were removed. In a departure from dominant frameworks at the existing UN World Conferences on Women and more broadly, they explicitly did so by invoking African girls.

One of the many outlets through which FEMNET's members recorded and circulated their girl-focused advocacy was the publication of a newsletter. Beginning in 1989, a year after the planning meeting at which FEMNET grew out of the African Women's Task Force, the NGO's staff began to publish *FEMNET News*. Initially published biannually and then quarterly, one thousand copies of each edition of *FEMNET News* circulated in English, and three hundred appeared in French by 1998.[1] Recipients were a mix of FEMNET members, donors such as UNICEF, and governmental and nongovernmental organizations in Africa and on other continents. In the late 1980s and early 1990s, publication of *FEMNET News* served to further the NGO's central mission, articulated by founding member Sara Hlupekile Longwe, to "create an infrastructure and channel through which NGOs will reach one another and share crucial information, knowledge and experiences, and therefore sharpen and improve their inputs to women's development in Africa."[2]

An early edition of *FEMNET News*, published in 1990, took aim at certain aspects of Girls in Development articulated from UNICEF's global headquarters in New York City. In February 1990, the International Conference on Popular Participation in the Recovery and Development Process took place in Arusha. Miriam Khamadi Were, a Kenyan medical doctor who served as UNICEF's chief health and nutrition officer in Addis Ababa, Ethiopia, spoke at the conference. *FEMNET News* circulated a description of Khamadi Were's speech and included a number of direct quotations from it, including this one: "Visualize a python squeezing a young girl to death while ordering her to sing. Africa, in her struggle towards economic recovery, faces a plight similar to the girl's." According to FEMNET's description of her speech, Khamadi Were argued that the education and employment of girls, the "brilliant daughters of Africa," were crucial components of the continent's prospects for economic growth and overall "development." The exclusion of girls and, in the future, women from full participation in development was, she claimed, a detriment to Africa's economic growth. The opposite was also true: poverty disproportionately impacted girls and women. In turn, it prevented them from being active participants in economic and political life.

In her speech, Khamadi Were named the culprit for both the suffocation of girls and Africa's economic woes as "international forces": the "foreign advisors" and institutions promoting economic austerity measures, exercising control over global financial markets, depressing prices of raw commodities, and moving decision-making processes away from supposedly community-based, "traditional," and gender egalitarian practices toward a small, power-wielding hierarchy of global elites. For Khamadi Were, this created a uniquely gendered, racialized, and generational form of poverty—one in which African parents struggled to educate girls, only to discover that their daughters had dismal job prospects and would be excluded from positions of economic and political power in the future. Miriam Khamadi Were argued that the global political order both harmed Africa economically and disproportionately impacted African girls and future women. In this equation, championing poverty reduction and addressing global economic inequalities were intimately intertwined with, and necessary precursors to, improving the situation of girls and women. They relied on the creation of a new geopolitical climate in which the needs and desires of African girls and women, boys and men drove the economic development process and high-level policymaking attached to it.[3]

While Miriam Khamadi Were depicted educated girls as essential to Africa's economic growth, according to FEMNET's description of her speech, she condemned the political action most commonly associated with that argument: that African nations, communities, and individual women were responsible for driving economic development from below. In her comparison of Africa's recovery from the economic crisis to a python squeezing a girl to death, Khamadi Were proclaimed, "International forces are squeezing Africa to death yet it is expected to sing. Africa is constantly being urged to pull itself together and pull itself up.... But how can it?" *FEMNET News* then stated that Khamadi Were encouraged African efforts to integrate women into development and overcome "myths" regarding gender roles that kept women "overworked" and in "bondage." She supported initiatives to fight "discrimination" in girls' education and women's employment and to convince "women themselves" to stop being "obstacles to their own development."

But even if all of those things were achieved, Khamadi Were argued, women's efforts to drive development from below were insufficient if not accompanied by high-level structural changes to the economic system and an end to the "bankrupt trend in Africa" of relying on "foreign advisors" to dictate development priorities. Describing women laboring to pull themselves up by their proverbial bootstraps, Khamadi Were said:

> Unfortunately these activities often resemble those of a caged mouse. No matter how active it becomes, it is still in the confines of a cage. Her situation is made even more complex in that the cage in which she lies is within a larger, entrapped barrel, that is, the entire African continent. It seems that just enough air is brought to it to facilitate breathing to keep the majority alive, but not do much more in terms of improving one's lot.

No matter how many girls became educated, how many women became employed, or how many attitudes and "traditional practices" were changed in Africa, according to Khamadi Were, Africa could not economically prosper, nor could its girls experience full justice. To achieve those things, a "burst [of] the barrel, and the cage"—contending with the legacies of colonialism within development planning and remaking the current macroeconomic and geopolitical order—had to be achieved.[4] For Khamadi Were, girls were not merely a simile through which to describe the stranglehold of the global economic system and economic austerity on African economies; the education and future employment of girls were tangibly harmed by systemic poverty that the geopolitical system manufactured and structural adjustment perpetuated, in part because of the gendered impacts of shrinking welfare state funding for public education, health care, and more.

A number of other *FEMNET News* articles argued that this metaphorical cage of reliance on "foreign advisors" and a corrupt international economic system perpetuated both poverty and gender-based disparities in ways that uniquely hurt girls in Africa and the broader Global South. The second edition of *FEMNET News* in 1990 included an editorial that explicitly claimed, "The root cause of Africa's under-development lies in the economic arena, which is largely dictated from the outside." That editorial framed the education of girls as essential not to develop human resources or combat ignorance but to make people less easily taken advantage of, given the increasing importance of written language in the world. FEMNET's editorial depicted formal education as a crucial tool for women to take control of their lives. But it argued that women's attainment and utilization of literacy relied on an end to structural adjustment programs, the forgiveness of African state-held debt, the stabilization of commodities prices, and a reduction in the high cost of manufactured imports. All of these practices, the editorial argued, were "part of the exploitative and unacceptable economic order that has impoverished Africa over the years.... Unless the economic situation both locally and globally changes, basic education for all will remain a dream, especially for African women."[5]

This editorial, like many articles in *FEMNET News*, did not list an individual author. However, Eddah Gachukia and Njoki Wainaina, discussed in chapter 2, remained the respective chairperson and coordinator of FEMNET after the 1988 programming conference that created the NGO out of the African Women's Task Force. They would stay in these roles until 1992, when Gachukia stepped down to become the founding executive director of the Forum for African Women Educationalists (FAWE), another Pan-African NGO focused on the education of girls and women in Sub-Saharan Africa. Gachukia remained involved in FEMNET after 1992 as part of the NGO's management committee. In Eddah Gachukia's place, Njoki Wainaina took over as FEMNET's chairperson in 1992. A series of women replaced Wainaina in her former role as coordinator, renamed executive director, between 1992 and 1994.

Beyond Gachukia and Wainaina, other people who were highly active in FEMNET in its early years—who likely contributed to various editions of *FEMNET News* and who certainly helped to shape the NGO's advocacy related to girls, women, and development—included women like Sara Hlupekile Longwe, a Zambian educator and activist. She helped to define and internationalize Gender and Development as a school of thought through the Longwe Framework for Gender Analysis, which she presented at the African Women's Task Force conference in 1988. Elizabeth Lwanga-Okwenje, a Ugandan development worker and employee of Oxfam in the late 1980s, was also important to FEMNET's early work. A 1989 article about Lwanga-Okwenje in the *Washington Post* quoted her criticism of "the [Global] South being dependent on the North. We've been so blinded by the power of the United States that even as we try to break this dependency, we don't know how."[6]

Leading FEMNET in the late 1980s and 1990s alongside Gachukia, Wainaina, Longwe, and Lwanga-Okwenje was Gladys M'Sodzi Mutukwa. From Zambia like Longwe, Mutukwa had recently conducted a study for the UN Economic Commission for Africa on the implementation of UN frameworks concerning discrimination against women. She would go on to have a leading role in the Zimbabwe-based NGO Women in Law and Development in Africa, or WiLDAF—another well-known Pan-African organization that focuses on women's rights. Aida Gindy, the Egyptian former head of UNICEF's Eastern and Southern Africa Regional Office in Nairobi, was a staple of FEMNET in its early years. So, too, was Coumba Ceesay Marenah, a diplomat from The Gambia who held a high-level role in the country's Women's Bureau. Marenah would go on to work with the UN Development Program and UN Women, among other agencies. Rounding out the group of women who played key roles in launching FEMNET and steering its early advocacy and operations was Norah Olembo. Introduced in chapter 2, Olembo was a Kenyan professor of biochemistry who helped to define laws governing environmental management and biodiversity in the country.

FEMNET's public advocacy concerning girls, women, and development, especially in *FEMNET News*, did not always attribute individual authorship to articles or particular lines of analysis. Key intellectual and political convergences and divergences existed among these women and the many other individuals and institutions that worked with and through FEMNET. Consistent in FEMNET's early advocacy, however, was that many of its members vociferously championed top-down changes to a global economic system that, they argued, had been forged through colonial and imperial violence and that nourished women's impoverishment in the Global South. As in Miriam Khamadi Were's speech and the 1990 anonymous editorial that *FEMNET News* circulated, girls became a lens through which many of FEMNET's members made these calls for structural change at the macroeconomic and national levels.

The individual beliefs of FEMNET's founders were not always anonymous when it came to fleshing out the relationships between girls and development. One of the 1990 editions of *FEMNET News* summarized a speech that FEMNET's coordinator Njoki Wainaina delivered at the UN World Conference on Education for All in Jomtien, Thailand. In her speech, Wainaina reportedly blamed structural adjustment policies for hurting girls' education. She condemned leaders of international agencies for supporting the programs.⁷ Her statement called for "major shifts of power, resources, control and decision-making" at the international level. In Jomtien, Wainaina reportedly argued that formal education and "literacy" were "not the first step along the road to development." Instead, the first step consisted of changing global economic policymaking and the work of international institutions to ensure "a minimum level of socio-economic development" in Africa and the rest of the world.⁸ When viewed in the context of the shift in development thinking and economic planning of the time away from social-welfare-based approaches toward capitalistic conceptions of empowering the individual to work her way to prosperity, Wainaina's advocacy, and FEMNET's decision to circulate a summary of her speech in its newsletter, represented clear rebukes.⁹

FEMNET News continued to put forth this argument in a variety of ways, and it often did so through the burgeoning language of children's rights. In one of the 1990 newsletters, the organization printed a letter allegedly written by a schoolboy in Bamako, Mali, to the head of the World Bank. "Dear Manager of the Big Bank," it began. "All the family sends you greetings. I hope that you, your wife and children are in good health. We have been told that we could write to you because over here, we are tired. The school-master told us what a debt is: it is when your mother goes to shop and has no money now but will pay later." The alleged schoolboy who wrote the letter then criticized the World Bank for the impact of the debt that it held for African countries—a thinly veiled reference to structural adjustment and to the high proportion of state-owned debt on the continent. "Everybody says that your bank must be reimbursed. As for us we suffer even more. People who work in the civil service are being sent home. They are told: the government has no money. Therefore, dear Manger of the Big Bank, please do not let people suffer like us. What we owe is too much, and we have not seen what use it has been."¹⁰

According to *FEMNET News*, this letter was similar to "hundreds of others written in English, French or Spanish from [children in] Third World countries." The NGO reported that many children delivered their letters, accompanied by beauty pageant queen Miss Zaire, during a demonstration against the World Bank in Washington, DC in 1989. In addition to addressing the destructiveness of foreign debt, "the children enclosed the amount of their 'small savings' in their letter" in an act of "symbolic solidarity." This all occurred as part of an apparently well-coordinated public relations campaign to emotionally portray children as the victims of structural adjustment and the African debt crisis.¹¹

Two years later, in 1992, another edition of *FEMNET News* continued to draw on ideas of children's rights in a similar vein. It cited a 1989 declaration from African heads of state in conjunction with the UN Convention on the

Rights of the Child. The African declaration blamed "the prevailing inequitable international economic order" and "man-made . . . disasters" for interfering with the "protection" of "children."[12] The same *FEMNET News* edition quoted a Nigerian philosophy professor who reportedly argued that the Convention on the Rights of the Child could not be implemented in Africa as long as "poverty" continued.[13]

One line of FEMNET's advocacy argued that debt uniquely hurt children by preventing their access to education, a critique of the idea that educated girls could help to drive development from below under the status quo of the international system. A cartoon printed in the newsletter, titled "No Excuse," argued "foreign debt" constituted a "burden of poor countries" that was "crushing their education programs." While much of the NGO's advocacy focused on continental Africa, this cartoon took a diasporic approach rooted in broader understandings of Blackness. It cited school closures in Jamaica, decried the firing of teachers in Zaire, and printed illustrations of a number of Black students.[14] The logic in all of these pieces, as well as many others in FEMNET's early newsletters and speeches that its members gave at sundry international conferences, fundamentally challenged the causality of UNICEF-backed strands of advocacy rooting economic underdevelopment in a lack of girls' education, cultural norms violating girls' rights, and a supposed failure to fully develop girls and women as Africa's human resources. Instead, according to FEMNET's foregrounding of foreign debt and global economic policies, poverty was to blame for girls' lack of education and broader rights. Whereas UNICEF's child revolution posited educated girls as the keys to overcoming poverty in a world of ongoing structural adjustment and economic crises, FEMNET published statements from African "experts" who claimed that children could not prosper as long as structurally driven poverty continued—and it did so in newsletters funded by UNICEF and written from an office based in UNICEF ESARO's headquarters in Nairobi.

Bottom-Up Visions of Development via Girls

Other forms of advocacy within FEMNET helped to flesh out parts of the core girl-focused narrative coming out of UNICEF's New York City headquarters. Only one issue after a 1992 edition in which *FEMNET News* ran a number of stories on the need for international economic changes to achieve children's rights, the front page of the newsletter featured an interview that FEMNET employee Winnie Ogana conducted with a Kenyan doctoral student in political science with the same first name, Winnie Mitullah. In the interview, Mitullah said, "External debts may be written off, but that will only solve the problem minimally. As long as Africa fails to make the best use of local, physical and material resources, the continent will continue to suffer." To Mitullah, "African women" needed to "fight" for their "rights"; for the government to "empower" women to "generate income"; and for a decrease in population growth.[15] It was rare for FEMNET's advocacy to dismiss the importance of high-level economic reforms, such as debt forgiveness, as Mitullah had done. However, this interview represents an important counterpoint to aforementioned uses of Girls in Development to demand macroeconomic changes. Within FEMNET, various lines of argumentation and political advocacy circulated. One agreed that mobilizing the human capital of girls, as future women, was essential to the promotion of bottom-up development frameworks within Africa and the Global South.

One strand of thought that FEMNET articulated in its early newsletters advocated for a form of technological solutionism in which schoolgirl scientists would learn the necessary tools to develop their societies out of poverty. The first edition of *FEMNET News* featured a photograph of three uniform-wearing schoolgirls running experiments in a chemistry lab. The caption under the photo read, "Girls should be equipped to face modern responsibilities."[16] The article accompanying the photo summarized a conference held in Nairobi in February 1989, which drew fifty participants from fourteen African countries to discuss the topic of improving the lives of young women and girls. In its coverage of the conference, *FEMNET News* claimed Timothy Thahane, who then worked for the World Bank, gave a speech arguing "women contribute heavily to the third world economies." Thahane claimed that the "status of women" must be "altered" in order to achieve the goals of economic development and "socially transforming the society."[17] At FEMNET, as at UNICEF and a connected group of actors, changing the status of women began with girls' education.

The second edition of *FEMNET News* similarly featured a photo of a young woman in a laboratory looking through a microscope, with the accompanying caption, "Women's role in the development of science has increased tremendously in recent years." The article next to the photo was called "Conquering the World through Science."[18] It discussed the formation of the Third World Organization for Women in Science at a conference in Italy in 1988. The article quoted Donald Leger, the director of the NGO Division of the Canadian International Development Agency, as arguing that women's unique characteristics would help them approach "the pursuit of truth" and scientific inquiry differently from men. The article concluded, "The prospects of women's full participation in society at all levels is one of the main hopes for a better order of affairs."[19] This participation would, according to FEMNET's summary and the accompanying photo of a girl with a microscope, occur by formally educating African girls in science, technology, math, and other STEM and vocational subjects so they could grow into women who would help their countries economically and socially develop via new technologies. Unlike UNICEF, much of FEMNET's policy prescriptions accompanying these articles called for an expansion of public education in Africa and an end to structural adjustment programs that often cut state funding for schools

According to a number of articles in the first few editions of *FEMNET News*, some but not all of which referenced UNICEF's work, children and women were not being effectively developed as human resources who could efficiently and productively contribute to economic growth. One of the main and most often repeated reasons *FEMNET News* named for this failure was patriarchy, displayed in cultural norms and traditions. Patriarchy, according to this line of thought, prevented girls from attending and succeeding in school. It also increased women's labor burdens without proper remuneration. A cartoon in a 1991 edition of *FEMNET News* showed an African man shouting, "Haraka" in Kiswahili, meaning "faster," while whipping a woman, presumably his wife, who resembled a beast of burden. The whipped woman had a human front half and the back half of an ox. She was on all fours with a baby strapped to her back, a pile of firewood and a basket of produce balanced on her head. She clenched a water pump and jug in one hand while cooking utensils protruded from a side bag attached to her torso. She was also pulling a plow to till the land behind her. Meanwhile, the man steered the plow as he whipped the woman and yelled at her to move faster.[20]

FEMNET News attributed the cartoon to the Kampala-based Action for Development (ACFODE) NGO, whose leaders attribute its 1985 creation to the UN Third World Conference on Women in Nairobi.[21] The headline and description of the cartoon make the meaning clear: "the African woman" performed an inordinate share of labor as a "beast of burden" controlled by the African man. The cartoon explicitly lamented that the African woman did not own the land on which she worked or have legal rights to custody of the children she birthed. It depicted the African man as the overbearing, violent, whip-wielding taskmaster who did not perform his fair share of the work—all while yelling at the woman to do more.[22]

FEMNET's newsletters regularly deployed such illustrations of African patriarchy to explain why women did not financially benefit from the fruits of their labor. These depictions also explored the causes of barriers to girls' educational access. Similar portrayals of endemic patriarchy often depicted girls as inherently vulnerable to the sexual predations of African men. One such article in a 1990 edition of *FEMNET News* described an "epidemic" of male teachers who lacked "professional ethics" and engaged in "sexual harassment of school-girls" in Uganda. These "innocent school-girls" fell victim to their teachers, according to the article, and often became pregnant, causing them to drop out or be forced out of formal education. The article argued, "Parents blame their daughters" instead of the real culprits—unmarried male teachers and educators who "lack professional ethics" and "use girls to satisfy their sexual demands." The article in *FEMNET News* portrayed girls as naive about the "repercussions of pre-marital sex." It then warned of schoolgirls who sought abortions while pregnant, "not knowing it may result in overbleeding and death or removal of an infected uterus." The stated solution to this dangerous and life-threatening violation of schoolgirls was for girls to report being "sexually harassed" and "turn to the law" for protection.[23]

Similar strands of thought in *FEMNET News* rooted the sexual violation of girls and barriers to their educational access in some combination of "culture," "custom," and "tradition"; in European colonialism in Africa; or in political and sexual corruption caused by powerful African men. In the process, debates about "Africanness" and who was supposedly to blame for Africa's economic and political crises of the 1980s were waged through discussions about African girls, their sexuality, their education, and their future labor as women. In the article that accompanied the photo of schoolgirls in a chemistry classroom in the first edition of *FEMNET News*, the NGO printed comments made by Eddah Gachukia at the aforementioned conference held in Nairobi in February 1989, Options for a Better Life for Young Women and Girls. FEMNET prefaced its recounting of Gachukia's speech by claiming, "It is crucial that young girls be guided and molded to be able to face their responsibilities." It affirmed the claim at the base of many of the NGO's discussions about girls: that their future productive and reproductive labor was essential to achieving economic and social development and that formal education was necessary to equip girls to fulfill those roles efficiently.

However, Gachukia reportedly argued that many African girls currently lacked the "rights" to be molded through education because of prevailing "socio-cultural attitudes and beliefs." Customs reportedly taught girls "to be obedient and submissive" as they grew up, which made them ill-equipped to rebuff the sexual "advances" of "a man who is old enough to be her father, and therefore one she treats with respect and obeys." The treatment of those girls' mothers and role models as "subordinates" and "inferior" to men compounded this problem, "especially ... where the colonial influence presented the man as the breadwinner. Even in schools, pictures and examples portray women in a subordinate role." On top of this damaging colonial legacy on the gendered division of labor, Gachukia argued that "traditional socio-cultural values" in Africa that "regulated adolescence and fertility" had endured a "breakdown." This echoed a common trope of colonial community development and woman-focused policymakers in Africa before and immediately after World War II.[24] Together, all of these factors reportedly led to a "dramatic rise" in schoolgirl pregnancies in Africa, allegedly causing a number of girls to seek dangerous abortions, face medical complications from early pregnancy, get married young, and drop out of school at alarming rates.[25] All of this, in Gachukia's view, hampered African development.

The first edition of *FEMNET News* built on its transcript of Gachukia's testimony at the girl-focused conference of 1989 to argue that female circumcision prevented girls from fully accessing education and harmed their health. The stated solution was for girls to learn about family planning and receive individual counseling about the "risks" of "sexual experiences." The article simultaneously argued that governments should censor pornography, offer "vocational training" for girls, outlaw female circumcision and "forced marriage," provide "free and compulsory education" for all children under the age of eighteen, and encourage girls to study "subjects with a science and technical bias." Together, these initiatives would address the currently "bleak and hopeless future for the [school] girl who becomes pregnant." They would help overcome the existence of harmful "socio-cultural attitudes and beliefs," address the damaging effects of colonialism on gender roles, and prepare girls to meet their "responsibilities," both productive and reproductive, in the service of achieving economic and social development.[26] In this formulation, FEMNET partially built on the logic of UNICEF's child revolution to argue that educated girls played a unique role in the achievement of economic and social development. The NGO furthered UNICEF's argument that cultural and traditional behaviors of parents led to the failure to develop girls as human capital. At the same time, it foregrounded the role of history, especially through colonialism, in posing additional barriers to girls' success.

FEMNET tended to place a much larger emphasis than UNICEF on the need to expand welfare state programming within Africa to protect and empower girls. Correspondingly, FEMNET's analysis placed less of an emphasis on individuals acting alone within the unit of the nuclear family or through targeted international programming. FEMNET's visions of bottom-up development via girl power, was, at its base, one that relied on a robust welfare state, unhampered by international constraints on topics such as debt forgiveness, to implement. A redistribution of global wealth through international assistance to fund public education was frequently a component of FEMNET's advocacy. Collectively, this strand of thought presented a girl-focused model of economic and social development of Africa that was driven from the bottom up through policy support from state and international levels. It intended to help African girls and communities scientifically innovate their way out of the economic crisis. At the same time, it preserved many of the calls of the first three World Conferences on Women that argued for robust welfare state services and significantly more international aid from developed countries, both of which ran counter to UNICEF's child revolution and structural adjustment programs.

Challenging the Underpinnings of Girls in Development

Yet other strands of advocacy within FEMNET challenged the very underpinnings of Girls in Development as a policy framework. Occasionally, *FEMNET News* ran articles questioning the use of educating girls, given the growth of formal education within Africa through the intertwined structures of colonial racism and capitalism. In this formulation, the formal education of girls was not always helpful for the joint pursuits of economic and gender justice; sometimes, it was downright harmful.

As one example, one of the 1990 editions of *FEMNET News* showed a photo of a teacher demonstrating something to two schoolgirls, mirroring earlier photos of schoolgirls performing science experiments. Yet the accompanying article, reprinted from the *Nation*, discussed the impact of the "global economic and political crisis" on formal education in Africa and the legacies of imperial influence "thirty years after most of the African states broke their colonial links." The piece argued that Africa's current "education crisis," defined by persistent barriers to many girls' and boys' access to education, traced "back to colonial rule" and had been exacerbated by poor policymaking since. It also questioned the very purpose of formal education: "Education for what? It no longer provides jobs." Education and the relationship between children and society must, the article argued, be rethought, decolonized, and repurposed to meet the genuine human needs—and not only the broad economic growth—of African societies.[27]

Another photo deviated from FEMNET's earlier endorsements of technological solutionism through girls' education in STEM. Showing a young woman bent over a computer, the image was reminiscent of FEMNET's earlier publication of photos of girl scientists alongside articles about how educating girls to make better use of science and technology would make women's labor more efficient and productive. Yet the caption next to the photo of the young woman using the computer read, "Much as women are eager to work on computers, lots of questions remain unanswered over their safety." The article underneath discussed the "negative consequences of technology."[28] While the excerpt did not wholly advise against the utilization of computers, it was nevertheless a marked departure from utopian visions of access to technology facilitating women's full and profitable integration into economic development. Another article from *FEMNET News* lamented the lost art of "traditional" midwifery in the face of the medicalization of childbirth, which FEMNET claimed began during colonialism. The article cast similar aspersions on the idea that access to science and technology would universally liberate girls and women and help their societies prosper.[29]

Still other strains of FEMNET advocacy challenged both UNICEF's child revolution and broader conceptions of Girls in Development by portraying the use of new technologies by capitalistic multinational corporations as inherently racist and exploitative of African girls and women. This logic further questioned the narrative that bottom-up change addressing traditional discrimination within African societies would promote both gender equality and an improvement in economic living standards. One cartoon in *FEMNET News* showed a Black woman speaking to a white man in a lab coat in the "Africa Sales Office" of a "European Drug Company." Recommending the Black woman use skin lightening products, the white male drug company employee said, "If blackness persists . . . consult a doctor!" The implication was that European drug companies treated Blackness as an illness, an ailment, a problem to be solved through the for-profit pharmaceutical and beauty industries targeting women. The accompanying article condemned "exploitative" British and other European cosmetic companies for profiting from racist beauty standards. It discussed alarmingly increasing rates of "young, 'sophisticated' African women" being admitted to hospitals with kidney failure and wide-ranging symptoms of mercury poisoning due to their use of skin lightening products.[30] Rather than helping their societies develop through education, social change, and access to new technologies, these young, modern, urban women were portrayed as the victims of technologies wielded by racist European corporations under the guise of modern medicine.

An editorial in the same edition of the newsletter expanded this discussion of skin lightening creams to a condemnation of pesticide manufacturers for "dumping" their "hazardous chemicals" in the "Third World." It depicted African women as the overworked victims of a capitalistic system that structurally promoted the exploitation of women in the Global South through new technological advances:

> The worst affected are agricultural workers, of whom women are the majority in Africa. . . .
>
> Instead of helping the poor eat better, this technology is exposing the poor to chemicals that cause cancer, miscarriages, still-births and other birth de-

fects, sterility, skin rashes and nerve damage, among other physical disorders. Severe cases of pesticide poisoning lead to death.

The multinationals who do roaring business with the Third World in the hazardous chemicals do not seem to take into account the human suffering inflicted by massive use of pesticides. Despite the dangers of this technology, few African countries have adequate regulations or the capacity to enforce them, thus giving the multi-nationals a free hand.[31]

In this formulation, technology wielded by multinational corporations hurt African women. National laws to regulate these corporations and protect women agricultural workers and the broader Third World was necessary.

Still another article in *FEMNET News* in 1992 fundamentally questioned the idea that "popular participation" of women and children was the key to development. Citing Christopher Lekyo, the executive officer of the National Council of Social Services in Kenya, and Dr. Swithun Mombeshora, Zimbabwe's minister of state for local government, the piece argued the benefits of scientific advancements in children's immunizations and broader development work had not been fully realized in Africa. It attributed the failures of technology to promote development in part to the elitism of the "technocrats" who oversaw development policymaking and of international NGOs and donors. These elites were allegedly removed from the communities in which they worked, expected change to occur too fast, and refused to devolve power. According to *FEMNET News*, Lekyo "asked how much power, therefore, leaders were willing to surrender to the people. 'Unless we surrender it we must not talk about popular participation.'"[32] In this genre of article that FEMNET circulated—an implicit criticism of UNICEF's GOBI-FFF initiatives outlined in the previous chapter—no amount of "participation" from girls, children, or women in development, and no application of new technologies, would fix the ineffective and corrupt centralization of power in the hands of foreign advisers, technocrats, and development experts.

Competing Frameworks

This 1992 edition of *FEMNET News* was particularly prophetic to the unfolding history of girl-focused development planning. First, it contained one of FEMNET's first uses of the term *girl child* in the NGO's newsletters. The final page of the spring 1992 edition contained a black box with the heading "The Girl Child." It argued that the UN Convention on the Rights of the Child of 1989 and the UN World Summit for Children of 1990 "made explicit commitments to strengthen the role and status of women, beginning with the needs of the girl child." "Education," the article continued, is "the foundation for improving the status of young girls and women." Portraying UNICEF's leadership of girl-focused developmentalism detailed in the last chapter as the result of the agency listening to criticism, the FEMNET article claimed that a number of national delegates to the UN conventions on children at the end of the Cold War beseeched UNICEF to support women to take a more active role in development by focusing on girls, rather than being the "passive beneficiaries of services."[33]

This idea of UNICEF leading the promotion of a plan of advocacy in which educating African girls was a crucial step to achieving African women's productive participation in economic development neatly encapsulated one strand of advocacy that appeared in *FEMNET News* in the late 1980s and early 1990s. It identified a main locus of change for economic development and poverty alleviation as educating African girls to labor their societies to prosperity. This would occur through national and local programs and the involvement of international NGOs and advisers who combated the supposedly harmful effects of African traditions in preventing sexually vulnerable or promiscuous girls from accessing school.

Next to that box on "The Girl Child" was a poem, "Roots," by the now-deceased Wandera-Chagenda, an artist "from East Africa who speaks for African youth." The poem hinted at another strand of advocacy, also often girl- and child-focused, that appeared throughout FEMNET's early newsletters. It grappled with the legacies of European colonialism and the meanings of tradition, culture, identity, and race in creating a decolonized Africa:

> Who are you
> Charcoal-black man?
> They ask.
>
> I am one
> Whose spirit you have exiled
> Still and hold in bondage
> . . .
> You shamed me
> Duped me, brought me
> Face to face with fear,
> Ramming down my throat
> Your civilization
>
> . . . you came
> Unprompted
> Uninvited
> Bent on sheer destruction

> I am not
> mere consumer of your culture,
> But I want to build
> And to create
> And to invent,
> I need my roots
> I need a firm foundation
> Point of swift departure.
> ...
> But I will not yield
> To your manipulation.
> In this changing world
> I need my own traditions.
> These are they
> That make me who I am
> Can you tell me who I am?[34]

On the other side of "The Girl Child" box, opposite Wandera-Chagenda's poem, was another poem from thirteen-year-old Tereziah Njoki, titled "The African Child." The child in the poem was "proud of his color," "fighting against the odds," and "hoping for a better future." The debate over what that future would look like was still unresolved, caught between calls for changes to an international economic and geopolitical order established in part through colonial violence, racism, and patriarchy versus those promoting economic growth from the bottom up through the empowerment of the educated and sexually vulnerable girl child.[35] These two strands of advocacy were not mutually exclusive, and FEMNET often embraced both while nuancing and challenging them in crucial ways. But only one of these two strands of advocacy would be written into the Beijing Platform for Action and entombed in norms guiding girl-focused interventions in the name of both human rights and economic development at the Fourth UN World Conference on Women in 1995.

A second reason that this 1992 edition of *FEMNET News* was prophetic to the future of girl-focused development is that it explicitly attributed bottom-up notions of Girls in Development to UNICEF, who had publicly promoted that line of thought in its child revolution of the 1980s, as the previous chapter argued. UNICEF was arguably FEMNET's most important donor in the first few years of FEMNET's existence. As the African Women's Task Force, later FEMNET, struggled to gain funding and legal recognition in the mid- to late 1980s, UNICEF ESARO provided the NGO with an organizational home until 1992. It also funded the publication of many editions of *FEMNET*

News. As FEMNET lacked money to pursue its own autonomous agenda in the late 1980s, its founders credited two organizations with providing financial support that allowed the NGO to stay afloat: beginning in 1990, the Canadian International Development Agency gave FEMNET money to carry out a series of gender sensitivity trainings among development planners and national bureaucrats, first in Kenya and then in other countries. Also in 1990, UNICEF commissioned FEMNET to work with it on the Girl Child Project, summarized in chapter 1 of this book. The erasures that occurred through the course of FEMNET's work with UNICEF on the girl child are essential to understanding the processes of exchange through which FEMNET's and UNICEF's conflicting and complementary streams of girl-focused advocacy were whittled into one dominant strand of logic by the time of the United Nations Fourth World Conference on Women in Beijing in 1995.

Conclusion

FEMNET's early networking advanced various political claims and ways of thinking about girls in the wake of the UN Third World Conference on Women in Nairobi. Within this work, ideas about girls and development often politically served to challenge free-market capitalism and to call for changes to the existing international economic order, as articulated in the previous three UN World Conferences on Women. On rare occasions, FEMNET's girl-focused advocacy promoted free-market frameworks that placed responsibility for development squarely on the shoulders of girls, their families, and their communities in Africa. More commonly, FEMNET advocated for some mix of the two approaches: top-down changes to the global economy, sometimes called for in the name of helping girls in the Global South, mixed with empowering girls to participate in development from below. Sometimes, FEMNET also put forth new strands of advocacy that questioned the very assumption that the education and labor of girls, facilitated through access to new forms of technology, would help develop the Global South out of poverty.

In all of these conceptions—some of them competing with and contradicting one another—discussions about girls were the crucibles through which broader debates about development, racism, and the mechanisms to decolonize both the UN and the global economic system were waged. These epistemologies and forms of advocacy represented a moment of possibility, and of creatively envisioning a new future, in the historically contingent trajectory of the internationalization of girl-focused development planning. It was not clear yet how the story would end—in the internationalization of neoliberal Girls in Development frameworks that placed blame and responsibility for development largely on the shoulders of individual girls, women, and their families, without top-down changes to the global economic system. Clear in this moment in the late 1980s and early 1990s, at the end of the Cold War, was that African girls and their real and imagined status became the terrain on which far-reaching debates about development and global economic inequalities were waged.

Understanding how neoliberal iterations of Girls in Development that sensationalized the sexual suffering of the African girl child became hegemonic requires an understanding of the disappearance of competing frameworks, both in support of and in challenge to Girls in Development. Chapter 1 of this book provided a case study of the erasures, silences, and silencing that accompanied this process as FEMNET and UNICEF worked together to generate information about girls' educational access in Eastern and Southern Africa between 1990 and 1992. The following chapter expands on the importance of bureaucratic practices of erasure, disappearance, and marginalization as particular frameworks of Girls in Development became cemented in the UN Fourth World Conference on Women in Beijing while others did not.

5

Crafting International Norms

The Girl Child and the Final UN World Conference on Women in Beijing

In September 1995, nearly fifty thousand people from almost every country in the world convened in Beijing and nearby Huairou, China, for the final United Nations World Conference on Women. Journalists attended the conference in the thousands and broadcast the convention's dramas and proceedings to audiences around the world through newspapers, radios, televisions, and the burgeoning internet. Gertrude Mongella, a Tanzanian diplomat, served as the conference's secretary general. Hillary Clinton, then First Lady of the United States, gave an acclaimed speech in Beijing on the importance of women's and girls' rights to human rights and economic growth. As many scholars and activists have noted, the widely celebrated, circulated, and commented-upon conference outputs—the Beijing Declaration and Platform for Action that delegates from all national governments in attendance voted to approve—set the blueprints for the linked movements for economic development and women's rights not only in 1995 but well into the present.[1]

Initially, a special section on girls was not going to be included in the Beijing conference outputs.[2] It did not appear in the official draft of the Platform for Action prepared by early 1995. Linda Tarr-Whelan, an official delegate to the UN conference under the administration of US president Bill Clinton, noted that the section on the girl child in the Beijing Platform for Action was belatedly included due to its "particular importance to African delegates."[3] In reality, the special section on girls was belatedly written into the Beijing conference outputs because of a lobbying campaign that representatives from UNICEF and FEMNET carried out, building on their work concerning girls and poverty since the 1980s discussed in the previous chapters. Employees of the Kenya Alliance for the Advancement of Children's Rights, another Nairobi-based NGO with links to both FEMNET and UNICEF, also supported the campaign.

The section on the girl child, or girls under the age of eighteen, in the Beijing Platform for Action focused on the capacity of girls to combat poverty and drive economic development when freed from the burdens of culturally rooted patriarchy. The outputs of the final UN World Conference on Women cemented the notion that empowering girls is a central way to overcome economic inequalities, especially in the Global South, without changes to macroeconomic systems perpetuating poverty and without the existence of robust welfare state programs. The Beijing Platform for Action wrote girl-focused economic development planning into a set of international norms that would guide not only United Nations policymaking but the work of numerous actors around the world through the popularization, dissemination, and endorsement of a certain set of ideas about the relationship between girls, poverty, the state, and patriarchy. While formal outputs of the Beijing UN World Conference on Women were not solely responsible for making free-market forms of gendered economic development planning into a dominant logic within powerful international spaces, they represent a fundamental step in this process.

This chapter examines the process of writing the girl child into the Beijing Platform for Action, largely through the fraught lobbying campaign that employees at UNICEF, FEMNET, and the Kenya Alliance for the Advancement of Children's Rights undertook. Much is often written about the conferences themselves. The pageantry, the spectacle, the emotional crescendos and inevitable fights that broke out have made for titillating reading, both in journalistic accounts from the time and in scholarly and public remembrances since.[4] Yet the nuts and bolts of the written conference outputs—the formal adoption of which marks the culmination of the World Conference on Women and, arguably, of two decades of the United Nations Women's Movement that preceded it—were worked out well in advance. The texts were written, revised, and negotiated at preparatory meetings and through various lobbying initiatives, such as the fraught girl-focused campaign. The campaign consisted of creating knowledge on the girl child and disseminating it at preconference preparatory meetings through position papers, short stories, and poetry. Lobbying also included attending meetings at which drafts of the conference texts were hammered out. This is not to discount the import of the conferences themselves; the events have historically generated tremendous connections, ruptures, and frictions. They have nourished social movements and influenced public policies.

The point here is to draw attention to the so far overlooked role of the bureaucratic wrangling and behind-the-scenes lobbying that went into preparing the texts of the formal conference outputs. Despite the ways in which international laws and norms have always been translated, retooled, and contested in their implementation, it is crucial to pay attention to the enormously influential written norms that each conference produced. These texts inspired sundry national laws, international protocols and frameworks, and nongovernmental, philanthropic, and corporate initiatives in the aftermath of the Fourth (and final) World Conference on Women. As the chapter shows, the formal conference texts, the Beijing Declaration and Platform for Action, were fiercely contested.

Tracing bureaucratic acts of knowledge production centered around drafting the Beijing Platform for Action requires going back to the regional conference on women in Africa that predated the Beijing conference. The African regional conference took place in Dakar in November 1994. As had been case for the previous World Conferences on Women, like the one in Nairobi discussed in chapter 2, each region had its own pre-Beijing preparatory conference. Their purpose was to bring delegates together at the official governmental plenary and concurrent NGO Forum to discuss crucial points of concern, strategize, and vote to adopt an official Regional Platform for Action. Regional conferences took place in 1994 for Asia and the Pacific in Jakarta (June), for Europe in Vienna (October), for Latin America and the Caribbean in Mar del Plata (September), for what actors at the time called the "Arab" Region in Amman (November), and for Africa in Dakar (November).

This chapter pays particular attention to the growth and circulation of specific ideas about the relationships among girls, poverty, the state, and patriarchy alongside the simultaneous erasure, minimization, and noncirculation of other ideas. It charts the spread of free-market ideas of girl-focused development—along with repeated attempts to contest and rebroaden conceptions of development to include antiausterity and decolonial logics—in the lobbying campaign that helped write girl-focused economic programming into a set of international norms that would become hegemonic through the Beijing Platform for Action. While the lobbying campaign was ultimately successful in placing girls at the heart of the joined international movements for economic development and women's rights, not all ideas that circulated among the campaign's participants made it into the Beijing Platform for Action. This chapter highlights how bureaucratic practices of knowledge deletion were central to the sculpting of girl-focused economic development into neoliberal logic that would become widely accepted as common sense. A major outcome of this process was making global economic inequalities and poverty seem like the result of universal yet locally and culturally rooted patriarchy rather than tangible economic policymaking—a hallmark of neoliberal feminism, among other things. Instead of spreading automatically, accidentally, or invisibly, as existing scholarship tends to suggest, free-market feminism grew into a set of international norms through repeated mundane acts of knowledge creation, erasure, and negotiation in bureaucratic spaces connected to the United Nations. It is within these spaces—in this case, in the acts of preparing for a major and well-publicized UN conference—that a fuller history of the growth and dominance of neoliberal feminism through girl-focused development, at the expense of competing alternatives, can be found.

Lobbying at the Regional and World Conferences on Women

FEMNET's leadership officially began to prepare for the UN Fourth World Conference on Women and the African regional conference that would precede it three years in advance. In 1992, FEMNET's staff, including Executive Director Njoki Wainaina and Chairperson Eddah Gachukia, hosted the NGO's First Programming Conference and General Assembly in Nairobi. The event reportedly drew more than one hundred participants from twenty-five African countries. One of the main outcomes of the Programming Conference and General Assembly of 1992 was FEMNET's decision to continue to mobilize for more effective representation of African women at the global and regional levels. To that end, the organization's staff began to plan for the UN Fourth World Conference on Women in Beijing in 1995 and the African Regional Conference on Women in Dakar in 1994.[5]

The first edition of *FEMNET News* published after the 1992 Programming Conference reminded its readership of tensions over who would represent African women going into the previous World Conference on Women in Nairobi in 1985. Discussing the African regional preparatory meeting in Arusha in 1984 detailed in chapter 2 of this book, an anonymous *FEMNET News* article recalled that a group of African women got "really angry" when UN-appointed NGO Forum heads Nita Barrow and Virginia Hazzard (also a former UNICEF official) tried to control the finalization of the African region's planning process going into the global NGO Forum in Nairobi. The women who were present at the African regional preparatory meeting in Arusha in 1984, *FEMNET News* reminded its readers in 1992, used their "frustration and anger" to birth the African Women's Task Force, which they demanded serve as the official organizing body for African NGOs surrounding the World Conference in Nairobi. It was this organization that morphed into FEMNET in 1988.[6] As Wainaina and Gachukia began to rally the proverbial troops to prepare for the upcoming UN Fourth World Conference on Women in Beijing, they reminded FEMNET's members and supporters of the battle concerning the previous World Conference in Nairobi—a battle that they won and wanted to channel as they prepared to go to the upcoming African regional and world conferences in Beijing. Commitments to promoting development by calling for changes to macroeconomic policymaking, more robust national programming in areas such as education and health care, and the empowerment of girls and women within families and communities underpinned FEMNET's mission in 1992 as it began preparations for the UN Fourth World Conference on Women in Beijing.

In March of 1993, at an NGO Committee planning meeting in Vienna, FEMNET gained formal responsibility for running the NGO Forum at the African Regional Conference on Women in Dakar in 1994 and for coordinating the continent's NGO presence at the World Conference on Women in Beijing the following year. FEMNET's mandate was to organize African women to participate in the conferences, coordinate with national and regional NGOs to that end, and prepare thematic subjects to be discussed and lobbied for inclusion in the Dakar and Beijing Declarations and Platforms for Action.[7]

FEMNET was also a member of the African Regional Coordinating Committee (ARCC) in charge of running the official African Regional Conference on Women for governmental delegates. ARCC comprised fifteen member states, the Organization of African Unity, and several UN agencies including UNICEF, the World Bank, and the United Nations Development Program. FEMNET was one of a handful of regional and Pan-African NGOs to sit on the committee.[8] In early 1993, the ARCC's outline for the Platform of Action to be debated in Dakar included four thematic issues, eight subthemes, and more than twenty categories. The girl child's socialization was mentioned in one of the categories. Other subthemes and categories in the document included the external debt crisis, structural adjustment programs, women's production capacities in the formal sector, employment, and women's access to land and natural resources—all high-level policy changes.[9]

An undated, initial draft of the African Platform for Action listed nine areas of focus that reportedly reflected "a broad-based consensus" of various constituent groups in the conference planning meetings.[10] The girl child was not indicated as one of the themes. Girls were mentioned a number of times in the details of discussions of those themes in the draft of the African Platform for Action but almost always as half of the phrase *women and girls*. For example, "The Platform emphasizes the need to analyze the roots of violence against women and girls, be they historical, social, cultural or religious in origin."[11] Girls were singled out for unique consideration on two issues: once when the document called on youth, "and especially girls," to take part in initiatives promoting peace in Africa; and the other when girls were discussed a handful of times on the topic of equal access to education.[12]

The draft African Platform for Action to be voted on in Dakar placed women in poverty at the top of its list of areas of focus. The proposed solutions for poverty and its impact on women varied. On one hand, the document endorsed the idea espoused by UNICEF and a growing number of organizations that the "participation . . . of women and girls" was necessary "to make full use of all human resources in the struggle against poverty."[13] It embraced a neoliberal emphasis on moving away from "the current welfare orientation" of development toward "the economic empowerment of women," which would enable women to labor their societies to prosperity from the ground up.[14]

However, the draft African Platform for Action on women located the causes of poverty not in discriminatory gender practices but in the "unequal distribution of wealth and income from global, regional, [and] sub regional to local levels." This poverty was perpetuated, the draft argued, by "crippling external debt" to foreign creditors.[15] The working document singled out the 1980s economic crisis for diminishing development and worsening the quality of life and health in Africa, and it decried the feminization of poverty in the globalizing economy.[16] In the draft of the African Platform for Action, solving poverty required more international and national expenditures on topics such as education and health care, and it necessitated the eradication of foreign debt in exchange for more spending on "social development."[17]

On the subject of culture, the draft document never mentioned the girl child. It instead noted that a set of "diverse cultures" existed in Africa and lamented the individuation of African society through the erosion of "collective identities." The proposed African Regional Platform for Action then called on the preservation of "welfare" and "social diversity" in an effort to promote a more equitable society.[18]

In an undated report calling for girls to be more explicitly included as their own area of focus in the African Platform for Action, UNICEF wrote that FEMNET was coordinating a campaign to include the girl child in the official frameworks adopted at both the African Regional and World Conferences on Women.[19] But in 1993 and most of 1994, the newsletters FEMNET published and various externally produced reports on the conference preparatory activities indicated the NGO made no concerted calls for girls' representation in the conference planning beyond what was already happening.

Before the African Regional Conference on Women in Dakar, FEMNET published thematic editions of *FEMNET News* in English and French to spread information about key topics that would be discussed at the NGO Forum and potentially written into the draft Declaration and Platform for Action. Its staff also began to publish an additional newsletter, *Our Rights*, in January 1994 in order to update its members specifically about the preparations for the African Regional Conference on Women in Dakar and the World Conference in Beijing. UNICEF's global headquarters and the Carnegie Corporation, both based in New York, funded the production of *Our Rights*.[20] Among the topics for which FEMNET provided in-depth examinations leading up to Dakar were women's relationships to democratization, peace, health, AIDS, the media, violence and economic crises, and population growth. Girls were initially not the main organizing principle in FEMNET's public advocacy leading up to the conference.[21]

The governments of African countries involved in writing the African Platform for Action were also not calling for an increased focus on the girl child, according to official UN documentation of the conference preparations. At a meeting of the African Regional Coordinating Committee in December 1993, delegates from seven African governments gave presentations on issues of concern for potential inclusion in the Platform for Action. None of them discussed girls. FEMNET's delegate presented a number of issues around which the NGO was advocating ahead of the conference. It mentioned the girl child as a subset of its broader lobbying on an expansive set of issues that called for various levels of change.[22]

UNICEF was the only other organization at the official planning meeting for Dakar that reportedly mentioned girls, and it did so in great detail. UNICEF's representative explicitly highlighted that the girl child was a mechanism to "break . . . the cycle of inequality and deprivation" for women and girls, due to the presumed ability of formal education to "empower" girls to fully participate in society as productive women. UNICEF's representative then distributed lobbying materials to the other attendees at the planning meeting and advocated for the utilization of a "life cycle perspective" emphasizing that women's oppression began from birth with discrimination against the girl child.[23]

The conference minutes do not name what materials UNICEF distributed at that meeting of the ARCC for the Conference on Women, but at some point—whether at that meeting or another one—UNICEF submitted a lengthy report, "The Situation of Girls in Africa," as preparatory materials for the ARCC to officially consider before the conference in Dakar.[24] "The Situation of Girls in Africa" repeated and reaffirmed the logic of the doctored report discussed in chapter 1 of this book. It began with the declaration that girls on the continent were not "wanted, valued and respected," "safe from harmful traditional practices," or "protected from the threats of early marriage, sexuality, pregnancy, disease, violence, and abuse." The report claimed that "thousands of girls" on the continent did enjoy those protections, but "millions" did not. The culprits for this widespread oppression, according to UNICEF, were "discriminatory attitudes and practices, deeply rooted in the cultures and traditions of African societies" that were indifferent to, and even "satisfied" with, the suffering of girls. The result was an alleged "apartheid of gender" in Africa that began with the victimization of the girl child.[25] This was a stark and likely deliberate choice of words, given the formal ending of apartheid as an institutionalized system of racist segregation in South Africa in the early 1990s.

The document that UNICEF's unnamed representative submitted to the ARCC sensationalized the sexual suffering of the African girl child. It engaged in an explicit and detailed description of "harmful traditional practices" against girls, such as "female genital mutilation." It argued that this practice led girls to "suffer from shock due to pain and bleeding, infections, damage to the urine and stool passages, chronic problems during sexual intercourse, difficult and risky child births, fetal loss, fetal brain damage, vesicovaginal and rectovaginal fistula, [and] psychological and psychosexual problems." Discussing the "pain," "powerlessness," and "untold suffering" of these "victims" to "male sexual exploitation," the report portrayed side effects of the most severe versions of female initiation rites as the norm under which most African girls lived and suffered.[26] Discussions of early marriage, early pregnancy, and violence against girls continued in the same vein.[27]

UNICEF's lobbying document for the inclusion of the girl child in the African Platform for Action built on the organization's advocacy surrounding girls from the late 1980s and early 1990s. In "The Situation of Girls in Africa," gender-based discrimination allegedly made girls "under-utilized" in the process of economic development. Due to girls' "very high demands on resources," this exacerbated "poverty." The document described the perpetual victimization of girls and women as the product of poor decision-making on the part of the continent, as "Africa cannot afford to continue wasting the potential of more than half its population."[28]

The UNICEF report then identified parents and communities as the culprits for girls' suffering and worsening poverty across Africa.[29] While men and boys were often portrayed as sexually violent and lascivious toward girls, women were depicted as fanatical "perpetrators of their own oppression" through the promotion of female genital mutilation and other harmful "traditions."³⁰ The solution to these abusive parent-child and community-child relationships was, in UNICEF's submission to the ARCC, the reeducation of parents and society and an alteration of children's "socialization process."³¹ Girls needed to be taught psychological "self-empowerment" and physical "self-defense" so they could resist their oppression and fully "participate" in economic development. According to "The Situation of Girls in Africa," the solution to poverty lay with the achievement of an interior change in the minds of girls, parents, and societies.³²

The Growth of a Lobbying Campaign

Beyond submitting that document to the official planning committee for the African Regional Conference on Women, UNICEF's lobbying to include the girl child in the African Platform for Action built on a collaboration with the Kenya Alliance for the Advancement of Children's Rights (KAACR).³³ UNICEF commissioned a concept paper for the Dakar NGO Forum on the importance of the girl child in Africa, which the development consultant Salome Muigai wrote and the KAACR published. Titled "The African Girl Child: Our Multiple Challenge," the paper painted the girl child as an "endangered species . . . from Cairo to Cape Town."³⁴ Likening African girls to endangered animals, like rhinos or elephants, the paper quoted UNICEF's 1990 report, "The Girl Child," when describing widespread discrimination against girls in Africa. It included large chunks of text that appeared verbatim in "The Situation of Girls in Africa," including the detailed and explicit description of the potential side effects of female genital mutilation.³⁵

Unlike UNICEF's narrative in "The Situation of Girls in Africa," however, the KAACR-published report explicitly blamed the World Bank and IMF's structural adjustment policies for exacerbating girls' plight by diminishing the provision of social services, increasing fees for public education, and forcing parents to choose between educating some of their children over others. "The African Girl Child" argued that this "freedom of choice" disadvantaged girls because of gendered labor divisions valuing girls' work in the home.³⁶ But in its proposed areas of action, "The African Girl Child" never called for an end or reworking of structural adjustment. It endorsed a few national-level actions, like affirmative action for the girl child in education. But the document, like UNICEF's study submitted to the regional coordinating commission, portrayed the girl child, her family, and her community as the primary loci of necessary change. Behavioral transformations were needed in the form of "empower[ing] the girl child to have a voice on all issues that affect her" and teaching parents how to more effectively communicate with their daughters.³⁷

The KAACR continued to take part in the campaign to write girls into the African Regional and then World Platforms for Action on Women. In October 1994, the KAACR published the booklet *Girls Are Not Passing Clouds*.[38] In March of that year, the NGO had included a solicitation in *Our Rights*, the monthly newsletter FEMNET published to detail organizational efforts going into the Dakar Regional and Beijing World Conferences on Women. The ad stated that the KAACR was coordinating the thematic focus on the girl child for the African Regional Conference on Women in Dakar and asked for contributions on girls' lives in areas such as "violence against girls in schools," "female genital mutilation," "abuse and sexual exploitation of girls," "rape," "childhood marriages," "prostitution," "physical assault," "education," and the "working girl child."[39]

Seven months later, the KAACR published *Girls Are Not Passing Clouds*, a booklet with articles attributed to girls under the age of eighteen from Kenya's primary schools and governmentally run "rehabilitation centers" for delinquent children. The articles were not written in response to the prompt the KAACR had included in FEMNET's *Our Rights*; the acknowledgments instead attribute the collection of the essays to Madeline Njeri, then a social worker with the Undugu Society of Kenya, an NGO started by a Dutch priest in the 1970s to help "rehabilitate" street children.[40] The topics covered in the booklet were similar to those listed in KAACR's solicitation for information on girls in FEMNET's newsletter, suggesting an intentional focus of the girl child campaign on girls' sexual, physical, and psychological suffering, often at the hands of family members.

Girls Are Not Passing Clouds printed one girl's poem beseeching her parents to "love me, accept me."[41] Another poet lamented that her mother treated her poorly through bottle-feeding instead of breastfeeding during her infancy and not being a supportive enough confidante thereafter, prompting the girl to go live on the streets.[42] One story told of a girl whose mother beat her if she talked to boys and chained her to the bed to make her do homework while another featured a girl with a cruel stepmother who read romance novels all day and made the girl clean the kitchen.[43] The stories ranged from the farcical to the mundane, and many differed from the narratives UNICEF and the KAACR put forth in their reports to the ARCC about girls as victims of extreme violence. However, a number of the stories in *Girls Are Not Passing Clouds* also fit that narrative by describing girls who were raped or forced into early marriage. Narratives denounced parents who beat their daughters and told of abused street girls being "rescued" and offered "protection" by NGO workers.[44] The booklet situated girls' suffering at the hands of parents and advocated for three solutions: girls "should have steel hearts to fight for our rights," parents should learn to properly "love" their daughters, and the legal system should prosecute adults who abuse girls.[45]

The foreword to *Girls Are Not Passing Clouds* lists Joyce Umbima as its author. When the booklet was published, Umbima was the chairperson of the KAACR. Umbima also headed the KAACR when the organization solicited feedback on girls through *Our Rights* earlier in the year. The ad listed Umbima as the thematic coordinator for "The Girl Child," one of many topics on which FEMNET organized NGOs to prepare presentations at the Dakar NGO Forum.[46] Before Umbima was the KAACR chairperson and oversaw the publication of *Girls Are Not Passing Clouds*, she had been FEMNET's interim director from January 1992 to January 1993—the period when FEMNET began its conference preparations for Dakar. Before that, Umbima served as the national executive director of the Child Welfare Society of Kenya from 1984 to 1992 and was at that organization when UNICEF's Kenya Country Office commissioned the Child Welfare Society to prepare a report on the situation of the girl child in Kenya.[47] In their aforementioned submission to the ARCC for Dakar, "The Situation of Girls in Africa," UNICEF staff recounted the history of the institution's mobilization on behalf of the girl child in Africa. It explicitly discussed its work with the KAACR and the Child Welfare Society of Kenya in the early 1990s, when UNICEF commissioned both organizations to produce situational reports on "female children."[48] These activities coincided with UNICEF ESARO's funding of FEMNET's participation in the Girl Child Project to assess the status of girls' education in Eastern and Southern Africa, discussed in chapter 1.

Adding to this critical mass of UNICEF-FEMNET, Nairobi-based mobilization for the girl child was the decision of the Lutheran World Federation to fund the publication of *Girls Are Not Passing Clouds* and other aspects of the KAACR's mobilization for the girl child going into Dakar. This was not a random occurrence: the Lutheran World Federation was also a donor to FEMNET. A representative from the Lutheran World Federation had attended FEMNET's 1992 Programming Conference, and representatives from the federation sat on the same preparatory boards as UNICEF and FEMNET for the African Regional Conference on Women. They also attended the same meetings as the two organizations for various UN activities in the mid-1990s.[49]

Taken together, these connections underscore the emergence of a Nairobi-based lobbying campaign focused on the girl child in the run-up to the African Regional Conference on Women in Dakar in 1994. UNICEF's ESARO and Kenya Country Office had headquarters in the same building at the United Nations compound in Nairobi, making it easy to coordinate their work. Those institutions connected to FEMNET, the KAACR, and the

Child Welfare Society of Kenya by funding the latter three organizations to produce studies on the girl child, promoting awareness about girls and setting some of the parameters surrounding why and how they should be analyzed in the first place. Joyce Umbima served as the executive director during part or all of each of those three NGOs' work with UNICEF on girls, attesting to the importance of people who moved through the revolving doors of the NGO world and took priorities and institutional connections with them. After Umbima left FEMNET for the KAACR, the two NGOs continued to work together to some extent to coordinate the thematic focus on the girl child going into Dakar, even though FEMNET's public lobbying on behalf of girls was one part of a larger set of advocacy between 1992 and 1994.

These institutional and individual connections may partially explain why FEMNET more publicly joined the lobbying campaign in late 1994. Just before the African Regional Conference on Women in Dakar, FEMNET's new executive director, Joyce Mangvwat, was listed as the coauthor of the *Platform for Action on the African Girl Child*. This was one of the last major publications resulting from the public lobbying campaign to include the girl child in the Dakar Platform for Action and to place a spotlight on the issue at the Dakar NGO Forum and official conference. UNICEF's New York headquarters funded FEMNET's publication of the *Platform for Action on the African Girl Child*, and FEMNET's staff distributed one thousand copies of the booklet at the meeting in Dakar. Joyce Umbima, FEMNET's former interim director, the former national executive director of the Child Welfare Society of Kenya, and then the chairperson of the KAACR, was listed as the coauthor alongside FEMNET's new head, Mangvwat.[50]

In a stark reversal of many of FEMNET's previous statements on women, girls, and development, the *Platform for Action on the African Girl Child* built on the narrative UNICEF had been promulgating about the girl child's subjugation in Africa. It portrayed girls as universally oppressed by "social and cultural factors," particularly in the form of physical, sexual, and psychological violence.[51] The document laid the origins of poverty and underdevelopment on familial and cultural factors, blaming women's alleged lack of contributions to economic development on girls' victimization under apparently timeless and inherent discrimination.[52] The solution, according to the FEMNET publication, was for individuals, communities, donors, and NGOs to "empower" girls by boosting their "self-esteem" and to "sensitize" parents and communities on the importance of treating their daughters better.[53] The document never discussed advocacy for resource allocation or political mobilization at the international or national levels, focusing instead on raising awareness and changing mindsets and interpersonal behaviors at the individual, familial, community, and cultural levels. Whereas FEMNET's earlier advocacy involved discussions of girls as part of broader calls for an end to structural adjustment policies to promote gender justice and combat poverty, the booklet the organization published with UNICEF funding and widely distributed in Dakar relied on "adjustments within gender relationships and behavior of men and women" to both promote girls' rights and alleviate poverty.[54]

Bottom-Up and Top-Down Change in the Dakar Declaration and Platform for Action

The campaign to write girls as a unique area of focus into the African Platform for Action adopted in Dakar proved successful; the last critical area of concern added to the document was the girl child. That section of the conference documents drew heavily from the Girl Child advocacy campaign and repeated a variation UNICEF's oft-repeated phrase since 1990: "the girl-child of today is the woman of tomorrow."[55] The African Platform for Action similarly repeated the claims of the girl child lobbying campaign that the girl child's "status [is] considered inferior right from birth" and that girls are uniquely vulnerable to sexual "exploitation."[56] The brief section on the girl child in the African Platform for Action articulated a broader view of causality for girls' plight than certain aspects of the narrative that UNICEF, and then the KAACR and FEMNET, promoted. It cited a range of factors, from "depressed economic conditions" and "high poverty" to "negative socio-cultural values," as causing girls' plight. To address girls' discrimination, however, the African Platform for Action was largely in line with the logic of the lobbying campaign that had written girls into it. The African Platform called for changes in attitude and practice at the individual and cultural levels. It specifically promoted the "elimination of negative cultural attitudes and practices against women and girls," the augmentation of girls' "self-esteem," and public campaigns to make men and boys, women and girls more "aware" of girls' plight.[57]

But the African Platform for Action did not only focus on bottom-up change through the figure of the girl child. Other revisions were made to the final version of the African Platform for Action: an increased focus on structural adjustment policies, foreign debt, widening inequalities in wealth under globalization, and the devastating impacts of the global economic crises of the 1970s and 1980s. All of these forces, the final document argued, had perpetuated the preexisting "marginalization of developing countries. Numerous, interrelated global factors therefore impinge on the lives of women in Africa, affecting both their productive and reproductive roles."[58] Diminished governmental expenditures and the increasing privatization of social services, the Platform for Action argued, "have compounded further the already disadvantaged situation of the women" through the erosion of educational and health care initiatives designed to combat "pre-existing conditions of inequality" on the continent.⁵⁹ To address poverty, the African Platform for Action demanded a relief of Africa's "crippling external debt" through direct loan cancellation and agreements to spend money owed on women's initiatives instead of repaying it to creditors.⁶⁰ The final platform also called for "the full participation and empowerment of women and girls in society to make full use of all human resources in the struggle against multidimensional poverty," especially through educational access, remunerated employment, health care, and family planning.⁶¹ In the official African Platform for Action adopted in Dakar, girls had a role to play in poverty alleviation. But they were called on to play that role with the support of national policies promoting robust, state-run programs on health care, education, and labor, and in a world in which foreign creditors forgave African debt and helped to ensure a more equitable distribution of global resources.

Adding Girls and Deleting Structural Adjustment from the Text of the Beijing Declaration and Platform for Action

In December 1994, FEMNET hosted a meeting to strategize for Beijing. In its status as the official UN-sanctioned coordinator of the Dakar NGO Forum and Africa Tent at the Beijing NGO Forum, FEMNET had been the head of the African Regional Steering Committee since the committee's inception in early 1994. Because of a lack of funding and personnel, however, FEMNET had difficulty orchestrating the meetings and various conferences, workshops, and other events it had hoped to conduct on a continental level.⁶² As a result, the Nairobi-based East Africa Sub-Committee of the African Regional Steering Committee made many of the official planning decisions for Dakar and Beijing. Also present on the committee and at the meeting in late 1994 were representatives from the KAACR, the Association of African Women in Research and Development, and the Council for Economic Empowerment of Women in Africa.

According to FEMNET's annual report for 1995, it was at the meeting in Nairobi in December 1994 that FEMNET, KAACR, and the two other NGOs mentioned above decided to attach a two-day African NGO caucus to an upcoming meeting in New York City of the UN Commission on the Status of Women. At the New York meeting, delegates from governments and international agencies were going debate the draft Beijing Declaration and Platform of Action and more generally plan for the conference. The linked NGO

Consultation Meeting in New York would prepare attendees for the World NGO Forum in 1995 that would run in parallel to the official governmental conference. Ahead of the New York City meeting, FEMNET's staff organized the African NGO caucus in order for delegates from the continent to lobby to include key issues from the African Declaration and Platform for Action in the emerging global framework that would be discussed in New York City. Attendees of the FEMNET-led session decided to focus the advocacy of the African NGO Caucus in New York on four key issues: poverty, peace, women in the democratization process, and the girl child.[63]

Of the four issues for which FEMNET lobbied in its capacity as the organizer of Africa's delegates to the caucus in New York, the only one that FEMNET's internal history and other preserved documents claim had a significant impact in the crafting of the Beijing Platform for Action was the girl child initiative. This was partially because, according to a US State Department summary of the New York City meeting, the US government's delegation strongly objected to language in the African Platform for Action from Dakar describing the "cause and effect" of structural adjustment policies, foreign debt, and poverty. The US delegates bracketed connected language in the draft Beijing Declaration and Platform for Action on foreign debt cancellation, "the allocation of resources," and macroeconomic policy.[64] Bracketing is a bureaucratic tactic employed in negotiations over draft UN documents. It allows governmental representatives to place in brackets sections they want removed or with which they disagree—a signal to other delegates that if not changed, the bracketed language may prevent that delegation from voting for the final document. Martha Alter Chen has referred to fights that broke out over bracketed language within the UN women's movement as a "battle of the brackets," invoking language used by activists and lobbyists.[65] This tongue-in-cheek reference belies a crucial tool within the mundane world of UN conference politics: the ability to delete things from being written into norms.

Alongside their bracketing of calls for high-level economic policy changes, US delegates supported the addition of language on "economic opportunities for women and inclusion of women in economic policy making," such as access to for-profit "credit and savings mechanisms."[66] The end result was that the version of the global Declaration and Platform for Action hammered out in New York City—and adopted, with relatively minor amendments, in Beijing—called for more studies on the effects of structural adjustment policies on women through "gender sensitive social impact assessments," despite the existence of a multitude of studies on the topic already.[67] Like bracketing, this was another technology of erasure at work in haggling over the content of the Beijing Declaration and Platform for Action: denying knowledge that already existed while calling for more studies on the subject. The finalized conference outputs for the UN Fourth World Conference on Women in Beijing would neither denounce structural adjustment, advocate for a cancellation of foreign debt owed by countries in the Global South, nor repeat the African Declaration and Platform for Action's stipulation for the more equitable distribution of global resources. As calls to improve the situation of women and girls by remaking the global economic system were bracketed and then erased from the document, endorsements of free-market and for-profit empowerment schemes for women, such as microfinance lending, remained and expanded.[68]

In contrast to their textual deletions and stonewalling of much of the African delegations' lobbying in New York City, the United States and European Union delegates were receptive to the inclusion of a special section on the girl child in the Beijing Declaration and Platform for Action. They reportedly worked to adapt the language to make it more universal and less specific to Africa.[69] According to a US Department of State summary, the United States then used pledges of financial resources for the implementation of the Beijing Platform for Action as negotiating chips to convince other countries, particularly in the Middle East, to overcome their reservations about the language involving the girl child's access to inheritance and private property rights and to secure the girl child as the twelfth area of concern agreed on in Beijing.[70] Among other things, this narrative positioned the United States as a champion of girls' and women's rights vis-à-vis particular countries in the Middle East after the Gulf War—a narrative that would continue and expand into the war on terror.[71]

Because members of African NGOs had not been able to convene since Dakar, aside from the small meeting at FEMNET's headquarters in Nairobi in December 1994, the outcome of the March–April 1995 caucus in New York City was that African NGOs were still reportedly not well organized to effectively mobilize in Beijing. FEMNET and other members of the steering committee met with the secretary general of the conference, Gertrude Mongella, who encouraged them to lobby governments to have their issues included in the Beijing Declaration and Platform for Action. The FEMNET-led African Steering Committee then organized two regional NGO meetings to take place within the continent before Beijing. This planning meant that a critical mass of NGOs went into Beijing feeling prepared and ready to convey an effective message.[72] The problem was, the Beijing Declaration and Platform for Action were written *before* Beijing, and the main opportunity to significantly alter the documents, aside from having national delegates to the official conference make basic proposed amendments in a highly politicized conference atmosphere, had been at the New York City planning meeting in March and early April.

Adopting the Beijing Declaration and Platform for Action

For two weeks in September 1995, delegates from 189 countries debated an official Declaration and Platform for Action that would set the agenda for the contemporary women's rights movement. More than 17,000 representatives from national governments, international agencies, and NGOs officially participated in the formal governmental plenary. Nearly a third of those attendees were journalists who kept audiences around the world apprised of the happenings in Beijing. Simultaneously, for ten days before and during the official conference, 30,000 advocates descended on the World Conference on Women's NGO Forum. The Chinese government had made a last-minute decision to move the location of the NGO Forum to Huairou, a district fifty kilometers north of Beijing, in an effort to marginalize the influence of NGO Forum attendees on both the governmental plenary and on internal politics within China. Heavy rain during the NGO Forum made Huairou wet and muddy, according to attendees, who spent hours commuting to and from the venue by bus. Attendees at the NGO Forum mixed high-level dignitaries from national governments, UN agencies, and international donors with advocates from a bevy of women's causes around the world.

"The Girl Child" was the twelfth and final strategic objective named in the Beijing Platform for Action. The document dramatically expanded the Dakar Platform for Action's comparatively brief analysis of girls. It directly borrowed the language and logic laid out in UNICEF's "The Situation of Girls in Africa" and in the lobbying materials released by KAACR and FEMNET ahead of the conferences. Proclaiming that "the skills, ideas and energy of the girl child" were necessary for the fulfillment of the World Conference on Women's three themes of equality, development, and peace, the Beijing Platform for Action stated that there was "worldwide evidence that discrimination and violence against girls begin at the earliest stages of life and continue unabated throughout their lives." Girls' inequality was especially pronounced in "sub-Saharan Africa and Central Asia," according to the document.[73] Because of this discrimination, and especially because of "sexual and economic exploitation, pedophilia, forced prostitution and possibly the sale of their organs and tissues, violence and harmful practices such as female infanticide and parental sex selection, incest, female genital mutilation and early marriage, including child marriage," the girl child, "the woman of tomorrow," could not "develop to her full potential."[74] Unlike the Dakar Platform for Action, the Beijing document did not emphasize poverty or economic circumstances as major factors contributing to girls' allegedly universal oppression. In a section not dealing with the girl child, the Beijing Platform for Action mentioned the negative impacts of structural adjustment programs on adult women "in Africa and the least developed countries." But it attributed those consequences to the programs' poor technical design and implementation. The Beijing conference outputs ultimately called structural adjustment programs "beneficial in the long term."[75] For girls, the causes of oppression were either described as cultural or had no root, as if they inherently existed in a state of nature.

To ease the plight of the girl child and create a more just and prosperous world, the Beijing Platform for Action recommended a series of actions at the community, family, and individual levels. Echoing iterations of the girl child lobbying campaign's calls for girls' liberation through psychological change, the Beijing Platform posited the necessity of the "elimination of intra-family discrimination against the girl child" and efforts to "sensitize the girl child, parents, teachers and society" on topics from good health care practices and intimate violence in the family to "customary practices," such as female genital mutilation, that hurt girls.[76] Through increased "awareness," the text argued, girls could also better "participat[e] in social, economic and political life" of their societies and promote the "development process."[77] Reflecting successful lobbying from the United States and countries in the European Union, the Beijing Platform for Action also included a broad emphasis on national legal frameworks promoting girls' access to individual rights such as inheritance and protection from abuse.[78]

Contested Legacies

There is tension in the archive about FEMNET's legacies on the UN Fourth World Conference on Women in Beijing. After the end of the historic conference, UNICEF's new executive director, Carol Bellamy, and the officer in charge of the United Nations Development Program's Regional Bureau for Africa, Emmanuel Dierckx de Casterle, both wrote to FEMNET to thank the NGO for its leadership in writing the girl child into the Global Platform for Action. FEMNET printed the letters in *FEMNET News*.[79] While they do not all mention FEMNET by name, reports also exist from all over the world crediting the African delegation to the New York Commission on the Status of Women meeting in March and April of 1995 for their effectiveness in lobbying to have a separate section on the girl child included in the document. Dorothy O. Helly of Hunter College and the Graduate School, CUNY called the addition a "brilliant strategy" for the broader women's rights movement because it brought conference attendees together around a relatively noncontroversial topic.[80] This is a striking statement. Shouting matches had arisen between delegates from Global North and South at the previous two UN World Conferences on Women over female circumcision and the real and imagined sexual suffering of girls and women in Africa, discussed in chapter 2. At the World Conferences on Women in Copenhagen in 1980 and Nairobi in 1985, some attendees protested that sensationalized accounts of the genitalia of girls and women in Africa distracted from calls for high-level action to address the economic realities that contributed to patriarchy within Africa.

What had been a divisive issue was now, in Helly's view and in the unanimously adopted Beijing conference outputs, an area of harmony. As these sensationalized depictions of the sexual suffering of girls in the Global South grew in volume, especially via the special section on the girl child, calls for high-level economic action disappeared from view.

An internal history of FEMNET produced in 2012 also portrayed the lobbying campaign to write girls into the Beijing conference outputs as a political victor. It called the organization's work with UNICEF on the girl child "the most unique area of African success in the process and outcome of the Africa and Beijing initiatives." It argued that "the findings, strategies, recommendations, materials and tools developed under [FEMNET's work with UNICEF on girls] became the source of ideas and concepts for the formulation of the Girl Child Action area in the African, and later Beijing, Platform for Action."[81]

FEMNET's internal documents from soon after the conference and in other areas of the 2012 internal history complicate these narratives. They place less of an emphasis on the girl child when discussing FEMNET's relationship with the UN Fourth World Conference on Women. In the NGO's annual report for 1995, published less than six months after Beijing, an anonymous article reflected on FEMNET members' participation in the event. While it briefly described the NGO's work with UNICEF and KAACR to lobby on behalf the girl child, it dedicated significantly more attention to participation in the events of the NGO Forum in Huairou. FEMNET's leadership coordinated the Africa Tent, which the report described as the home base to the nearly four thousand African women and men who participated in the nine-day forum. Under FEMNET's leadership, the tent hosted an African cultural night, talks, meetings, dances, and other forms of advocacy and socialization. Those activities, FEMNET's report reminisced, highlighted the "rich and varied cultures and traditions" on the continent and foregrounded the techniques African women used to respond to an "unstable world situation." The Africa Tent also hosted a different theme on each day of the forum, with the various thematic committees FEMNET set up before the Dakar conference in charge of each day. The themes covered were, in order, Environmental Issues; Women and Democracy; Women, Violence, and Human Rights; Women and Peace; Education; the Girl Child; Women's Health; Gender Training and Poverty (combined themes); and Women and the Media and Women, Art, Culture, and Sports (combined themes).[82] In this lineup, the girl child was once again a component in the middle of a greater and varied whole of FEMNET's mobilization, which explicitly broadcast women's vast range of circumstances and experiences and posited a variety of solutions to the interconnected problems of economic and gender justice on the continent.

FEMNET's 1995 annual report went into particularly rich detail when describing the Program of Plenaries, "a site for setting the agenda for the global women's movement" within the NGO Forum. The unnamed Africa region presenter at the Program of Plenaries, according to FEMNET, praised the end of apartheid in South Africa, condemned ongoing wars in Angola and Rwanda, decried multiparty politics as failing to be truly democratic, and paid particular attention to the consequences of "a move from primary production to a global/free market. She emphasized the weakening of African economies due to economic globalization, declaring that weaker economies needed protection for survival." In FEMNET's description, the speaker condemned structural adjustment policies in Sub-Saharan Africa for disproportionately hurting women in the name of "'third-world' debt" repayment. In light of growing global inequalities between "North and South," the speaker called for a new world order, the remaking of international trade protocols, and "the need to restructure in order to address poverty."[83] She also promoted "indigenous systems of communal property rights . . . instead of privatizing all property." FEMNET reported that the speech condemned "the expansion of free market capitalist economies" not only for increasing inequalities between rich and poor but, "most of all, [for] an increasing poverty of women."[84]

This African delegate speaking at the Program of Plenaries reportedly followed her discussion of capitalism, poverty, gender, and North-South divides by questioning "the rights of NGOs to speak for" African women and communities. Echoing many of the themes put forth back in FEMNET's 1992 Programming Conference, the speaker advocated changing NGO boards to involve input from "constituents" rather than viewing them merely as "beneficiaries" of policies. Without this, she allegedly said, the "women's movement" would stay isolated and overly elitist. FEMNET recounted how the speaker condemned the need for NGO accountability to donors, given that foregrounding donor priorities actively led NGOs to work against the best interests of their communities. The speaker called on NGOs to renegotiate their relationships with donors in the short term and to push for self-reliance in the long term through initiatives such as the establishment of donor trust funds. FEMNET portrayed the speech of the African delegate to the Program of Plenaries as reflecting deep concern about NGOs having not maintained their "autonomy" while taking money and projects from international agencies and national governments.[85] In its four-page, single-spaced, detail-laden recounting of the NGO plenaries and the African NGO's proposed plan of action moving forward, FEMNET mentioned "girls" exactly once, in passing, in a section on expanding women's and girls' educational access.[86]

When reflecting on the Third World Conference on Women in Nairobi, Gachukia remarked the NGO Forum is where "real issues within the women's movement" were debated, compared with more sanitized and whitewashed official conference.[87] In Beijing, those "real issues" continued to concentrate on topics of racism, economic inequality, North-South tensions, and patriarchy. They did not primarily focus on female circumcision or forms of intimate, sexually explicit oppression—topics Gachukia would describe as efforts from white women in the Global North "to go under our skirts to identify our problems" at the expense of discussions of economic and other structural causes of the suffering of women and girls in the Global South.[88] But the Beijing Platform for Action, which delegates from all 189 countries in attendance at the World Conference on Women voted unanimously to approve, explicitly put forth a vision of economic growth and social justice that rested on going under the skirts of girls and into the minds of girls in order to help the Global South develop. Ironically, the inclusion of the girl child as the twelfth and final agenda item within the Beijing Platform for Action came to be viewed as evidence that the African delegates had finally had their say in the crafting of the global women's movement. A reflection from US delegate Linda Tarr-Whelan demonstrates this irony and the broader economic stakes involved in the way in which the girl child was written into the Beijing Platform for Action. Whelan's reflection was published in *Human Rights*, the quarterly magazine published by the American Bar Association's Section of Civil Rights and Social Justice:

> The Beijing Platform for Action . . . created benchmarks for achieving women's empowerment and advancement as an investment for societies. Here was a road map for women's full participation in every aspect of society—economic and employment opportunities, health and education, prevention of violence against women, the "Girl Child" (of particular importance to African delegates), land and inheritance rights, family law, participation in decision-making, and the role of the media. . . .

Most impressive to me was watching a new mindset take hold that women are the most underutilized resource in the world—seeing the power and potential of women's talents and skills as essential for countries to succeed. . . .

Providing education for girls and opening up economic opportunity, particularly through microenterprise lending; focusing attention on safe motherhood; and stopping human rights abuses and the spread of HIV-AIDS in women have become global phenomena. . . .

Where does this leave us? There is an inexorable wave of change to advance and empower women as a matter of human rights and economic reality.[89]

It was in the context of trying to adjust to the "economic reality" of structural adjustment programs and the spread of neoliberal capitalism in the wake of the global economic crash that the global women's movement focused on the girl child and her sexual suffering.

Conclusion

Scholars and activists have noted that the outputs of the UN Fourth World Conference on Women in Beijing promoted neoliberal feminism while the outcomes of the three prior UN World Conferences on Women that took place during the Women's Decade between 1975 and 1985 were more economically leftist in their calls for high-level, structural economic changes, such as their embrace of the New International Economic Order. One way to read this history is that the Cold War nominally ended between 1989 and 1991, removing the leftist economic impulses—socialist states and their delegations to the conferences—that kept the rise of US-backed neoliberal capitalism at bay from the outputs of the previous conferences. This is Kristen Ghodsee's reading of the situation: in Beijing, "a certain brand of liberal, bootstrap-pulling, entrepreneurial feminism predominated over the state-focused activism that had influenced previous UN women's conference documents." She continues, "Although there were still many leftist and socialist women in attendance at the Beijing conference (most from the developing world), they no longer enjoyed the same power and influence without the financial backing of the Eastern Bloc and the context of superpower rivalry."[90]

Without discounting the crucial role that the end of the Cold War and the rise of the United States as the world's supposed sole superpower—a narrative that can be complicated in a variety of ways but that matches up with dominant optics of the situation at the time, at least from certain vantage points—this chapter has shown how such large-scale dynamics in international relations played out at the mundane levels of bureaucratic policymaking. Doing so shifts the narrative and complicates it in crucial ways. As Linda

Tarr-Whelan observed, it was not the US delegation that was most directly responsible for writing girls into the Beijing Platform for Action. The special section on the girl child resulted instead from a lobbying campaign among people at UNICEF, FEMNET, and KAACR. Portraying girls as universally oppressed, especially in the Global South, and depicting their real and imagined sexual suffering through sensationalized accounts were central to the lobbying campaign. Calling for the emotional empowerment of girls, a change in parental mindsets, and the altering of local cultures were the named solutions for the intertwined problems of patriarchy and economic development.

At the same time, the United States did play a large role in writing other sections *out* of the Beijing Platform for Action—sections that FEMNET and a broader set of lobbyists from Africa wanted included alongside the section on the girl child. These deletions removed pointed criticisms of structural adjustment as worsening the status of women in the Global South. They also erased calls for policy changes at the macroeconomic level, such as the forgiveness of state-held debt. It is this simultaneous process of circulation and erasure that made the outputs of the Beijing Platform for Action emblematic of the kind of neoliberal feminism that would, in the period after 1995, dominate international norms and policymaking. While the end of the Cold War provides a crucial backdrop against which this process took place, it becomes visible only when focusing on the quotidian bureaucratic haggling through which the texts of both the African Regional Platform for Action and the Beijing Platform for Action were written, negotiated, and adopted.

6

Empowering African Girls through Corporate Sponsorships?

The Afterlives of the Beijing Platform for Action

In 1995, Mercy Musomi was one of roughly fifty thousand people to converge in Beijing, China, for the final United Nations World Conference on Women. As a delegate to the conference's NGO Forum, Musomi constituted part of a group of people who successfully lobbied to make girl-focused economic programming, or Girls in Development, a central focus of the historic event. By supporting the inclusion of Section L, "the girl-child," in the conference outputs and raising awareness about it at the ten-day-long NGO Forum that ran parallel to the official event, Musomi and her peers helped to make Girls in Development a dominant international framework for economic programming, women's rights, and children's rights. The adoption of Section L in Beijing would have consequences not only within the United Nations but in a mix of institutions and advocacy groups around the world.

Reflecting on the importance of the Beijing conference nearly two decades later, Musomi recalled, "That is the moment, because the Platform for Action was developed and everything else ... that was the time that girls' issues came to an international forum. And from then it has been the issues of girls" that have dominated Musomi's own work and that of a number of human rights and economic development practitioners around the world.[1] Musomi is far from being alone in the assessment of Section L's ripple effect in the Beijing conference outputs. Heather Switzer has called the Beijing Platform for Action "significant" for being "the first ... global agenda-setting platform and multilateral agreement to single-out girls as a discrete demographic disaggregated from 'women' and 'children.'" The Beijing conference results, Switzer notes, were "widely circulated" and inspired the codification of Girls in Development in the UN's Millennium Development Goals, in a host of "corporate responsibility" initiatives and public-private partnerships, in the work of NGOs all over the world, and more.[2]

This chapter focuses on the period after the adoption of Girls in Development in the Beijing Platform for Action. It unpacks how these norms translated into practice with a representative case study following the Girl Child Network, the girl-focused NGO that Musomi would go on to help found and lead in Nairobi after she returned from Beijing. There are many possible case studies to choose from to demonstrate the impacts of Section L's inclusion in the final UN World Conference on Women—too many to fit into a single monograph. Focusing on the Girl Child Network in Nairobi serves at least three purposes. First, the involvement of Musomi and the other founders in Beijing shows direct causality between the 1995 World Conference on Women and the growth of tangible girl-focused programming in its wake. Musomi's own recollection and the written records of the NGO make clear that it was the success of the girl-focused lobbying campaign detailed in the previous chapter that inspired the Girl Child Network's creation and activities. As one of many examples, the minutes from a meeting of the Girl Child Network in 1998 show that members of the NGO referred to the Beijing Platform for Action and encouraged one another to bring hard copies of the platform to future meetings as they discussed the organization's operations and future plans.[3]

Beijing was more than a mere space of debate and public spectacle where governmental delegates voted to adopt an agenda that had no legally binding enforcement mechanisms. The UN Fourth World Conference on Women in Beijing and the inclusion of the section on the girl child within the official conference outputs directly led to the creation of institutions like the Girl Child Network and the programming that its staff would undertake. Not all girl-focused institutions and initiatives created after the conference had such direct links to it, of course; the norms adopted in Beijing rippled outward in various ways. The Girl Child Network serves as an important reminder, however, that direct causality between the conference and subsequent girl-focused programming did indeed exist. It further provides a case study as to how people like Mercy Musomi translated the norms adopted in Beijing into actual on-the-ground programming in ways that interacted with actual girls and their families.

Second, for the purposes of the particular story that this book tells—one that centers both Nairobi and actors such as Musomi in a global history of girl-focused economic development—following the story back to Nairobi from Beijing shows that Nairobi was more than a hub of thought and activism for the growth of Girls in Development. It and the country of Kenya were also prime laboratories in which staff of the Girl Child Network enacted, tested, and refined girl-focused initiatives.[4] As is usually the case in human-focused programming, Nairobi and broader Kenya were spaces in which donors, the public, parents, teachers, and girls themselves engaged with Girls in Development. They participated in girl-focused programs, pushed back against them, expanded and appropriated them, and otherwise creatively engaged with the meanings of girl-focused development planning as it touched their own lives.[5]

Focusing back on Nairobi in this way shows the dual nature of cities like Nairobi and countries like Kenya in histories of development, humanitarianism, and the creation of international norms. They have simultaneously served as hubs of thought and as places to test out this thought through policy implementation. In this history, it was not only internationally mobile women like Eddah Gachukia, Njoki Wainaina, and even Mercy Musomi who shaped Girls in Development and helped internationalize this approach into a far-reaching set of norms. Lower-level NGO workers, girls, their parents, community members, and others have impacted and continue to impact the meanings of Girls in Development, especially as it is constantly renegotiated through its implementation in particular schemes and in specific locations across time and space.

At the same time, the story to come is not merely a celebratory tale of agency nor of girls and other people creatively appropriating Girls in Development for their own ends.[6] A red thread throughout this book has been the ways in which Girls in Development has served as a vehicle for the global expansion of free-market feminism and the sublimation of calls for structural changes to the global economy into calls for the internal psychological empowerment of individual girls and their families in order to pull themselves up out of poverty by their proverbial bootstraps and serve as engines of economic growth from below. This free-market feminism propelled by and embodied in Girls in Development has often contained coded forms of racialization and a particular geography. It has most often focused on Black, Brown, and Indigenous girls living in Africa, Asia, and South America.

This brings us to the third and final reason this chapter follows the story back to Nairobi through the Girl Child Network in the wake of final UN World Conference on Women in Beijing in 1995. Despite the uniqueness of this particular history, the tale of the Girl Child Network is emblematic of a broader trend in Girls in Development: the growing importance of sponsorships from corporations and representations of the sexually suffering girl child to campaigns that have been able to attract long-term donor funding. The history of the Girl Child Network is one that ends in the recent past and present, with the (re)creation of sexualized and racialized formulations of the suffering African girl child in need of rescue from multinational corporations.

One way the history of Girls in Development has often been told to date focuses on the 2008 financial collapse and the roles of campaigns led by the Nike Foundation, the Clinton Global Initiative, Warren Buffett's NoVo Foundation, Girl Rising, and more.[7] And yet, in the years surrounding the 2008 global financial crisis, these predominantly North America–based, capitalistic actors did not manufacture Girls in Development out of thin air and single-handedly impose it in places like Kenya in a last-ditch bid to save capitalism from calls for structural change and/or increased regulations. Instead, these actors often tapped into preexisting initiatives, many of them connected to Beijing and its wake.

This is, then, neither a simple story of the imposition of free-market, racialized feminism from multinational corporations and North Atlantic–based actors nor a celebratory tale of the agency of girls and their communities in spaces like Nairobi as they appropriated Girls in Development from below. It is instead a story that takes place in the frictions in between, as women like Mercy Musomi navigated their options for, as Dorothy Hodgson has eloquently put it, "effective political action in a world shaped by the legacies of colonialism and the contemporary policies and practices of neoliberalism."[8] The inclusion of the girl child in the Beijing Platform for Action reimagined what these forms of political action might look like in a world in which bold, structural changes to the global economic system had been eclipsed by calls for changes to girls' internal mindsets and an expansion of the very global economic system that had been under such intense scrutiny within the UN women's movement and beyond through calls for a New Economic Order and other changes since the mid-1970s. In this post–Cold War world of the 1990s and early 2000s, people like Musomi and institutions like the Girl Child Network tested, refined, and expanded newly cemented norms of fighting poverty and patriarchy from below via a focus on the girl child. They faced particular forms of constraints, found new opportunities, and, in the process, remade and re-created understandings of the sexually suffering African girl child who supposedly could, paradoxically, be rescued by neoliberal globalization and shield her community from its sharpest edges.

Founding the Girl Child Network

The Girl Child Network was founded by twenty-five Kenyan women who attended the UN World Conference on Women in Beijing in 1995.[9] "Amid discussions of poverty, health, violence, and education," notes a recent history of the NGO, these women "encouraged delegates to consider the unique experience of the girl child. They knew that issues like child marriage, female genital mutilation, and lack of access to education were all too real for girls they knew and girls around the world." Afterward, "when they left Beijing in September of 1995, these women had the Beijing Declaration and Platform for Action. . . . They also had a plan for making these objectives a reality in East Africa: create a unified and informed network of organizations and individuals working with girls."[10] Thus, the Girl Child Network was born. This origin story has been repeated in different iterations on the Girl Child Network's website, on social networking platforms such as LinkedIn and Facebook, and in press releases such as a UNESCO newsletter announcing the Girl Child Network as the 2020 recipient of the UNESCO Laureate Prize for Girls' and Women's Education.[11]

While it contains the narrative flourishes that origin stories often gain over time, this tale is largely supported by the proverbial receipts in founding documents and early NGO records that have been preserved at the Girl Child Network's headquarters in Nairobi. The UN Fourth World Conference on Women ended in September 1995. Within six months, by March 1996, a group of at least fifteen individuals representing fourteen different NGOs were conducting monthly meetings in Nairobi under the auspices of the Girl Child Network. At these meetings, they set parameters for the running of their new organization and kept detailed minutes to record their activities.[12]

The founders conceived of the Girl Child Network as "a national forum" whose membership would be made up of "NGOs, government organizations and other interested parties"[13] In practice, the earliest members of the Girl Child Network were a mix of local, national, and international NGOs and advocacy groups concerned with children, women, girls, economic development, and human rights. There was some overlap with the leadership of the lobbying campaign that had written girl-focused economic programming into the Beijing conference outputs. The Kenya Alliance for the Advancement of Children's Rights, where Mercy Musomi worked when she traveled to Beijing to represent the NGO at the event, was one of the NGOs most directly involved in creating the Girl Child Network and had been involved in the lobbying campaign that the previous chapter in this book details. Eddah Gachukia, FEMNET's cofounder and former chairperson, also discussed at various points in this book, presented at a meeting of the Girl Child Network in 1998 when she helped screen a video titled *Send Your Girl Child to School*.[14] The NGO for which Gachukia had served as the founding executive director since 1992, the Forum for African Women Educationalists, hosted the meeting of the Girl Child Network where Gachukia spoke. By then in her early sixties, Gachukia was a matron of Kenyan society. She was a former member of Parliament, founder of her own network of private schools, former leader of the UN women's movement, and well-known advocate for education. Staff at UNICEF also attended some meetings for the Girl Child Network and presented at one of the monthly meetings of the new NGO's members. These meetings initially took place at the offices of CARE Kenya and then rotated each month among the various NGOs that supported the network.[15]

Despite these connections with the lobbying campaign that wrote Girls in Development into the Beijing conference outputs, many of the founders and early supporters of the Girl Child Network constituted a new younger generation of advocates. They often worked for other nongovernmental organizations that arose during the global NGO boom since the 1970s in Nairobi, which continued to grow as a hub of developmentalist thought and programming on the continent.[16] People like Jane Mbugua from the African Network for the Prevention and Protection against Child Abuse and Neglect (ANPPCAN, est. 1986), Edwin Onyancha from the Center for the Study of Adolescence (est. 1988), Rosemary Wanjiku Mbugua from the Collaborative Center for Gender and Development (est. 1996), and Lydiah Anjiah from Action Aid Kenya (est. 1972) helped to craft the Girl Child Network into a new NGO and dictated its programming.[17]

Older international institutions beyond UNICEF that worked on many continents were also in the mix. CARE Kenya and its staff members like Jennifer Mpungu and Genga Idowu played particularly important roles in the foundation of the Girl Child Network. Established in 1946 as the Cooperative for American Remittances to Europe, CARE soon expanded its scope and geographical focus beyond supporting people living in the immediate aftermath of World War II. By the early 1960s, members of the international NGO were working in South and East Asia, Latin America, and Africa, and they opened the Kenya offices in Nairobi in 1968.[18] The Canada branch of Save the Children (est. 1919 in London in the wake of World War I) employed their own staff members in Nairobi who were also early supporters of the Girl Child Network.[19]

While Kenya-based NGOs and international NGOs with offices in Kenya constituted most of the founding membership of the Girl Child Network, some governmental agencies and state-funded institutions were also involved. Many of these agencies had been founded during colonialism and then nationalized after Kenya gained formal independence from the United Kingdom in 1963. Bisi Adebayo and other researchers at the University of Nairobi—a public institution of higher education founded in 1961—participated in early meetings, as did members of the Child Welfare Society of Kenya, a state-run agency founded during the Mau Mau war in 1955.[20] The Kenyan government was not the only state supporter of the Girl Child Network. Henk van Beers was an active member in the founding of the network, eventually joining the executive committee. Van Beers worked for the SNV Netherlands Development Organization, founded in 1965 by the Dutch Ministry of Foreign Affairs.[21] By 1998, the Canadian International Development Agency (CIDA)—an avid proponent of Women in Development and then Gender and Development frameworks—had joined the network, as did the United Kingdom's Department for International Development.[22]

In the early Girl Child Network meetings, the founders set forth a few purposes for the organization. They wanted the NGO to "articulate initiatives and concerns through advocacy," foster the "facilitation of information," and bring about a "strengthening of girl child programming in Kenya."[23] In various meetings held in 1996, they reproduced and expanded language from the Beijing Platform for Action by arguing that "the Girl Child has unique problems" and systemically faced a "disadvantaged situation."[24] She was "overshadowed by women" in programming led by "the GAD framework"—the Gender and Development framework that had built on and often replaced the Women in Development framework for economic growth and gender justice since the early 1990s. Women in Development, discussed in chapter 3, argued that economic development programs needed to more explicitly focus on women and tap into their under-recognized human capital.[25] Gender and Development approaches, which gained steam in the early 1990s but had roots in the 1980s, held that gender was a socially constructed relation of power in spaces such as the family, the home, and institutions. According to Gender and Development as a school of thought, gender could be both reinforced and challenged through economic development frameworks.[26] While the founders of the Girl Child Network, like the crafters of the Beijing Platform for Action, drew from both paradigms in their work, they argued that both Women in Development and Gender and Development were too focused on adult women and overlooked the girl child. On the other hand, the NGO's early members also argued that in "child specific programs," the girl child "is overshadowed by the boy children."[27] The Girl Child Network's founders therefore articulated a need to focus their NGO on the girl child and to remove her from the shadows at the nexus of women's rights, children's rights, and economic development.

Bureaucratic Hurdles and Funding Troubles

For its first few years of operation, the Girl Child Network was not registered as a formal legal entity, did not have its own offices, and operated through the

CARE Kenya secretariat in Nairobi. As in the founding story of FEMNET detailed in chapter 2 of this book, it has been a common strategy for new NGOs to be hosted by other larger NGOs in their first few years of operation. This arrangement gave the Girl Child Network's creators the ability to legally operate through the institutional registration documents of CARE Kenya, which, in turn, allowed them to legally solicit and receive donations to get the new institution up and running.

At the same time, nestling the Girl Child Network within the legal and operational auspices of CARE Kenya produced confusion and frustration among some of the new organization's members. In November 1996, Nazim Mitha, an employee of UNICEF's Kenya Country Office, raised concerns in a meeting of the network that there was not enough "clarity" between the operations of Girl Child Network and CARE Kenya. According to the meeting minutes, "The argument was, why could it not be construed that CARE was using the Network to get funds for other purposes? This argument was valid according to Nazim, because UNICEF, for example would be asking such questions. As he put it, there was a possibility that UNICEF would be interested in providing counterpart funding to the Network." Other attendees reportedly agreed, particularly in response to the announcement that CARE Kenya planned to use the future coordinator of the Girl Child Network both to oversee the network and to run some of CARE's own girl-focused programming. The result of these complaints was the argument that "a mechanism be sought to make the GCN [Girl Child Network] independent" from CARE both financially and in terms of the future staff who would oversee the network's operations.[28]

These tensions over how to legally and financially position the Girl Child Network as an institution took place against the backdrop of ongoing tensions within Kenya, and in many other countries in the post–Cold War world, about the relationship of NGOs to democratization and national sovereignty. One-party states like that of Kenya's Daniel arap Moi no longer received the same support that they had formerly enjoyed from the United States, the Soviet Union, and/or other nations whose governments treated countries in Africa and beyond as frontline states in the global Cold War. Kenya would become an increasingly important ally for the United States and Israel, and vice versa, in the growing war on terror in the late 1990s and early 2000s.[29] However, the 1990s was a decade in which the Moi regime and similar one-party governments were under increasing pressure to democratize and open up multiparty elections—which Kenya did for the first time in 1992.[30] As the 1990s wore on, pro-democracy activists in Kenya and internationally framed NGOs like the Girl Child Network as an essential part of the democratization process and as important for the creation a viable "civil society" that could advocate for the public interest and serve as counterweights to unchecked state power. In turn, people within the Moi administration and beyond often viewed NGOs, funded largely by foreign donors, as vehicles for undermining state sovereignty.[31] The Moi administration—and, after Moi left power in 2002, the Kibaki and then Kenyatta administrations—often changed or threatened to change the laws governing how NGOs like the Girl Child Network had to register with the state and report international donations in order to legally operate.[32]

The registration process for the Girl Child Network reflects this fraught and constantly changing political landscape. In 1998, it was officially registered as a nongovernmental organization; in 2000, it became a community-based organization; in 2006, it legally registered as a Charitable Trust Deed; and in 2012, it once again legally registered as an NGO.[33] Without going into all of the intricacies of what these legal changes in status meant, the Girl Child Network's written records make clear that its organizers sometimes felt as though they were wading through ever-expanding political cobwebs as they tried to legally position themselves to operate and receive donations—all without running afoul of a national government that not only changed its laws but also continued to intermittently disappear, torture, detain, and engage in various harassment tactics against human rights advocates. The government's forcible closures of multiple human-rights-focused NGOs and publications in 1995 and the firebombing of another NGO office—not officially a government act but speculated to be sanctioned by the Moi regime—attest to the political climate in which the Girl Child Network arose.[34]

And yet, the founders of the Girl Child Network did not see the government of Kenya merely as a source of bureaucratic stress or as an existential threat should the institution be perceived as politically dangerous. In many cases, early meeting minutes reflect a desire to work with the government of Kenya and to lobby certain ministries to fulfill their commitments to funding priorities in education, health care, and children's rights. As mentioned above, individual members and various institutions run or funded by the government of Kenya supported the Girl Child Network and worked alongside them in various ways. And despite its hostility to certain NGOs, the Moi administration also recognized that nongovernmental organizations funneled vast sums of money into the country. The government of Kenya declared NGOs an essential aspect of Kenya's national development strategy on multiple occasions throughout the 1990s and early 2000s. It has partnered with them in various capacities, from colonial times through early independence to the present.[35]

The perils of navigating the national bureaucracy as an NGO was not the only reason that CARE Kenya hosted the Girl Child Network within the former's Nairobi offices during the latter's first years of existence. As with many other NGOs, including FEMNET, funding constraints were the most frequently mentioned problems that the Girl Child Network faced early on. Financial reports, meeting minutes, and other documents from the Girl Child Network's secretariat make clear that the organization struggled to find financial footing. The NGOs that constituted the Girl Child Network's early members and donors often had limited funding themselves. Many would not or could not commit to reliable, long-term donations. More, many potential donors changed their plans every few years. Buzzwords and priorities in international development frequently shifted, making sustained, consistent programming difficult. While the Girl Child Network's staff began to publish a magazine in English for NGO workers and girls, *Binti* ("Daughter" in Kiswahili), in 1998, the network's more tangible girl-focused programming was initially next to impossible—its records are full of lamentations of late editions of the magazine, canceled meetings, and delayed events with stakeholders because of a lack of money and the fact that most people working with the Girl Child Network had other full-time jobs and were involved on a volunteer-only basis.

"The Launching Pad to Greatness" (and Institutional Autonomy): Corporate Sponsorships, International Donors, and the Sanitary Pads Campaign

The Girl Child Network did indeed separate from CARE Kenya over time, becoming its own legal entity in 1998, gaining Mercy Musomi as its full-time executive director in 2000, and boasting its own offices in 2001. However, the NGO continued to struggle to find financial footing and to create initiatives that directly engaged with girls. It was not until the Girl Child Network embraced corporate sponsorships, particularly with wealthy multinational corporations like Procter & Gamble, and attracted more overseas donors such as the Irish charity Aidlink that the NGO's funding stream became robust and reliable enough to hire multiple full-time staff members and create direct programming beyond *Binti* magazine. The initiative that helped the Girl Child Network establish these corporate and philanthropic partnerships and that has remained the NGO's flagship program into the present is the Sanitary Pads Campaign. Since its inception in 2005, the campaign has reportedly distributed menstrual pads, underwear, and other hygiene items to millions of Kenyan schoolgirls.

The logic guiding the campaign since its inception is that schoolgirls often miss classes when they are menstruating due to a lack of access to sanitary pads, a lack of knowledge of how to appropriately handle menstruation, and cultural and familial biases. This, the logic goes, disadvantages girls in formal education vis-à-vis boys. In turn, girls' human capital is allegedly not sufficiently developed, and girls are not sufficiently empowered to become profitable and self-confident entrepreneurs and workers as future women. More, the logic of the Sanitary Pads Campaign has contended, girls who miss class due to their periods are more likely to drop out of school and experience early marriage and gender-based violence. A 2007 article in *Binti* sums up this logic guiding the Sanitary Pads Campaign, calling it the "launching pad to greatness." Printed above a letter allegedly written by a schoolgirl named Nasieku, the slogan portrays the sanitary pad as a metaphor of a rocket launch pad that will propel the girls into lucrative futures, first as empowered schoolgirls and then as empowered, profitably laboring women who are fully in control of their own labor, reproductive and otherwise.[36]

The Sanitary Pads Campaign was rooted in partnerships with local and national businesses at its inception in early 2005. It was then bolstered by a mix of national and international governmental and nongovernmental organizations, according to the NGO's financial records and internal reports from the early 2000s. This included the supermarket chain Uchumi until its closure led the staff of the Girl Child Network to its rival chain, Nakumatt. The NGO's members also worked with Marvel Five, a Nairobi-based manufacturer of sanitary pads and diapers, to source products to distribute to schoolgirls. National shipping companies helped transport the pads for free from Nairobi to places like Mombasa. Twiga Chemicals, the Kenya branch of the Forum for African Women Educationalists (the NGO that Gachukia helped establish a few years before), and USAID also supported the campaign.

As time went on, however, work with wealthy multinational corporations and international donors became at least as important as the NGO's work with local and regional entities. By mid-2006, the Girl Child Network had reportedly distributed pads to fifty-five thousand schoolgirls across eight regions of Kenya. Most of the pads reportedly came from Procter & Gamble, a US-based multinational consumer goods company that sells sanitary pads and feminine hygiene products under globally distributed and widely recognizable brands like Always, Whisper, Oil of Olay, and Gillette. In 2006, the first year that Procter & Gamble donated to the Girl Child Network, it became the NGO's single greatest donor and increased the organization's annual budget by nearly 50 percent. This funding and other money that came into the NGO explicitly to support the Sanitary Pads Campaign allowed the organization to significantly increase its expenditures on program costs and hire more staff.[37]

This all occurred after some hiccups in getting the Sanitary Pads Campaign going. Working primarily with Marvel Five Investments to provide pads and cash for their distribution reportedly did not provide enough financial support to run the campaign. Early on, Girl Child Network staff had tried soliciting donations directly from individuals through drives at a local supermarket and at the Nairobi International Trade Fair. In employee-authored reports that the NGO kept on file, these drives consistently failed to yield sufficient donations. They also led staff of the Girl Child Network to receive disgruntled comments from grocery store shoppers, some of whom argued that the government—not individuals—should provide pads directly to schoolgirls. Other shoppers distrusted the campaigns or criticized their discussions of menstruation for being "taboo" and "unprofessional."[38] Partnering with Procter & Gamble proved to be lucrative for the NGO and allowed it a degree of unprecedented institutional autonomy and stability—which, in turn, allowed the Girl Child Network's employees to reach out to more corporate and international donors with new promotional materials and increasingly sophisticated public relations campaigns focused on girl power.

This corporate outreach snowballed. Also in 2006, the NGO's staff organized a motor sport race in Nairobi to raise money and awareness for the Sanitary Pads Campaign. Staff created promotional materials to deliberately target "car dealers, petroleum, [and] oil" companies and held the rally at a racetrack run by the East African–owned Portland Cement Company. Hyundai Motors was one of many donors to give through the rally. Also in 2006, Shell Oil Company, British Petroleum, and Boeing became donors to the Girl Child Network's Sanitary Pads Campaign.[39]

Three years later, by 2009, the Irish charity Aidlink had joined the fray and became another major long-term donor to the Girl Child Network. It, too, did so explicitly in order to support the Sanitary Pads Campaign. The Girl Child Network's budget continued to grow exponentially. Because of the success of the menstrual hygiene efforts in attracting wealthy large-scale donors, anxieties about whether the NGO would survive, be able to hire multiple full-time staff, or ever get its own girl-focused programming off the ground gave way to a well-established institution with fifteen full-time staff members and a budget that had grown by 400 percent, to roughly US$1.25 million in 2009. According to the NGO's annual reports and financial audits, the vast majority of this budget derived from publicity related to the Sanitary Pads Campaign and, in turn, was spent to allow the campaign to continue.[40]

Just as multinational corporations and international donors became increasingly crucial to the successes of the Girl Child Network and its flagship initiative, the promotional materials the NGO produced, and its communications to donors, became increasingly standardized and sophisticated. As one example, from 2006 onward, promotional materials generally included images or videos of girls receiving not only the sanitary pads but also accompanying pairs of underwear and, in some cases, a "wallet" in which the girls were supposed to keep their pads and other hygiene items. Calling the carrying cases for the pads "wallets" is symbolic of linkages of girls' genitalia, sexual health, and hygiene to financial investments and future wealth in the campaign materials and the broader, global discourses of Girls in Development that it represented after Beijing.[41]

Relaying the emotional response of the girls or their parents upon receipt of the items was another crucial component of this increasingly standardized script as the campaign became better funded and the promotional materials more curated. One annual report told donors that excursions to distribute pads to Somali girls in northeastern Kenya led to a particularly emotional exchange: "The experience was remarkable as mothers to the girls receiving the packs broke into tears." Promotional materials containing images often began with serious, abject-looking schoolgirls as the materials described the plight of menstruating and more generally oppressed girls across the continent. The campaign literature would then shift to images of beaming or dancing schoolgirls holding up pairs of underwear and menstrual pads for the camera to see, evidence for donors that their money was hard at work in the service of girl power.

Religion and ethnicity often played a part in these visual materials. Girls were shown in hijabs or other headscarves commonly associated with Islam, a dominant religion in Kenya's Somali communities. The campaigns partially focused on these communities during a time when Kenya's role in the war on terror vis-à-vis neighboring Somalia was escalating. Girls in photos similarly often wore clothing and beaded jewelry that signified to an informed viewer their status as Maasai or Kalenjin—two ethnicities long seen in Kenya as less developed and supposedly more oppressive to girls and women than others that had existed in closer proximity to missionary and state-led development, welfare, and education initiatives in the former British colony turned nation-state. Campaign literature often thanked God and mentioned various Protestant Christian and Catholic partner organizations.

In some cases, the staff of the Girl Child Network facilitated dramatized video shoots. The Irish charity Aidlink sent videographers to Nairobi to film volunteer actors from the United States International University pretending to be adolescent menstruating schoolgirls who missed school and faced bullying because of their lack of access to sanitary pads. In the film script, the university students acted out finding empowerment and self-esteem once they began to use the pads. When the students proposed to shoot the campaign video on their university's campus—reportedly after finding inspiration in their own staging of the feminist play *The Vagina Monologues* on campus—the Girl Child Network staff instead set up a video shoot at a nearby primary school. This was in order to make the setting more realistic for the viewer. These staged performances—ones the Girl Child Network's staff savvily crafted to appeal to particular donor sensibilities and that university students creatively enacted as they were engaged in their own global conversations about gender, sex, and the nature of systemic oppression—were an essential part of the Sanitary Pads Campaign and, in turn, of the NGO thriving as an institution.

Friction with the Past

This history of the Girl Child Network and its flagship operation contains continuities with girl-focused welfare and development work in various parts of Africa and beyond during colonialism in the first half of the twentieth century and early independence in the 1960s. It fixates on the sexual suffering of girls; it holds up education and consumer goods, offered through capitalist charity and then, presumably, the girl's own purchasing of Procter & Gamble's menstrual pads from supermarkets like Uchumi and Nakumatt, as the solution; and it elides notions of history—the various technologies and techniques through which people managed menstruation in the region and beyond for thousands of years of human existence before the early 2000s has been erased from view. It also promotes various narratives of saviorism and uplift with a mix of racial, ethnic, religious, regional, and gendered subtexts, although in this case a Nairobi-based NGO led by a team of Kenyan, Christian, and often Kikuyu staff headed by Musomi were the uplifters of girls in Somali, Kalenjin, Maasai, Muslim, and non-Christian communities.

In other ways, however, this story is unique to the post-1990, post–Cold War moment; the prior narrative of continuity, while likely familiar to historians of colonialism and early nationalism, is incomplete. It particularly fails to grasp how capitalism, and in this case neoliberal capitalism and the growth of multinational corporations, has been an essential part of girl-focused economic programming since the 1990s. In turn, Girls in Development has arguably been an important component of the economic growth and public relations of multinational corporations. In 2015, a decade after the launch of the Sanitary Pads Campaign, Procter & Gamble's subsidiary Always reportedly accounted for 65 percent of menstrual hygiene products sold in Kenya, edging out local companies like Marvel Five while drawing the ire of local feminist doctors and environmentalists for using harmful plastics and other chemicals that can reportedly endanger the health of their users and of the planet. It is worth noting that the composition of sanitary pads that Always sells in Africa is different from its pads currently sold in the Global North.[42]

The centrality of plastic as an ingredient in the manufacturing of sanitary pads may provide clues as to why companies like Shell and British Petroleum—members of the oil and gas industries that are essential to, and profit from, the production of plastics and that have deliberately escalated their support for the use of plastics in global manufacturing in the wake of declining profits from fossil fuels[43]—have been such central donors to the Sanitary Pads Campaign. The corporations and corporate foundations that support Girls in Development have often used this support in their own public relations, advertising, and promotional materials, insulating themselves from calls for more financial oversight in the wake of the 2008 financial crisis and the ongoing climate crisis in the process.[44]

Yet collapsing this history into a mere tale of co-optation from multinational corporations also misses crucial parts of the story. Returning to Dorothy Hodgson's writing on the ways in which neoliberalism and gender-based development work in East Africa grew in and through one another in fraught ways, in a "world shaped by the legacies of colonialism and the contemporary policies and practices of neoliberalism," Musomi and her colleagues at the Girl Child Network found both constraints and new opportunities.[45] The constraints were financial, they were bureaucratic, and they often required the NGO's staff to maneuver in a complex web that was suspended between the nation-state, the international system, and Nairobi as a physical hub of planning and enacting development. Over time, partnering with wealthy multinational corporations and international donors offered funding opportunities and institutional security that working with national and local NGOs, businesses, and governments could not.

In the process, donors received, and likely expected, particular emotional experiences of uplifting supposedly abject African girls from universal sexually based forms of oppression. Empowering girls through access to consumer goods facilitated by globalizing capitalism was an essential ingredient. Christianity as an uplifting force hovered not far in the background. All of this took place on the African girl child's genitalia as an imagined and often highly fetishized site of economic investment, gender-based empowerment, and development intervention. The focus on affective and psychological transformations within individual girls through discussions of empowerment and self-esteem, locating the roots of girls' real and imagined suffering within sexual biology and a lack of local knowledge, and framing the solution as integration into capitalistic markets as current consumers of pads and future laborers as educated and empowered women are all typical ingredients of globalizing narratives of "girl power" post-Beijing. A number of scholars have written about initiatives that have followed this script or similar ones since 2008, from Brazil to Malaysia, Tanzania, and many other locales.[46]

Conclusion

The Girl Child Network was established as a direct result of the inclusion of a special section on the girl child in the Platform for Action of the UN Fourth World Conference on Women. A history of the Nairobi-based Girl Child Network complicates existing scholarly tendencies to treat neoliberal forms of Girls in Development as stemming primarily from the work of corporate philanthropies and their Global North–based allies who are active the world of free-market development planning. The Girl Child Network's history is not one in which multinational corporations unilaterally imposed girl-focused programming onto people in spaces like Nairobi and broader Kenya. It is one of local actors situated within international and transnational networks, like the founders of the Girl Child Network, searching for ways to consistently fund their interest in working with girls. These actors found economic opportunities by partnering with multinational corporations and international donors, opportunities that allowed them to stabilize their institutions, hire more staff, and expand programming.

Such partnerships with donors came with strings that helped reproduce and remake long-standing images of the sexually suffering African girl child. Advocacy campaigns commodified images of girls for interlaced forms of economic, religious, emotional, racial, and ethnic consumption in the contexts of the global expansion of neoliberal capitalism, the escalating war on terror, and ongoing tensions in Kenyan state-making. African girls' genitalia served as fetishized sites of intervention for free-market development schemes in the process. Empowering girls meant integrating them into global markets as consumers and future entrepreneurs. These are the frictions inherent to Girls in Development as it has been implemented in a neoliberal, postcolonial, and post–Beijing conference world. When viewed in the context of the kinds of development planning called for in the outputs of the UN Third World Conference on Women in Nairobi in 1985, discussed in chapter 2—a new international economic order, large-scale debt forgiveness for countries in the developing world, renegotiated terms of trade, a distribution of wealth globally and within individual countries, and making women's labor more visible, less burdensome, and better compensated—the difference is stark. As calls for high-level action disappeared from view, a focus on the most intimate aspects of life for girls in Africa and the broader Global South through free-market frameworks replaced them.

Conclusion

The Platform for Action adopted at the UN Fourth World Conference on Women in Beijing was the first official output from a UN World Conference on Women that did not call for the creation of a new international economic order or demand some other form of large-scale, structural change to the global economic system. It also cemented into international norms a particular form of girl-focused programming as a central part of the linked pursuits for development and gender-based rights. These two events were not coincidental.

In the 1980s, staff at UNICEF led the turn to Girls in Development. They did so in the context of a perceived crisis in child well-being in the wake of the global economic crash and the turn to economic austerity via structural adjustment programs. Politically, UNICEF's platform served as an alternative to appeals for a reworking of global systems of economic exchange that caused poverty and increased mortality rates. Through the vehicle of girl-focused development, people connected to the agency shifted attention to bottom-up methods of economic growth and improving people's quality of life, rather than top-down structural changes. A focus on the real and imagined discrimination that girls faced in their homes and communities, which prevented their development as human capital or as a savvy financial investment in the name of economic growth, arose instead. In UNICEF's advocacy, an increasing focus on girls, their education, and their status—especially in the Global South—furthered a political platform that naturalized the effects of neoliberal economic policymaking and economic crisis as the results of patriarchy rooted within the nuclear family and local cultures. Girls, once singled out as victims of growing poverty and mortality, were now identified as the resources whose education and future labor were necessary to overcome poverty and broader forms of injustice.

While the focus on Girls in Development that initially grew within UNICEF in the 1980s would become hegemonic by the turn of the new millennium, staff at UNICEF did not single-handedly drive the internationalization of girl-focused programming. Instead, its global spread was the result of a lobbying campaign led by UNICEF and the African Women's Development and Communication Network, or FEMNET, which traces its origins to the lead-up to the UN Third World Conference on Women in Nairobi in 1985. A group of women from across Africa founded it as an explicitly Pan-African NGO meant to mobilize women on the continent surrounding development-related issues and to advocate for them within United Nations and the broader international system.

Nairobi occupied a particularly important space within this girl-focused FEMNET-UNICEF lobbying campaign. The Kenyan capital city housed FEMNET's headquarters, UNICEF's compound for its Eastern and Southern Africa Regional Office, and UNICEF's Kenya Country Office. Beginning in the 1950s, UNICEF's leadership increasingly expanded the institution's center of power from New York City to its field offices around the world. By the mid-1990s, Nairobi reportedly hosted 245 UNICEF employees, the largest number of personnel in the entire organization except for the US-based offices, which included the New York City headquarters.[1] It is within UNICEF's Nairobi hub and FEMNET's headquarters—initially housed at the UNICEF office compound as a young NGO—that one must situate the growth of multiple forms of advocacy surrounding girls, austerity, and development in the late 1980s and early 1990s.

It may be tempting to retrospectively view the girl-focused logic put forth in the Beijing Platform for Action of 1995—the version of girl power that would become hegemonic—as the inevitable outcome of UNICEF's activism and the dominance of neoliberal capitalism within international institutions after the end of the Cold War. However, the scope of the burgeoning Girls in Development movement and its political implications were deeply contested in the late 1980s and early 1990s. Various forms of political action and ideas arose through these negotiations. As FEMNET's girl-focused advocacy makes clear, a range of actors across Africa and beyond focused on girls as a way to call for the reworking of global economic and political structures forged through colonialism and capitalism. These forms of advocacy sometimes rejected the bottom-up, girl-focused visions of development that UNICEF put forth in its child revolution of the 1980s. They often called for structural, top-down changes to the global economic system in the name of girls and their well-being. At other times, FEMNET's advocacy embraced or built upon the girl-focused logic in UNICEF's work. Common across conversations was that adults invoked girls in order to justify, critique, and otherwise engage with capitalism and (de)colonization. The real and imagined status of girls, and in particular of African girls, served as the battleground on which far-reaching debates about a perceived crisis in capitalism, shrinking social welfare programs, and the unkept promises of decolonization took place.

How did these conflicting strands of girl-focused advocacy become whittled down and internationalize into a dominant version? The working of multiple ideas into one cohesive logic is not merely a history of the spread of knowledge within a transnational circuit; it is also a history of its erasure. The Girl Child Project provided a case study of how knowledge suppression and amplification emerged hand in hand as particular logics concerning girls and development became hegemonic. It offered key examples of how conflicting forms of knowledge about girls were selectively suppressed, silenced, and streamlined into a singular narrative through UNICEF and FEMNET's work together.

Here, the story drew from feminist histories of science and global intellectual histories that foreground agnotology, or the study of the production of forgetting, erasure, ignorance, or doubt. An agnotological approach focused on how, why, and under what conditions the erasures of certain ideas and actors connected to girl power as a set of economic frameworks occurred as others rose to ascendancy. Such discussions showed the intentionality and bureaucratic labor that went into erasing particular frameworks of gender-based rights and development, and the bodies of data and knowledge underpinning these frameworks, from circulation. Quotidian bureaucratic practices of knowledge creation, deletion, revision, and dissemination were critical to this coproduction of circulation and noncirculation, of knowing and unknowing, of amplification and suppression.

An agnotological approach also highlighted the importance of political contexts to determining which knowledge spread from the UNICEF-FEMNET lobbying campaign and became adopted as common sense and which knowledge was covered up, forgotten, or rendered obsolete. In this case, the institutional reliance of FEMNET on UNICEF for survival in a world of funding shortfalls and state-led political repression served as the crucible in which some knowledge about girls and development spread while others were erased or fell by the wayside. Multiple levels of silence and silencing characterized this process. The result was an increasingly singular iteration of girl power disseminated from the same FEMNET-UNICEF network in which multiple earlier visions clashed with one another about the necessary location of change to bring about a more just and prosperous world.

This streamlined vision of Girls in Development spread out to a geographically diffuse set of international, governmental, and nongovernmental institutions and individual actors. It did so in part through its inclusion in the final UN World Conference on Women in Beijing in 1995. As a direct result of the lobbying campaign, a special section on the girl child, Section L, was written into the conference outputs. Bureaucratic practices of knowledge deletion and the power of particular nation-states—especially the United States in a post–Cold War world—further molded Girls in Development into a system of thought that became common sense through its adoption in the culminating conference of the UN-based women's movement.

A major outcome of this process was making global economic inequalities and poverty seem like the results of universal yet culturally rooted patriarchy enacted within families, rather than the partial products of high-level economic policymaking. The Beijing Platform for Action served as a major touchstone in the shift of mainstream international feminisms from a focus on structural to individual causes and solutions to gender-based discrimination, poverty, and economic inequalities. Instead of demanding macro-level changes from above, as portions of the outputs of the previous three UN World Conferences on Women had done, the official outputs of the UN Fourth World Conference on Women focused on adjusting the mindsets and behaviors of girls and their kin within the idealized unit of the nuclear family. Girls' genitalia increasingly became a primary location for the linked pursuits for gender-based rights and development. Some of the language contained in the Beijing Platform for Action placed the blame for gender injustice, economic stagnation, and rising inequalities on apparently inherent and timeless "cultural" practices and beliefs within the Global South.

It is difficult to overstate the importance of the UN Fourth World Conference on Women in Beijing and the ideas it put forth about girls, patriarchy, poverty, development, education, and the labor of women. The booming field of girlhood studies has drawn attention to the various girl power schemes since the mid-1990s that have been promoted by actors such as the World Bank, billionaire Warren Buffet's NoVo Foundation, the Clinton Global Initiative, the Nike Foundation, and the governments of countries on every continent inhabited by humans. Yet the dominance of ideas put forth in the Beijing Platform for Action is not only evident in the activities of these institutional actors, these usual suspects in histories of free-market feminism. The norms adopted in Beijing have guided the work of smaller-scale organizations based in various parts of the world, such as the Girl Child Network. Inspired by the inclusion of the special section on girls in the UN Fourth World Conference on Women in Beijing, Mercy Musomi and her peers in Nairobi founded the Girl Child Network as an NGO with the goal of drawing more attention to the unique needs of girls in society. Yet they quickly butted up against some of the same realities that FEMNET's members encountered: financial constraints and the need to attract consistent donors in a world structured by neoliberalism and colonialism. Pursuing sponsorships from multinational corporations, many of them connected to the oil, gas, and plastics industries, and attracting funding and public attention from Christian organizations in a religious environment shaped by the war on terror in the Horn of Africa offered institutional stability and new opportunities for the staff of the Girl Child Network.

The narratives that increasingly came out of the Girl Child Network's campaigns—such as its flagship Sanitary Pads Campaign—often rooted girls' oppression within their sexual suffering. They tended to portray the solution to this suffering as capitalist and Christian charity, which would "empower" the girls to control their own sexuality by using sanitary pads manufactured by multinational corporations. The result was the post-Beijing entrenchment of the African girl child's genitalia as an imagined and often highly fetishized site of development intervention, investment, and profit-making for the corporations sponsoring the Girl Child Network's work.

While some of the particulars of the story may be unique, the Girl Child Network is hardly alone. Girl-focused development programming has flourished around the world since the end of the UN Fourth World Conference on Women in 1995. It has done so through the growth of NGOs and their work with a mix of governmental, corporate, religious, and international agencies from Liberia to Brazil, Indonesia, and Pakistan, to name just a few.[2] The 2008 financial collapse that rocked much of the world breathed new life into girl power programming as corporations seeking protection from calls for oversight turned to girl-focused public relations campaigns.[3] Yet multinational corporations did not invent these campaigns out of thin air. They often grabbed onto preexisting norms and models that had been cemented in Beijing and in the lobbying campaign that led up to it.

Historians have often been more comfortable depicting Girls in Development as schemes of control driven primarily by for-profit corporations, rooted in logics promoted by known promoters of neoliberal capitalism, such as the World Bank, than they have been in recognizing the fraught alliances that gave birth to the idea that girls are a crucial site of free-market investment. In the histories of girl-focused developmentalism that exist, corporations and institutions such as the Clinton Global Initiative serve as the initiators of Girls in Development schemes. The Clintons have, after all, become synonymous with neoliberal capitalism, and the name Hillary Clinton has become shorthand for *neoliberal feminism* to many. The problem with these stories is that they are not fully accurate. And, in their oversimplicity, they erase institutions such as FEMNET and the people who built it—a self-described group of Pan-African women advocating around issues related to women in development in Africa—from view.

An alternative or complementary script to the one above, of Girls in Development as a product of the unilateral imposition from large corporations and their institutional and governmental allies, is one that highlights the ways in which girls and other people in their communities have resisted and creatively appropriated girl-focused programming from below. This is also a familiar script and, for many historians, a comfortable one. We, and I include myself in this, have often been comfortable telling simple stories of imposition from the Global North and idealized resistance from Global South.

A familiar connected script—an alternative approach to writing this book—would have foregrounded the agency of girls in spaces like Nairobi as they have responded to girl power programs. It is vital to recognize that people targeted by dominant visions of rights-based development and other hegemonic frameworks have always creatively engaged with such programming. Yet highlighting girls' agency in response to Girls in Development does not help us to understand the high-level history of girl power and how it came to be so entrenched around the world. More, and as scholars such as Shirin M. Rai, Kalpana Wilson, and Sumi Madhok have noted, the commitment to agency as a concept has often reproduced the neoliberal developmentalist fetishization of individual actors perpetually resisting structural oppression from below.[4] In the process, overuse of the concept has written particular economic politics of the 1980s and 1990s, and their lingering colonial residues, into scholarly productions in the present (a time fraught with various politics and residues of our own). There is also a particular kind of "performance" and emotional labor at work in such stories of agency, as Walter Johnson argued. They often do more to make the author (often white, usually based at an institution within the Global North) "feel better and more righteous" than they accurately reflect the complexities of the past or "make the world better or more righteous."[5]

Tales of South-South resistance networks and collaborations earn particular romanticization in existing scripts of scholarly writing. Another way to write this book would have been through a triumphalist narrative centering how FEMNET as a Pan-African women-in-development NGO and African women as a largely self-organized, self-identifying collective successfully lobbied to include girls in the Beijing Platform for Action. This narrative would have shown how they shaped a major outcome of the UN women's movement and connected international movements for development and women's rights.

Such a narrative would have slotted neatly into debates that criticize existing scholarship of international norms and dominant frameworks—like human rights—for being overly Eurocentric. Going back to Johnson's observations about the emotional role that agency has often served, such a narrative of Pan-African feminist triumphalism might also feel good to someone trying to perform allyship in the age of Black Lives Matter and ongoing calls to decolonize academia. Yet this narrative, seductive as it may be, is also not the whole story. It would be, in the words of Lynn Thomas, another case of agency serving "as the impoverished punch line" of a story that is much more complex and "empirically rich."[6] In this case, telling a triumphalist narrative of FEMNET's members like Eddah Gachukia and Njoki Wainaina successfully shaping the creation of international norms through the inclusion of girls in the final UN World Conference on Women—and making this the romantic culmination of the story—would reproduce the silences and silencing inherent to the history of Girls in Development. It would fail to include how and why many of the political commitments attached to early visions of Girls in Development within FEMNET's Pan-African women's organizing were systematically removed from circulation and inclusion into an international set of norms. It would also artificially erase UNICEF and the US government, and the way that power operated in and through these institutions, in a late Cold War and then post–Cold War world from the story.

What remains is neither a Eurocentric narrative of one-dimensional imposition of girl-focused norms of development, in which African women are absent, nor a rosy and one-dimensional story of resistance or triumph. We have instead a story that grew through the cracks. "Frictions" and "irritative, chafing, edgy, uneasily friendly" alliances characterized the emergence of Girls in Development from the FEMNET-UNICEF lobbying campaign and its implementation in the work of NGOs like the Girl Child Network.[7] This campaign was characterized as much by silences and suppression as it was by amplification and mutual encouragement.[8] And, in the words of Amina Mama, it is at its core a story of "complexity, nuance and multiplicity" as well as of "power relations."[9]

The history of Girls in Development insists on paying attention to bureaucratic spaces and methods of silencing. Silencing does not happen naturally, and silence is not always an innate state; it takes work. A major outcome of the UN women's movement to date—neoliberal feminism—was not a natural, unwitting, or invisible process that followed the end of the Cold War. The emergence of free-market feminism is traceable through quotidian, mundane acts of knowledge creation and deletion through the writing of Girls in Development into the UN women's movement. The UNICEF-FEMNET lobbying campaign provides one case study as to how and where these erasures became visible. For the most part, such erasures occurred not in high-profile, sexy speeches of international politicians or in explosive fights but in behind-the-scenes writing, revising, and dissemination of knowledge. They appeared in horse trading over the languages of conference texts months before the conference itself and in the loud silences that arose in response to these bureaucratic acts of suppression. Such erasures were entrenched as staff at NGOs such as the Girl Child Network built on the hegemonic narrative that emerged from Beijing and adjusted their own development- and rights-focused activities to attract consistent funding in the overlapping contexts of neoliberal capitalism, (post)colonialism, and the war on terror.

Beyond its quest to understand how free-market feminism internationalized into a dominant ideology through the vehicle of girl-focused development, this book is a request to pay attention to the boring and the mundane in the creation of knowledge and hegemonic norms. Sometimes searches for brute force from above, or for romantic resistance narratives from below, distract from the messy—and often tediously bureaucratic—in betweens.[10] It is in these in betweens that much of the past and the present have unfolded. Rather than trying to avoid the discomfort that such narratives may provoke, they require us to sit with histories that "estrange us from, as much as attach us to, celebratory, 'happy' narratives of the past."[11] They also sometimes require us to toss rote scripts that guide how we write and view history aside as we grab onto other methods.

Acknowledgments

Many people supported the creation of this book, and I am grateful to them. Rachel Kagoiya, the former head of communications at FEMNET, spent years curating and maintaining the FEMNET archive. Thank you for showing me the ropes during my visits. The very fact of a Pan-African women's NGO having its own robust, publicly accessible archive dating back decades is noteworthy given how power—including financial constraints—shapes the work of archiving. Thank you to Mercy Musomi, Florence Annan, and all of the staff at the Girl Child Network for allowing me to access the NGO's records and for more generally supporting the research underpinning this book. I am grateful to all of you.

I thank Dr. Sangai Mohochi and Dr. Maurice Amutabi for providing me with affiliation at Maseno University and the Catholic University of East Africa during the two years I lived in Kenya while researching this book. Thank you to the broader Mohochi and Masero families for a decade and a half of friendship and intellectual engagement. Special thanks go to Anastasia Masero for talking through certain aspects of this project with me and for various forms of camaraderie. Ouko Erustus has contributed to this book in multiple ways, first as a Kiswahili teacher and then as a dear friend. I am grateful to the many people who shared their time and energy as I researched this book, whether through formal interviews or informal conversations. Thank you for sharing your stories—often personal, sometimes painful. I hope that I have done them, and you, justice.

Jean Allman intellectually shaped this book in innumerable ways. I am particularly grateful to Jean for the encouragement to analytically lean into the silences and erasures in this story and for the critical rigor with which she approaches academic knowledge production and teaching. Thanks to Shefali

Chandra for helping me foreground the stakes of this project. I am grateful to Elizabeth Borgward, Tim Parsons, Andrea Friedman, Nancy Reynolds, and Sowande' Mustakeem for their various forms of support and feedback as I got this project off the ground. Thank you to Adwoa Opong, Stephanie Heger, Amanda Scott, Waseem bin Kasim, and Ethan Bennett for your friendship and intellectual exchanges during our mutual years in St. Louis.

I cannot adequately convey the impact that Dorothy Hodgson and Pamela Scully have had on my thinking surrounding this book and my broader academic career. Thank you for your scholarship, mentorship, advice, and friendship. I am grateful to and for you both. Thanks, as well, to our entire Gender Justice in the Era of Human Rights SSRC DPDF group, and especially to fellow historians Elise Franklin and Alex Ruble. The community that I found with you all sustained and inspired me during the highs and lows of producing this book.

It still makes me giddy to be able to converse with many of the scholars whose work has inspired my own. Abosede George, Antoinette Burton, Lynn Thomas, Heather Switzer, and Abou Bamba have provided feedback and advice on various aspects of this project in its later stages. Thank you for the intellectual generosity and grace you have extended to me. Thank you, as well, to Karishma Desai and Emily Bent for talking through certain aspects of this project with me, including the ethics involved. Cassandra Mark-Thiesen, Elora Shehabuddin, Glenda Sluga, Antoinette Burton, and Renisa Mawani gave talks that I facilitated in the Berlin Global History Colloquium while I was finishing the book. Their visits, both in person and virtual, and our conversations surrounding them deepened my thinking on various aspects of the project, for which I am grateful. Corrie Decker and Sarah Duff peer reviewed the book manuscript for the University of Chicago Press. Their incisive and generous feedback made the final product stronger—I am indebted to you both.

Sebastian Conrad, Margrit Pernau, and Andreas Eckert pushed me and this book in new directions during my time as a junior faculty member in Berlin. I am grateful for their intellectual contributions and for welcoming this aggressively friendly American into the fold at the GraKo for Global Intellectual History. I have benefited from a thriving academic community in Berlin, including at the Global History platforms that Sebastian Conrad hosts. Dozens of mentors, colleagues, and graduate students have provided feedback on segments of this book at sundry conferences and workshops. I owe you all my thanks: Lucija Bakšić, Edna Bonhomme, Lea Börgerding, Samuël Coghe, Serawit Debele, Sonja Dolinsek, Franziska Exeler, Michael Facius, Frank Gerits, Michael Goebel, Martin Hamre, Minu Haschemi Yekani, Nadin Heé, Lisa Hellman,

Sacha Hepburn, Franziska Hermes, Patricia Hertel, Valeska Huber, Christian Jacobs, Christoph Kalter, Florian Keller, Bridget Kenny, Sophie-Jung Hyun Kim, Nadja Klopprogge, Stephanie Lämmert, Dörte Lerp, Ismay Milford, Ben Miller, Vicente Gomez Murillo, James Musonda, Thục Linh Nguyễn Vũ, Timothy Nunan, Avner Ofrath, Adwoa Opong, Friederike Philippe, Joseph Ben Prestel, Elisa Prosperetti, Felicitas Remer, Clare Richardson, Esra Sarioglu, Marcia Schenck, Susanne Schmidt, Pascale Siegrist, Nader Sohrabi, Gayatri de Souza, Yorim Spoelder, Fidel Tavarez, Mikko Toivanen, Sébastien Tremblay, and Julia Wambach. Enormous thanks to Camilla Bertoni, Maggie Crisp, and Carmen Cuevas Alonso for keeping the Global History program running so seamlessly and for the many forms of labor—bureaucratic, intellectual, emotional, and more—that you perform.

Thank you to everyone at the Margherita von Brentano Center for Gender Studies at the Free University of Berlin, especially Heike Pantelmann and Dilara Aksoy. You have provided intellectual support, enthusiasm, and kindness as I started a new job as a junior research group leader during my final months of book revisions. Genevieve Leach and Adèle Etard-Quinson worked as research assistants and helped me track down key sources in libraries at the beginning and end of this project. I am grateful to you both. Sincere thanks to Dylan Montanari, Fabiola Enríquez Flores, Mary Al-Sayed, and the entire team at the University of Chicago Press for helping this book come alive. Gratitude goes to Anja Berkes for creating the index.

Beyond being great colleagues, Sophie-Jung Hyun Kim, Lea Börgerding, Disha Karnad Jani, Thục Linh Nguyễn Vũ, and Susanne Schmidt have sustained me with their friendship as I finished this book. Thank you to the graduate students whom I have had the immense pleasure of mentoring, teaching, and in many cases befriending in Berlin. Special thanks to my graduate students, colleagues, and chairs who have been allies in the fight to interrogate and dismantle the violent power structures that continue to pervade academia, including sexual harassment. I am grateful to Anne-Marie Harrison for editing this book manuscript, for her friendship, and for her commitment to many of the ethics that underpin my own motivations as a historian.

A number of institutions have funded the research and writing of this book: the United States Department of Education, the Social Science Research Council, the German Research Foundation, the Volkswagen Foundation, the Berlin University Alliance, P.E.O. International, and the Spencer T. and Ann W. Olin Fellowship at Washington University in St. Louis.

Thank you to my mom (Karen Bellows), dad (David Blakely), and stepmom (Liz Blakely) for your encouragement, love, and support. You paved the way for me to write this book. Thank you, Anne, for everything. You helped me finish. Loraine Björendahl, Kelley Van Towle, Enumale Agada, and Viviane Bréfort are treasured friends or family who deserve acknowledgment for keeping me going during the marathon of book production. Clément Quinson has worn more hats than anyone else connected to this book: beta reader, editor, rubber duck (a person against whom one bounces unfinished ideas), emotional support, chef, dog coparent, friend, partner, and spouse. I cannot thank you enough, or the entire Quinson clan, for everything you do. And, okay, while we're at it: thank you, Ripley. Vive l'équipe BBQ.

Material in this book was previously published as follows: Sarah Bellows-Blakely, "Girlhood in Africa," in *The Oxford Research Encyclopedia of African History* (Oxford: Oxford University Press, 2020), © 2020 by Oxford University Press; Sarah Bellows-Blakely, "Empowering African Girls? Capitalism, Poverty, and Silencing in the Writing of History," *American Historical Review* 128, no. 3 (2023): 1182–1210, © 2023 by the author, published by Oxford University Press on behalf of the American Historical Association.

Notes

Introduction

1. FEMNET gained formal consultative status with the UN Commission on the Status of Women in 1996. However, its members regularly attended and played leading roles in CSW planning meetings leading up to the Fourth UN World Conference on Women in Beijing. See, for example, *FEMNET at CSW63: Report March 2019* (Nairobi: FEMNET, 2019), 7, https://www.femnet.org/wp-content/uploads/2019/06/FEMNET-Report-on-CSW63-final.pdf.

2. See, for example, Sally Engle Merry, *Human Rights and Gender Violence: Translating International Law into Local Justice* (Chicago: University of Chicago Press, 2006); Kristen Ghodsee, "Conclusion," in *Second World, Second Sex: Socialist Women's Activism and Global Solidarity during the Cold War* (Durham, NC: Duke University Press, 2019); Charlotte Bunch and Susana Fried, "Beijing '95: Moving Women's Human Rights from Margin to Center," *Women's Human Rights* 22, no. 1 (Autumn 1996): 200–204; Elisabeth J. Friedman, "The Effects of 'Transnationalism Reversed' in Venezuela: Assessing the Impact of UN Global Conferences on the Women's Movement," *International Feminist Journal of Politics* 1, no. 3 (1999): 357–81; and Linda Tarr-Whelan, "The Impact of the Beijing Platform for Action: 1995 to 2010," *Human Rights* 37, no. 2 (2010), accessed April 29, 2017, https://www.americanbar.org/groups/crsj/publications/human_rights_magazine_home/human_rights_vol37_2010/summer2010/the_impact_of_the_beijing_platform_for_action/.

3. Tarr-Whelan, "The Impact of the Beijing Platform for Action." Other mentions of the roles of African delegates in conceptualizing and popularizing the section on the girl child in the Beijing Platform for Action include Dorothy O. Helly, "Beijing '95: The Fourth World Conference on Women," *NWSA Journal* 8, no. 1, Global Perspectives (Spring 1996): 171; and HRNet, "Women's Conference in Dakar," posted in Google Group misc.activism.progressive, January 12, 1994, accessed July 22, 2024, https://groups.google.com/g/misc.activism.progressive/c/O2cgIg6e6Vo/m/RCnYoZiKgfgJ.

4. Heather Switzer has noted, "girls as a category for development targeting initially found its most widely circulated articulation in the production and dissemination of Section L" of the Beijing Platform for Action; Switzer, *When the Light Is Fire: Maasai Schoolgirls in Contemporary Kenya* (Champaign: University of Illinois Press, 2018), conclusion, footnote 7. See also Navtej Purewal, "Interrogating the Rights Discourse on Girls' Education: Neocolonialism, Neoliberalism, and the Post-Beijing Platform for Action," *IDS Bulletin* 46, no. 4 (2015): 47–53; and Kathryn

Moeller, *The Gender Effect: Capitalism, Feminism, and the Corporate Politics of Development* (Oakland: University of California Press, 2018).

5. See, for example, Anne Sisson Runyan, "Women in the Neoliberal 'Frame,'" in *Gender Politics in Global Governance*, ed. Mary K. Meyer and Elisabeth Prügl (Lanham, MD: Rowman & Littlefield, 1999), 210–20; Ghodsee, *Second World, Second Sex*; and Gayatri Chakravorty Spivak, "'Woman' as Theatre: United Nations Conference on Women, Beijing 1995," *Radical Philosophy* 75 (1996): 2–4.

6. Ghodsee, *Second World, Second Sex*, 18, 92, 236, 239–40.

7. Nancy Fraser, "Feminism, Capitalism, and the Cunning of History," *New Left Review* 56 (2009): 110–11. Ghodsee reprints this quotation from Fraser in *Second World, Second Sex*, 18. Other key works on the historical convergence of feminism with neoliberal capitalism include Nancy Fraser, *Fortunes of Feminism: From State-Managed Capitalism to Neoliberal Crisis* (London: Verso, 2013); Michelle Murphy, *The Economization of Life* (Durham, NC: Duke University Press, 2017); Kathryn Moeller, *The Gender Effect*; Chandra Talpade Mohanty, "Transnational Feminist Crossings: On Neoliberalism and Radical Critique," *Signs: Journal of Women in Culture and Society* 38, no. 4 (2013): 967–91; and Catherine Rottenberg, "The Rise of Neoliberal Feminism," *Cultural Studies* 28, no. 3 (2014): 418–37.

8. Citing Mohanty, Akosua Adomako Ampofo, Josephine Beoku-Betts, and Mary J. Osirim have argued that a key feature distinguishing "transnational and Black feminism" from "western feminism" is that the former "challenge[s] the complicity of western feminism on issues of racism and colonialism. . . ." Akosua Adomako Ampofo, Josephine Beoku-Betts, and Mary J. Osirim, "Researching African Women and Gender Studies: New Social Science Perspectives," *African and Asian Studies* 7 (2008): 1–2, accessed July 30, 2024, https://core.ac.uk/download/pdf/303062658.pdf. See also Chandra Talpade Mohanty, *Feminism without Borders: Decolonizing Theory, Practicing Solidarity* (Durham, NC: Duke University Press, 2003).

9. For examples, see Kalpana Wilson, "'Race,' Gender and Neoliberalism: Changing Visual Representations in Development," *Third World Quarterly* 32, no. 2 (2011): 315–31; Kalpana Wilson, "Towards a Radical Re-appropriation: Gender, Development and Neoliberal Feminism," *Development and Change* 46, no. 4 (2015): 803–32; Shirin M. Rai, *Gender and the Political Economy of Development: From Nationalism to Globalization* (New York: John Wiley & Sons, 2001); Shirin M. Rai, "The History of International Development: Concepts and Contexts," in *The Women, Gender and Development Reader*, ed. Nalini Visvanathan, Lynn Duggan, Nan Wiegersma, and Laurie Nisonoff, 2nd ed. (London: Zed, 2011); Shirin M. Rai, "Gender and Development: Theoretical Perspectives," in *The Women, Gender and Development Reader*, 2nd ed.

10. Dierdre N. McCloskey, "Other Things Equal: Free-Market Feminism 101," *Eastern Economic Journal* 26, no. 3 (Summer 2000): 363–65, https://www.deirdremccloskey.com/docs/pdf/Article_314.pdf.

11. A few of the many existing critiques of the term *neoliberalism* include Rajesh Venugopal, "Neoliberalism as Concept," *Economy and Society* 44, no. 2 (2015): 165–87; Gabriel Chouhy, "Rethinking Neoliberalism, Rethinking Social Movements," *Social Movement Studies* 19, no. 4 (2020): 426–46; Jamie Peck and Nik Theodore, "Still Neoliberalism?," *South Atlantic Quarterly* 118, no. 2 (2019): 245–65; Giandomenica Becchio and Giovanni Leghissa, *The Origins of Neoliberalism: Insights from Economics and Philosophy* (London: Taylor & Francis, 2016); and Taylor C. Boas and Jordan Gans-Morse, "Neoliberalism: From New Liberal Philosophy to Anti-Liberal Slogan," *Studies in Comparative International Development* 44 (2009): 137–61.

12. Chandra Talpade Mohanty, "Under Western Eyes: Feminist Scholarship and Colonial Discourses," *Feminist Review* 30, no. 1 (1988): 61–88. For examples of debates on neoliberalism and feminism, see Özlem Aslan and Zeynep Gambetti, "Provincializing Fraser's History: Feminism and Neoliberalism Revisited," *History of the Present* 1, no. 1 (2011): 130–47; Lyn Ossome, "In Search of the State? Neoliberalism and the Labour Question for Pan-African Feminism," *Feminist Africa* 20 (2015): 6–25; Kristen Loveland, "Feminism against Neoliberalism: Theorising Biopolitics in Germany, 1978–1993," *Gender & History* 29, no. 1 (April 2017): 67–86; Joan Sangster and Meg Luxton, "Feminism, Co-optation and the Problems of Amnesia: a Response to Nancy Fraser," *Socialist Register* 49 (2013); and Johanna Oskala, "Feminism, Capitalism, and Ecology," *Hypatia* 33, no. 2 (2018): 216–34. Examples of debates on feminisms and women's movements within African and Black feminisms include Delia Kumavie, "Ama Ata Aidoo's Woman-Centered Pan-Africanism: A Reading of Selected Works," *Feminist Africa* 20 (2015): 57–68; Pinkie Mekgwe, "Theorizing African Feminism(s)," *Quest: An African Journal of Philosophy/Revue Africaine de Philosophie* 20, no. 1–2 (2008): 11–22; Agnes Atia Apusigah, "Is Gender Yet Another Colonial Project? A Critique of Oyeronke Oyewumi's Proposal," *Quest: An African Journal of Philosophy/Revue Africaine de Philosophie* 20, no. 1–2 (2008): 23–44; Rose M. Brewer, "Black Feminism and Womanism," in *Companion to Feminist Studies*, ed. Nancy A. Naples (Hoboken, NJ: Wiley Blackwell, 2021), 91–104; Ampofo, Beoku-Betts, and Osirim, "Researching African Women and Gender Studies"; and Patricia Hill Collins, "What's in a Name? Womanism, Black Feminism, and Beyond," *Black Scholar* 26, no. 1 (1996): 9–17.

13. Heather Switzer, Karishma Desai, and Emily Bent, eds., *Girls in Global Development: Figurations of Gendered Power* (New York: Berghahn, 2023); Switzer, *When the Light Is Fire*; Switzer, "(Post)Feminist Development Fables: The Girl Effect and the Production of Sexual Subjects," *Feminist Theory* 14, no. 3 (2013): 345–60; Switzer, "Disruptive Discourses: Kenyan Maasai Schoolgirls Make Themselves," *Girlhood Studies* 3, no. 1 (2010): 137–55; Farzana Shain, "'The Girl Effect': Exploring Narratives of Gendered Impacts and Opportunities in Neoliberal Development," *Sociological Research Online* 18, no. 2 (2013): 181–91; Lesley Pruitt, "'Fixing the Girls': Neoliberal Discourse and Girls' Participation in Peacebuilding," *International Feminist Journal of Politics* 15, no. 1 (2013): 58–76; Emily Bent, "Girl Rising and the Problematic Other: Celebritizing Third World Girlhoods," in *Feminist Theory and Pop Culture*, ed. Adrienne Trier-Bieniek (Rotterdam: Sense, 2015), 89–101; Purewal, "Interrogating the Rights Discourse on Girls' Education"; Emily S. Mann, "Latina Girls, Sexual Agency, and the Contradictions of Neoliberalism," *Sexuality Research and Social Policy* 13, no. 4 (2016): 330–40; Sylvia Chant, "Galvanizing Girls for Development? Critiquing the Shift from 'Smart' to 'Smarter Economics,'" *Progress in Development Studies* 16, no. 4 (2016): 314–28; Moeller, *The Gender Effect*; and Murphy, *The Economization of Life*.

14. Selected works on agnotology include Londa Schiebinger, "Agnotology and Exotic Abortifacients: The Cultural Production of Ignorance in the Eighteenth-Century Atlantic World," *Proceedings of the American Philosophical Society* 149 (2005): 316–43; Robert N. Proctor, *Cancer Wars: How Politics Shapes What We Know and Don't Know about Cancer* (New York: Basic, 2005); Robert N. Proctor and Londa Schiebinger, eds., *Agnotology: The Making and Unmaking of Ignorance* (Stanford, CA: Stanford University Press, 2008); Michael Betancourt, *The Critique of Digital Capitalism: An Analysis of the Political Economy of Digital Culture and Technology* (Brooklyn, NY: Punctum, 2016); and Manuela Fernández Pinto, "Tensions in Agnotology: Normativity in the Studies of Commercially Driven Ignorance," *Social Studies of Science* 45, no. 2 (April 2015): 294–315.

15. Jean Allman, "The Disappearing of Hannah Kudjoe: Nationalism, Feminism, and the Tyrannies of History," *Journal of Women's History* 21, no. 3 (2009): 13–35; and Joel Cabrita, *Written Out: The Silencing of Regina Gelana Twala* (Athens: Ohio University Press, 2023).

16. Samuel Moyn, "On the Nonglobalization of Ideas," in *Global Intellectual History*, ed. Samuel Moyn and Andrew Sartori (New York: Columbia University Press, 2013), 187–204. See also Sophie-Jung Hyun Kim, "Between World-Imagining and World-Making: Politics in Fin-de-Siècle Universalism and Transimperial Indi-US Brotherhood," *Journal of World History* 35, no. 1 (2024): 53–83.

17. Michel-Rolph Trouillot, *Silencing the Past: Power and the Production of History* (Boston, MA: Beacon, 1995). Other relevant works on silencing, erasure, and forgetting include Ann Laura Stoler, "Colonial Aphasia: Race and Disabled Histories in France," *Public Culture* 23, no. 1 (2011): 121–56; Maxine Molyneux, "Gender and the Silences of Social Capital: Lessons from Latin America," *Development and Change* 33, no. 2 (2002): 167–88; Lisa Lowe, *The Intimacies of Four Continents* (Durham, NC: Duke University Press, 2015); and Sarah Bellows-Blakely, "Empowering African Girls? Capitalism, Poverty, and Silencing in the Writing of History," *American Historical Review* 128, no. 3 (2023): 1182–1210.

18. Saidiya Hartman, "Venus in Two Acts," *Small Axe* 26, no. 2 (2008): 1–14; and *Lose Your Mother: A Journey along the Atlantic Slave Route* (New York: Farrar, Straus and Giroux, 2008). A critical reflection on the need for what Hartman terms "narrative restraint" in attempts to contend with historical erasures is Serawit Debele, "The Politics of 'Queer Reading' an Ethiopian Saint and Discovering Precolonial Queer Africans," *Journal of African Cultural Studies* 34, no. 1 (2022): 98–110.

19. For a few of many examples, see Amina Mama and Hakima Abbas, "Editorial: Feminism and Pan-Africanism," *Feminist Africa* 20 (2015): 1–5; Athambile Masola, "African Women's Letters as Intellectual History and Decolonial Knowledge Production," in *The Palgrave Handbook of African Women's Studies*, ed. Olajumoke Yacob-Haliso and Toyin Falola (Cham, Switzerland: Palgrave Macmillan, 2020), https://doi.org/10.1007/978-3-319-77030-7_163-1; Athambile Masola, "The Politics of the 1920s Black Press: Charlotte Maxeke and Nontsizi Mgqwetho's Critique of Congress," *International Journal of African Renaissance Studies* 13 (2018): 59–76; Brenda Nyandiko Sanya and Anne Namatsi Lutomia, "Archives and Collective Memories: Searching for African Women in the Pan-African Imaginary," *Feminist Africa* 20 (2015): 69–76; Gabi Mkhize and Kalpana Hiralal, "Editorial: Women's History and Subjectivity: Reflections on Liberation Narratives," *Alternation: Interdisciplinary Journal for the Study of the Arts and Humanities in Southern Africa* (2019): 1–13; and Allman, "The Disappearing of Hannah Kudjoe."

20. Various critiques of the concept of agency can be found in Walter Johnson, "On Agency," *Journal of Social History* 37 (2003): 113–24; Kalpana Wilson, *Race, Racism and Development: Interrogating History, Discourse and Practice* (London: Zed, 2012), 45–68; Sumi Madhok and Shirin M. Rai, "Agency, Injury, and Transgressive Politics in Neoliberal Times," *Signs: Journal of Women in Culture and Society* 37 (2012): 645–69; Sumi Madhok, Anne Phillips, and Kalpana Wilson, eds., *Gender, Agency and Coercion* (London: Palgrave Macmillan, 2013); Sumi Madhok, *Rethinking Agency: Developmentalism, Gender and Rights* (New Delhi: Routledge, 2013); Lynn M. Thomas, "Historicising Agency," *Gender & History* 28 (2016): 324–39; Bellows-Blakely, "Empowering African Girls?"; and Sarah Bellows-Blakely, "Review Essay: Disentangling Feminisms from the Cold War," *Gender & History* 32, no. 1 (2020): 247–58.

21. Kalpana Wilson, "'Race,' Gender and Neoliberalism: Changing Visual Representations in Development," *Third World Quarterly* 32, no. 2 (2011): 315–31.

22. Evoking language from Nancy Fraser and Sonia E. Alvarez, among others, Jocelyn Ol-

cott notes that since the 1990s, NGOs have often been seen "as the handmaidens of neoliberalism rather than as the vehicles for radical grassroots democracy, generating the pejorative term 'NGO-ization.'" Jocelyn Olcott, *International Women's Year: The Greatest Consciousness-Raising Event in History* (Oxford: Oxford University Press, 2017), 250. Further discussions of the "NGO-ization" of the women's movement and the relationships between women NGO activists and neoliberalism can be found in Sonia E. Alvarez, "Advocating Feminism: The Latin American Feminist NGO 'Boom,'" *International Feminist Journal of Politics* 1, no. 2 (1999): 181–209; Sonia E. Alvarez, "Beyond NGO-ization? Reflections from Latin America," *Development* 52 (2009): 175–84; Sonia E. Alvarez, "Latin American Feminisms 'Go Global': Trends of the 1990s and Challenges for the New Millennium," in *Cultures of Politics/Politics of Cultures: Re-visioning Latin American Social Movements*, ed. Sonia E. Alvarez, Evelina Dagnino, and Arturo Escobar (Boulder, CO: Westview, 1998), 293–324; Nancy Fraser, "Feminism, Capitalism, and the Cunning of History"; Srila Roy, "Politics, Passion and Professionalization in Contemporary Indian Feminism," *Sociology* 54, no. 4 (2011): 587–602; and Catherine Eschle and Bice Maiguashca, "Theorizing Feminist Organizing in and against Neoliberalism: Beyond Co-optation and Resistance?," *European Journal of Politics and Gender* 1, no. 1–2 (2018): 223–39. Tehila Sasson provides a history of the growth of NGOs and neoliberalism in the context of British decolonization in *The Solidarity Economy: Nonprofits and the Making of Neoliberalism after Empire* (Princeton, NJ: Princeton University Press, 2024).

23. Dorothy Hodgson has provocatively theorized about the relationships between individual choices and structural oppression by posing the following question: "what are the possibilities for effective political action in a world shaped by the legacies of colonialism and the contemporary policies and practices of neoliberalism?" *Being Maasai, Becoming Indigenous: Postcolonial Politics in a Neoliberal World* (Bloomington: Indiana University Press, 2011), introduction. Elizabeth Ngutuku and Auma Okwany argue for the importance of "going beyond the narratives of victimhood" to instead "present women's emergent, incomplete, and incongruent agency" in Kenya and the broader Global South in "Beyond Colonial Politics of Identity: Being and Becoming Female Youth in Colonial Kenya," *Genealogy* 8, no. 47 (2024): 1–24. Jennifer Nash has innovated new methods in Black Feminist Theory and its relationships to loss and beauty in *How We Write Now: Living with Black Feminist Theory* (Durham, NC: Duke University Press, 2024).

24. See, for example, Amina Mama and Hakima Abbas, eds., "Feminism and Pan Africanism," *Feminist Africa* 20 (2015); Masola, "African Women's Letters as Intellectual History and Decolonial Knowledge Production"; Masola, "The Politics of the 1920s Black Press"; Susan Geiger, *TANU Women: Gender and Culture in the Making of Tanganyikan Nationalism, 1955–1965* (Portsmouth, NH: Heinemann, 1997); Mkhize and Hiralal, "Editorial: Women's History and Subjectivity"; Keisha N. Blain and Tiffany M. Gill, eds., *To Turn the Whole World Over: Black Women and Internationalism* (Urbana: University of Illinois Press, 2019); and Allman, "The Disappearing of Hannah Kudjoe." For scholarship on the centrality of women (African and otherwise) to histories of internationalism and/or global intellectual histories, see, for example, Kumari Jayawardena, *Feminism and Nationalism in the Third World* (London: Zed, 1986); Leila Rupp, *Worlds of Women: The Making of an International Women's Movement* (Princeton, NJ: Princeton University Press, 1998); Elora Shehabuddin, *Sisters in the Mirror: A History of Muslim Women and the Global Politics of Feminism* (Oakland: University of California Press, 2021); Glenda Sluga, "Women, Feminisms and Twentieth-Century Internationalisms," in *Internationalisms: A Twentieth-Century History*, ed. Glenda Sluga and Patricia Clavin (Cambridge: Cambridge

University Press, 2017), 61–84; Ghodsee, *Second World, Second Sex*; Lucy Delap, *Feminisms: A Global History* (Chicago: University of Chicago Press, 2020); Francisca de Haan, Margaret Allen, June Purvis and Krassimira Daskalova, eds., *Women's Activism: Global Perspectives from the 1890s to the Present* (New York: Routledge, 2013); Francisca de Haan, Krassimira Daskalova and Anna Loutfi, eds., *A Biographical Dictionary of Women's Movements and Feminisms: Central, Eastern, and South Eastern Europe, 19th and 20th Centuries* (Budapest: Central European University Press, 2006); and Elisabeth Armstrong, "Before Bandung: The Anti-Imperialist Women's Movement in Asia and the Women's International Democratic Federation," *Signs: Journal of Women in Culture and Society* 41, no. 2 (2016): 305–31. For examples of scholarship on African and Black Internationalisms, see Adom Getachew, *Worldmaking after Empire* (Princeton, NJ: Princeton University Press, 2019); Rita Abrahamsen, "Internationalists, Sovereigntists, Nativists: Contending Visions of World Oder in Pan-Africanism," *Review of International Studies* 46, no. 1 (2020): 56–74; Ismay Milford, *African Activists in a Decolonising World* (Cambridge: Cambridge University Press, 2023); Jake Hodder, "Toward a Geography of Black Internationalism: Bayard Rustin, Nonviolence, and the Promise of Africa," *Annals of the American Association of Geographers* 106, no. 6 (2016): 1360–77; Tiffany Florvil, *Mobilizing Black Germany: Afro-German Women and the Making of a Transnational Movement* (Champaign: University of Illinois Press, 2020); Keisha N. Blain, *Set the World on Fire: Black Nationalist Women and the Global Struggle for Freedom* (Philadelphia: University of Pennsylvania Press, 2018); and Leslie M. Alexander, *Fear of a Black Republic: Haiti and the Birth of Black Internationalism in the United States* (Urbana: University of Illinois Press, 2022).

25. Ama Ata Aidoo, "Literature, Feminism, and the African Woman Today," in *Reconstructing Womanhood, Reconstructing Feminism: Writings on Black Women*, ed. Delia Jarrett-Macauley (London: Routledge, 1995), 157–76; Filomina Steady, "African Women: Re-centering the Issues for the 21st Century," in *Africa in the 21st Century*, ed. Ama Mazama (New York: Routledge, 2007), 133–53; Ampofo, Beoku-Betts, and Osirim, "Researching African Women and Gender Studies"; Mohanty, "Under Western Eyes"; and Chandra Talpade Mohanty, "'Under Western Eyes' Revisited: Feminist Solidarity through Anticapitalist Struggles," *Signs: Journal of Women in Culture and Society* 28, no. 2 (Winter 2003): 499–535.

26. Anna Lowenhaupt Tsing, *Friction: An Ethnography of Global Connection* (Princeton, NJ: Princeton University Press, 2005); and Antoinette Burton, *Africa in the Indian Imagination: Race and the Politics of Postcolonial Citation* (Durham, NC: Duke University Press, 2016), introduction, chap. 4, and epilogue. Burton builds on the work of anti-apartheid activist and historian of the movement Phyllis Naidoo in *Footprints in Grey Street* (Durban, South Africa: Ocean Jetty, 2002); and *156 Hands That Built South Africa* (Durban, South Africa: Art Printers, 2006). Jocelyn Olcott also uses the concept of friction to explore the 1975 UN Women's Conference in Mexico City in *International Women's Year*, 12 and 262.

27. Burton explores the importance of the verticality of transnational networks—the messy power dynamics that disrupt uncomplicated horizontal alliance building while creating fraught new affinities—in *Africa in the Indian Imagination*. A longer lineage of debates about the emancipatory potential of transnational networks versus their inherent limitations and complexities can be found in the introduction of Hodgson's *Being Maasai, Becoming Indigenous*.

28. Njoki Wainaina, comp., *HerStory: Our Journey; Advocating for the Rights of African Women*, concept and interviews by Fatma Alloo, ed. Rachel Kagoiya (Nairobi: African Women's Development and Communication Network/FEMNET, 2012), 92, https://femnet.org/wp-content/uploads/2020/07/FEMNET-Herstory-Book-2012.pdf.

29. Emails to the author from a UNICEF employee, July 11 and 13, 2012, and https://www.unicef.org/history/archives, accessed May 1, 2021.

30. Christopher S. Wren, "Unicef Says Fraud Cost $10 Million," *New York Times*, May 26, 1995, https://www.nytimes.com/1995/05/26/world/unicef-says-fraud-cost-10-million.html.

31. Select sources on semi-structured interviews and oral histories include Anne Galletta, *Mastering the Semi-structured Interview and Beyond: From Research Design to Analysis and Publication* (New York: NYU Press, 2013); Kathleen M. Blee and Verta Taylor, "Semi-structured Interviewing in Social Movement Research," in *Methods of Social Movement Research*, ed. Bert Klandermans and Suzanne Staggenborg (Minneapolis: University of Minnesota Press, 2002), 92–117; Sherna Berger Gluck and Daphne Patai, eds., *Women's Words: The Feminist Practice of Oral History* (New York: Routledge, 1991); Katrina Srigley, Stacey Zembrzycki, and Franca Iacovetta, eds., *Beyond Women's Words: Feminisms and the Practices of Oral History in the Twenty-First Century* (Abingdon, UK: Routledge, 2018); and Susan Geiger, "Women's Life Histories: Method and Content," *Signs: Journal of Women in Culture and Society* 11, no. 2 (1986): 334–51.

32. Ngũgĩ wa Thiong'o, *Decolonizing the Mind: The Politics of Language in African Literature* (London: James Currey, 1986); Simon Gikandi, "Ngũgĩ's Conversion: Writing and the Politics of Language," *Research in African Literatures* 23, no. 1 (1992): 131–44; Mama and Abbas, "Editorial: Feminism and Pan-Africanism," nn. 1, 5; and Mahmood Mamdani, "The African University," *London Review of Books* 40, no. 14 (July 19, 2018), https://www.lrb.co.uk/the-paper/v40/n14/mahmood-mamdani/the-african-university.

33. A sample of many works in the booming fields of African, Black, and global girlhood studies include Corinne T. Field, Tammy-Charelle Owens, Marcia Chatelain, Lakisha Simmons, Abosede George, and Rhian Keyse, "The History of Black Girlhood: Recent Innovations and Future Directions," *Journal of the History of Childhood and Youth* 9, no. 3 (2016): 383–401; Abosede George, *Making Modern Girls: A History of Girlhood, Labor, and Social Development in 20th Century Colonial Lagos* (Athens: Ohio University Press, 2014); Relebohile Moletsane, Claudia Mitchell, Ann Smith, and Linda Chisholm, *Methodologies for Mapping a Southern African Girlhood in the Age of Aids* (Rotterdam: Sense, 2008); Lynn M. Thomas, *Politics of the Womb: Women, Reproduction, and the State in Kenya* (Berkeley: University of California Press, 2004); Jennifer Helgren and Colleen A. Vasconcellos, eds., *Girlhood: A Global History* (New Brunswick, NJ: Rutgers University Press, 2010); Switzer, *When the Light Is Fire*; Switzer, Desai, and Bent, *Girls in Global Development*; Corrie Decker, "Reading, Writing, and Respectability: How Schoolgirls Developed Modern Literacies in Colonial Zanzibar," *International Journal of African Historical Studies* 43, no. 1 (2010): 89–114; Ruby Lal, *Coming of Age in Nineteenth-Century India: The Girl-Child and the Art of Playfulness* (Cambridge: Cambridge University Press, 2013); Ngutuku and Okwany, "Beyond Colonial Politics of Identity"; and multiple volumes of the journal *Girlhood Studies*, which Berghahn has published since 2008 and which Claudia Mitchell edits.

34. For example, see recent debates on the utility of the term *Global South* in Dan Banik, interview with Sara Stevano, "Shifting Paradigms: The Global South and Feminist Political Economy Unveiled," *In Pursuit of Development*, podcast audio, January 17, 2024, https://t.co/hH5sgFkE2Z; Miriam Prys-Hansen, "The Global South: A Problematic Term," *Internationale Politik Quarterly*, June 29, 2023, https://ip-quarterly.com/en/global-south-problematic-term; Stewart Patrick and Alexandra Huggins, "The Term 'Global South' Is Surging. It Should Be Retired," Carnegie Endowment for International Peace, August 15, 2023, https://carnegieendowment.org/2023/08/15/term-global-south-is-surging.-it-should-be-retired-pub-90376; C. Raja Mohan, "Is

There Such a Thing as a Global South?," *Foreign Policy*, December 9, 2023, https://foreignpolicy.com/2023/12/09/global-south-definition-meaning-countries-development.

35. Switzer, Desai, and Bent, *Girls in Global Development*; Switzer, *When the Light Is Fire*; Switzer, "(Post)Feminist Development Fables"; Switzer, "Disruptive Discourses"; Purewal, "Interrogating the Rights Discourse on Girls' Education"; Shain, "'The Girl Effect'"; Pruitt, "'Fixing the Girls'"; Bent, "Girl Rising and the Problematic Other"; Mann, "Latina Girls, Sexual Agency, and the Contradictions of Neoliberalism"; Murphy, *The Economization of Life*; Moeller, *The Gender Effect*; Chant, "Galvanizing Girls for Development?"; Jackie Kirk, Claudia Mitchell, and Jacqueline Reid-Walsh, "Toward Political Agency for Girls: Mapping the Discourses of Girlhood Globally," in *Girlhood: A Global History*, ed. Jennifer Helgren and Colleen A. Vasconcellos (New Brunswick, NJ: Rutgers University Press, 2010), 14–30; Cynthia M. Caron and Shelby A. Margolin, "Rescuing Girls, Investing in Girls: A Critique of Development Fantasies," *Journal of International Development* 27, no. 7 (2015): 881–97; Sydney Calkin, "Disrupting Disempowerment: Feminism, Co-optation, and the Privatised Governance of Gender and Development," *New Formations*, no. 91 (Summer 2017): 69–86; Calkin, "Globalizing 'Girl Power': Corporate Social Responsibility and Transnational Business Initiatives for Gender Equality," *Globalizations* 13, no. 2 (2016): 1–15; Calkin, "Post-feminist Spectatorship and the Girl Effect: 'Go on, Really Imagine Her,'" *Third World Quarterly* 36, no. 4 (2015): 654–69; Sydney Calkin, *Human Capital in Gender and Development* (London: Routledge, 2018); Andrea Cornwall, "Unpacking 'Participation': Models, Meanings and Practices," *Community Development Journal* 43, no. 3 (2008): 269–83; Andrea Cornwall, Elizabeth Harrison, and Ann Whitehead, eds., *Feminisms in Development: Contradictions, Contestations and Challenges* (London: Zed, 2007); and Elisabeth J. Croll, "From the Girl Child to Girls' Rights," in *The Politics of Rights: Dilemmas for Feminist Praxis*, ed. Andrea Cornwall and Maxine Molyneux (London: Routledge, 2007).

36. George, *Making Modern Girls*; Pamela Scully, "Gender, History, and Human Rights," in *Gender and Culture at the Limit of Rights*, ed. Dorothy L. Hodgson (Philadelphia: University of Pennsylvania Press, 2011), 17–31; Nakanyike Musisi, "The Politics of Perception or Perception as Politics? Colonial and Missionary Representations of Baganda Women, 1900–1945," in *Women in African Colonial Histories*, ed. Jean Allman, Susan Geiger, and Nakanyike Musisi, 95–115 (Bloomington: Indiana University Press, 2002); Benjamin N. Lawrence and Richard L. Roberts, eds., *Trafficking in Slavery's Wake: Law and the Experience of Women and Children* (Athens: Ohio University Press, 2012); Roland Sintos Coloma, "White Gazes, Brown Breasts: Imperial Feminism and Disciplining Desires and Bodies in Colonial Encounters," *Paedagogica Historica* 48, no. 2 (2012): 243–61; Lata Mani, *Contentions Traditions: The Debate on Sati in Colonial India* (Berkeley: University of California Press, 1998); Leila Ahmed, "Discourse of the Veil," in *Women and Gender in Islam* (New Haven, CT: Yale University Press, 1992), 144–68; and Antoinette Burton, *Burdens of History: British Feminists, Indian Women, and Imperial Culture, 1865–1915* (Chapel Hill: University of North Carolina Press, 1994).

37. Ulrike Lindner, "The Transfer of European Social Policy Concepts to Tropical Africa, 1900–50: The Example of Maternal and Child Welfare," *Journal of Global History* 9, no. 2 (2014): 208–31; Jean Allman, "Making Mothers: Missionaries, Medical Officers and Women's Work in Colonial Asante, 1924–1945," *History Workshop Journal* 38, no. 1 (1994): 23–47; Deane Van Tol, "Mothers, Babies, and the Colonial State: The Introduction of Maternal and Infant Welfare Services in Nigeria, 1925–1945," *Spontaneous Generations: A Journal for the History and Philosophy of Science* 1, no. 1 (2007): 110–31; Philippa Mein Smith, *Mothers and King Baby: Infant Survival and Welfare in an Imperial World: Australia 1880–1950* (London: Macmillan, 1997); Molly

Ladd-Taylor, *Mother-Work: Women, Child Welfare, and the State, 1890–1930* (Urbana: University of Illinois Press, 1994); Alisa Klaus, *Every Child a Lion: The Origins of Maternal and Infant Health Policy in the United States and France, 1890–1920* (Ithaca, NY: Cornell University Press, 1993); and Carol Summers, "Intimate Colonialism: The Imperial Production of Reproduction in Uganda, 1907–1925," *Signs: Journal of Women in Culture and Society* 16, no. 4 (1991): 787–807.

38. Liat Kozma, "Girls, Labor, and Sex in Precolonial Egypt, 1850–1882," in *Girlhood: A Global History*, ed. Jennifer Helgren and Colleen A. Vasconcellos (New Brunswick, NJ: Rutgers University Press, 2010); George, *Making Modern Girls*; Edward Ross Dickinson, *The Politics of German Child Welfare from the Empire to the Federal Republic* (Cambridge, MA: Harvard University Press, 1996); and Donald Quataert, "Labor and Working Class History during the Late Ottoman Period c. 1800–1914," in *Workers, Peasants and Economic Change in the Ottoman Empire, 1730–1914* (Istanbul: Isis, 1992), 185–96.

39. Tambe, *Defining Girlhood in India*; Ishita Pande, "Vernacularizing Justice: Age of Consent and a Legal History of the British Empire," *Law and History Review* 38, no. 1 (2020): 267–79; Dorothy L. Hodgson, *Gender, Justice, and the Problem of Culture: From Customary Law to Human Rights in Tanzania* (Bloomington: Indiana University Press, 2017); Annie Bunting, Benjamin N. Lawrence, and Richard L. Roberts, eds., *Marriage by Force? Contestation over Consent and Coercion in Africa* (Athens: Ohio University Press, 2016); Paul Ocobock, *An Uncertain Age: The Politics of Manhood in Kenya* (Athens: Ohio University Press, 2017); and Brett L. Shadle, *Girl Cases: Marriage and Colonialism in Gusiiland, Kenya, 1890–1970* (Portsmouth, NH: Heinemann, 2006).

40. Omni El Shakry, *The Great Social Laboratory: Subjects of Knowledge in Colonial and Postcolonial Egypt* (Stanford, CA: Stanford University Press, 2007); Nancy Rose Hunt, *A Colonial Lexicon: Of Birth Ritual, Medicalization, and Mobility in the Congo* (Durham, NC: Duke University Press, 1999); Nancy Rose Hunt, "'Le Bébé en Brousse': European Women, African Birth Spacing and Colonial Intervention in Breast Feeding in the Belgian Congo," *International Journal of African Historical Studies* 21, no. 3 (1988): 401–32; and Thomas, *Politics of the Womb*.

41. Obioma Nnaemeka, ed., *Female Circumcision and the Politics of Knowledge: African Women in Imperialist Discourses* (Westport, CT: Praeger, 2005); Thomas, *Politics of the Womb*; Elisabeth Bekers, ed., *Rising Anthills: African and African American Writing on Female Genital Excision, 1960–2000* (Madison: University of Wisconsin Press, 2010); Hodgson, *Gender, Justice, and the Problem of Culture*; and Sarah Bellows-Blakely, "Girlhood in Africa," in *The Oxford Research Encyclopedia of African History* (Oxford: Oxford University Press, 2020).

42. Corrie Decker, *Mobilizing Zanzibari Women: The Struggle for Respectability and Self-Reliance in Colonial East Africa* (New York: Palgrave Macmillan, 2014); Mary O'Dowd and June Purvis, eds., *A History of the Girl: Formation, Education and Identity* (London: Palgrave Macmillan, 2018); Samuel S. Thomas, "Transforming the Gospel of Domesticity: Luhya Girls and the Friends Africa Mission, 1917–1926," *African Studies Review* 43, no. 2 (September 2000): 1–27; and John L. Rury and Eileen H. Tamura, *The Oxford Handbook of the History of Education* (Oxford: Oxford University Press, 2019).

43. For more on Jolly's role in the growth of poverty reduction campaigns before and during his time at UNICEF, see Joanne Meyerowitz, *A War on Global Poverty: The Lost Promise of Redistribution and the Rise of Microcredit* (Princeton, NJ: Princeton University Press, 2021), chaps. 1–2 and 5.

44. Daniel Branch, *Defeating Mau Mau, Creating Kenya: Counterinsurgency, Civil War, and Decolonization* (Cambridge: Cambridge University Press, 2009); Caroline Elkins, *Imperial*

Reckoning: The Untold Story of Britain's Gulag in Kenya (New York: Henry Holt and Company, 2005); David Anderson, *Histories of the Hanged: Britain's Dirty War in Kenya and the End of Empire* (London: Weidenfeld and Nicholson, 2005); E. S. Atieno Odhiambo and John Lonsdale, eds. *Mau Mau and Nationhood: Arms, Authority, and Narration* (Oxford: James Currey, 2003); Wunyabari Maloba, *Mau Mau and Kenya: An Analysis of a Peasant Revolt* (Bloomington: Indiana University Press, 1993); and Tabitha Kanogo, *Squatters and the Roots of Mau Mau, 1905–63* (Oxford: James Currey, 1987).

45. Cora Ann Presley, *Kikuyu Women, the Mau Mau Rebellion, and Social Change in Kenya* (Boulder, CO: Westview, 1992); Audrey Wipper, "The Maendeleo Ya Wanawake Organization: The Co-option of Leadership," *African Studies Review* 18 (1975): 99–120; and Branch, *Defeating Mau Mau*.

46. I have reconstructed Jolly's time in Kenya by comparing the contents of published interviews with Jolly from the 2000s with textual documents from governmental and missionary archives of colonial Kenya and the United Kingdom in the 1950s and secondary sources. The interviews include Thomas G. Weiss, interview with Richard Jolly, "Transcript of Interview of Richard Jolly," transcribed by Ron Nerio, in *United Nations Intellectual History Project* (New York: Graduate School and University Center, 2005), 9; and John Toye, interview with Richard Jolly, "The Achievements of a Cheerful Economist," January 2012, accessed April 21, 2021, https://johntoyedotnet.wordpress.com/papers. Documentary sources from the 1950s include the National Archives of the UK (TNA), Public Record Office (PRO), Colonial Office (CO) 822/1138, Social Welfare in Kenya, 1954–1956; TNA PRO CO 822/652, Community Development in Kenya, 1951–1953; and the National Library of Scotland (NLS), Church of Scotland Mission (CSM) Papers, Acc. 7548/B 265, Presbyterian Church of East Africa (PCEA) General Administration Committee minutes, June 19–20, 1957. Secondary sources include Presley, *Kikuyu Women*; Wipper, "The Maendeleo Ya Wanawake Organization"; and Branch, *Defeating Mau Mau*.

47. Eddah Gachukia, "Dr. Eddah Gachukia, FEMNET Founding Member and Chairperson (1984–1992)," interview by Fatma Alloo and Carlyn Hambuba, in Wainaina, comp., *HerStory: Our Journey*, 47–48; "Educationist: Dr. Eddah Wacheke Gachukia," *Daily Kenya*, August 9, 2012, accessed May 1, 2021, http://dailykenya.blogspot.com/2012/08/educationist-dr-eddah-wacheke-gachukia.html.

48. Eddah W. Gachukia, "Forum '85 Report" (Nairobi: Kenya NGO Organizing Committee, 1987); "The Birth of a Network," *FEMNET News* 1.1 (May–July 1989): 3; and "FEMNET's Advance into the Future," *FEMNET News* 2.1 (December 1992–March 1993): 4; and Wainaina, comp., *HerStory: Our Journey*, 13, 47–49.

Chapter One

1. As one of many examples, see Republic of Kenya Central Bureau of Statistics, Ministry of Finance and Planning; and UNICEF, *Situational Analysis of Children and Women in Kenya* (Nairobi: ManGraphics, 1984).

2. James P. Grant, *The State of the World's Children 1984* (Oxford: Published for UNICEF by Oxford University Press, 1983), 59–61; "Statement of UNICEF Director, 'Focus on the Girl Child,'" in "Executive Board Policy Decisions: A Compilation of Decisions Taken by the Executive Board, 1986–1990," UN Economic and Social Council, UNICEF Executive Board, November 26, 1993, 5; "1990/17: Focus on the Girl Child," in "Executive Board Policy Decisions," UNICEF Executive Board, November 26, 1993, 50–51, accessed April 29, 2017, https://www.unicef

.org/about/execboard/files/86-90-L1309-Add4-Compilation_English.pdf; UNICEF, "'The Girl Child': An Investment in the Future," in *Draft: Children and Development in the 1990s: A UNICEF Sourcebook on the Occasion of the World Summit for Children, 29-30 September 1990* (New York: UNICEF, 1990), 152–55; and Algeria et al., "Focus on the Girl Child: Implementation of UNICEF Policy on Women in Development: Draft Proposal" (New York: United Nations, 1990).

3. J. Pulane Lefoka, "Educational Research Network in Eastern and Southern Africa (ERNESA)," *NORRAG News* 32 (August 2003): 110–11.

4. In three of the countries studied—Madagascar, Botswana, and Kenya—ERNESA's researchers produced original research on girls' educational experiences and collated existing evidence into in-depth studies. Researchers from five other countries—Burundi, Ethiopia, Mozambique, Rwanda, and Somalia—compiled existing data on girls' schooling. ERNESA's members wrote their country reports in a mix of French and English.

5. Sheila Parvyn Wamahiu, "The Pedagogy of Difference: An African Perspective," in *Equity in the Classroom: Towards Effective Pedagogy for Girls and Boys*, ed. Patricia F. Murphy and Caroline V. Gipps (London: UNESCO and Falmer, 1996), 57; Anna P. Obura, "Learning the Gender Bias Early: Primary School Textbooks," *CERES FAO Review* 19 (1986): 3; Anna P. Obura, *Changing Images: Portrayal of Girls and Women in Kenyan Textbooks* (Nairobi: African Centre for Technology Studies), 1991; and Anna P. Obura, "The Needs of Third World Children in International Schools Away from Home," *International Schools Journal* (Spring 1985): 17.

6. Girls continued to outnumber boys in the first three years of secondary school. At the senior secondary level, those statistics flipped, with boys narrowly outnumbering girls. Lydia Nyati-Ramahobo, Agnes F. Njabili, Sana Mmolai, Ontiretse Selepeng-Tau, and James Taole, comps., *The Girl Child Study: Opportunities and Disparities in Education, Part One of Two, The State of the Art Review*, compiled for the Botswana Educational Research Association, UNICEF, FEMNET, and ERNESA (Gaborone, Botswana: Botswana Educational Research Association, February 1992), 70–72.

7. In Rwanda, roughly 49.8 percent of recorded primary school students were girls in 1990. For Madagascar, girls made up 48.81 percent of reported primary school students versus 51.19 percent boys. In secondary school, the proportion of girls grew to 49.13 percent. In Kenya, 48.7 percent of reported primary school students were girls in 1990. Figures from Anna P. Obura, comp., "Synthesis Report: The Girl Child; Opportunities and Disparities in Education," Unpublished Report Compiled for FEMNET and UNICEF ESARO, FEMNET Documentation Center, Nairobi, 1992, 58–59; Suzy Ramamonjisoa, *Possibilités et disparités éducatives entre fillettes et garçons à Madagascar* (Tsimbazaza, Madagascar: UNICEF Madagascar), 16–17; and Sheila P. Wamahiu, Fred A. Opondo, and Grace Nyagah, comps., *Educational Situation of the Kenyan Girl Child*, compiled for the Educational Research Network in Kenya (ERNIKE) and UNICEF ESARO (Nairobi: ERNIKE, March 1992), 10–15, FEMNET Archive.

8. "Burundi," in Obura, "Synthesis Report," Appendix; "Mozambique: Enrolments [sic] in Primary Education by Grade—1989," in Obura, "Synthesis Report," Appendix; "Ethiopia, Table 2, Enrolment [sic] by Sex in Primary School," in Obura, "Synthesis Report," Appendix; "Enrolment [sic] in Somali Primary Schools," in Obura, "Synthesis Report," 54.

9. "Rwanda Girl Child Study," in Obura, "Synthesis Report," Appendix.

10. *Studies on Disparities and Prospects for Girls' Basic Education in Burundi* (Bujumbura, Burundi: UNICEF, 1991), in Obura, "Synthesis Report," 72.

11. "Mozambique Girl Child Study," in Obura, "Synthesis Report," Appendix.

12. Nyati-Ramahobo et al., *The Girl Child Study, Part One*, 72.

13. Ramamonjisoa, *Possibilités et disparités*, 22.
14. Obura, "Synthesis Report," 8–9, 54, 70.
15. Obura, "Synthesis Report," 7–11, 31–33, 39, 44–46.
16. "Somalia Girl Child Study," 15–16, in Obura, "Synthesis Report," 54–55, 70, and Appendix.
17. Catharine B. Hill, Kenneth M. Kletzer, and Arunkant A. Shah, "The Effects of Public Expenditures on Kenya's Macroeconomy," in *The Evaluation of Public Expenditure in Africa*, eds. Henry J. Bruton and Catharine B. Hill (Washington, DC: World Bank, 1996), 150–52.
18. Wamahiu et al., *Educational Situation of the Kenyan Girl Child*, 21, 36, 77–78, 84–85, 98.
19. Wamahiu et al., *Educational Situation of the Kenyan Girl Child*, 98.
20. Ramamonjisoa, *Possibilités et disparités*, 23.
21. Ramamonjisoa, *Possibilités et disparités*, 3, 14, 38.
22. Nyati-Ramahobo et al., *The Girl Child Study, Part One*, Botswana, 13.
23. Nyati-Ramahobo et al., *The Girl Child Study, Part One*, Botswana, 13.
24. Lydia Nyati-Ramahobo and Sana Mmolai, comps., *The Girl Child Study: Opportunities and Disparities in Education, Part Two: Botswana in Depth Case Study*, compiled for the Botswana Educational Research Association, UNICEF, FEMNET, and ERNESA (Gaborone, Botswana: Botswana Educational Research Association, July 1992), 3, FEMNET Archive.
25. Nyati-Ramahobo and Mmolai, *The Girl Child Study, Part Two*, 33–34.
26. Nyati-Ramahobo and Mmolai, *The Girl Child Study, Part Two*, 48–50.
27. Nyati-Ramahobo and Mmolai, *The Girl Child Study, Part Two*, 8–46.
28. Nyati-Ramahobo et al., *The Girl Child Study, Part One*, Botswana, 3.
29. Nyati-Ramahobo et al., *The Girl Child Study, Part One*, Botswana, 3; Nyati-Ramahobo and Mmolai, *The Girl Child Study, Part Two*, 47–52.
30. Wamahiu et al., *Educational Situation of the Kenyan Girl Child*, 10.
31. Wamahiu et al., *Educational Situation of the Kenyan Girl Child*, 10.
32. Wamahiu et al., *Educational Situation of the Kenyan Girl Child*, 21–22.
33. Wamahiu et al., *Educational Situation of the Kenyan Girl Child*, 20.
34. Wamahiu et al., *Educational Situation of the Kenyan Girl Child*, 32.
35. Wamahiu et al., *Educational Situation of the Kenyan Girl Child*, 34.
36. Wamahiu et al., *Educational Situation of the Kenyan Girl Child*, 98.
37. Wamahiu et al., *Educational Situation of the Kenyan Girl Child*, 75.
38. Wamahiu et al., *Educational Situation of the Kenyan Girl Child*, 36.
39. Wamahiu et al., *Educational Situation of the Kenyan Girl Child*, 98.
40. Wamahiu et al., *Educational Situation of the Kenyan Girl Child*, 86.
41. Wamahiu et al., *Educational Situation of the Kenyan Girl Child*, 86–88.
42. Wamahiu et al., *Educational Situation of the Kenyan Girl Child*, 80.
43. Wamahiu et al., *Educational Situation of the Kenyan Girl Child*, 77–78.
44. Obura, "Synthesis Report," Unpublished, 53, 68, 70.
45. Obura, "Synthesis Report," Unpublished, 70.
46. Ethiopia Girl Child Study, 2–5, in Obura, "Synthesis Report," 8, 13.
47. Obura, "Synthesis Report," Unpublished, 54.
48. Obura, "Synthesis Report," 19.
49. Somalia Country Study 7–9, in Obura, "Synthesis Report," Unpublished, 18; Mozambique Country Study 2, 4–5, 16 in Obura, "Synthesis Report," 22; Ethiopia Country Study, in Obura, "Synthesis Report," 68.
50. Obura, "Synthesis Report," 4.

51. Rwanda Girl Child Study, 1, in Obura, "Synthesis Report," Unpublished, 31; *Studies on Disparities and Prospects for Girls' Basic Education in Burundi*, 1–3, in Obura, "Synthesis Report," 39, 44.

52. Obura, "Synthesis Report," 7, 9–11.

53. Obura, "Synthesis Report," 7.

54. Obura, "Synthesis Report," 9–11.

55. Obura, "Synthesis Report," 4.

56. Anna P. Obura and D. Komba, comps., *The Girl Child: Opportunities and Disparities in Education, Workshop and Country Studies Synthesis Report* (Nairobi: UNICEF ESARO, 1992), 53.

57. UNICEF, "'The Girl Child': An Investment in the Future," 152–55.

58. Wamahiu et al., *Educational Situation of the Kenyan Girl Child*, 1.

59. Obura, "Synthesis Report," 24–25.

60. Obura and Komba, *The Girl Child*, 61.

61. Obura and Komba, *The Girl Child*, 57–59.

62. See, for example, Obura, "Synthesis Report," Appendix; Obura and Komba, *The Girl Child*, Annex.

63. Obura and Komba, *The Girl Child*, 1–111.

64. Obura and Komba, *The Girl Child*, 7–9.

65. Obura and Komba, *The Girl Child*, 36–39.

66. Obura and Komba, *The Girl Child*, 12.

67. Obura and Komba, *The Girl Child*, 18.

68. Obura and Komba, *The Girl Child*, 21.

69. Obura and Komba, *The Girl Child*, 18–19, 24.

70. Obura and Komba, *The Girl Child*, 24.

71. Obura and Komba, *The Girl Child*, 26.

72. See, for example, UNICEF, "The Situation of Girls in Africa," in *Volume 2: Conference Papers on Priority Issues, Part II B: Education, Health and Social Issues*, UN Economic Commission for Africa, African Centre for Women, Fifth African Regional Conference on Women, Dakar, Senegal, November 16–23, 1994, 43–75 (E/ECA/ACW/RC.V/EXP/WP.3B), accessed April 29, 2017, http://repository.uneca.org/bitstream/handle/10855/2624/Bib-21097.pdf?sequence=1.

73. Christopher S. Wren, "Unicef Says Fraud Cost $10 Million," *New York Times*, May 26, 1995, https://www.nytimes.com/1995/05/26/world/unicef-says-fraud-cost-10-million.html.

74. Daniel Baheta, interviewed by author, Nairobi, October 26, 2014.

75. Obura and Komba, *The Girl Child*, 5.

76. Sara Hlupekile Longwe, comp., *Towards an African Women's Network: A Report of the African Women's Task Force Meeting Held in Nairobi on 11–15th April 1988* (Nairobi: FEMNET, 1988), 17, 23, 43–44; "The Birth of a Network," *FEMNET News* 1.1 (May–July 1989): 3; "FEMNET's Great Advance," *FEMNET News* 2.1 (December 1992–March 1993): 2; and Norah K. Olembo, ed., "African Women's Development and Communication Network (FEMNET) Report on First Programming Conference, 5th–7th October, 1992" (Nairobi: FEMNET, 1993), 6–7, 10–11.

77. Longwe, comp., *Towards an African Women's Network*, 2, 23, 119–20; Olembo, ed., "African Women's Development and Communication Network (FEMNET) Report on First Programming Conference," 2–3; "FEMNET's Advance into the Future," *FEMNET News* 2.1 (December 1992–March 1993): 4; and Wainaina, comp., *HerStory: Our Journey*, 14–15, 22–25.

78. "FEMNET's Advance into the Future," *FEMNET News* 2.1 (December 1992–March 1993): 4.

79. Longwe, comp., *Towards an African Women's Network*, 120; Wainaina, comp., *HerStory: Our Journey*, 15, 23.

80. Esther Kamweru, interview with Njoki Wainaina, "African Women Speak Out," *FEMNET News* 4.4 (October–December 1994): 13–14.

81. The history of Wangari Maathai and the NGO she founded, the Greenbelt Movement, provide an interesting case study of how the leadership of another Nairobi-based organization mobilized vis-à-vis the government of Kenya and the international community in the 1980s–1990s. Namulundah Florence, *Wangari Maathai: Visionary, Environmental Leader, Political Activist* (New York: Lantern, 2014); Patrick Luganda, "Tribute to Wangari Muthaai: The Green Belt Movement," *Network of Climate Journalists of the Greater Horn of Africa*, September 26, 2011; Rebekah Cockram, "Agents of Rights-Based Justice: Wangari Maathai and Kenya's Green Belt Movement," *Global Africana Review* 1, no. 1 (Spring 2017), 3–12.

82. Wainaina, comp., *HerStory: Our Journey*, 16.

83. Wainaina, comp., *HerStory: Our Journey*, 16, 23.

84. Audrey Wipper, "The Maendeleo Ya Wanawake Organization"; Cora Ann Presley, "The Mau Rebellion, Kikuyu Women, and Social Change," *Canadian Journal of African Studies* 22 (1988): 519–20; National Archives of the UK, Public Record Office, Colonial Office, Kew Gardens, England 822/652, Community Development in Kenya, 1951–1953; and TNA PRO CO 822/655, Deputy Governor Crawford at Jeanes School Speech Day, December 2, 1953.

85. Marilyn Muthoni Kamuru, "Maendeleo ya Wanawake and the Politics of Silencing Women," *The Elephant*, February 21, 2020, https://www.theelephant.info/features/2020/02/21/maendeleo-ya-wanawake-and-the-politics-of-silencing-women.

Chapter Two

1. Olcott, *International Women's Year*, 5; Ghodsee, *Second World, Second Sex*; Lea Börgerding, "Staging Emancipation and its Limits: East German Cultural Diplomacy, the German Democratic Women's League, and the 1975 World Congress of Women in East Berlin," *Women's History Review* (2023): 1–19.

2. UN General Assembly Resolution 3201 (S-VI), "Declaration on the Establishment of a New International Economic Order," Resolutions Adopted on the Report of the *Ad Hoc* Committee of the Sixth Special Session, May 1, 1974, 3–5, https://digitallibrary.un.org/record/218450?ln=en&v=pdf.

3. Ruth Bacon, "U.S. Center for IWY 1975, Newsletter No. 3-75," June 1, 1975, 3, Sheila Weidenfeld Files, box 47, folder "Women—International Women's Year Conference," Gerald R. Ford Presidential Library, https://www.fordlibrarymuseum.gov/library/document/0126/1489978.pdf.

4. Bacon, "U.S. Center for IWY 1975," 3.

5. See, for example, Margaret Fulton, "Copenhagen—Mid-Decade World Conference on Women 1980," *Atlantis: Critical Studies in Gender, Culture & Social Justice* 6, no. 2 (1981): 195; Olcott, *International Women's Year*, 13, 45; and Ghodsee, *Second World, Second Sex*, introduction and chap. 1.

6. "Re: Mexico City, Gen. Skocroft Conversation," undated, Sheila Weidenfeld Files, box 47, folder "Women—International Women's Year Conference," Gerald R. Ford Presidential Library, https://www.fordlibrarymuseum.gov/library/document/0126/1489978.pdf.

7. "Draft Message from Mrs. Ford to IWY Conference, Mexico City, to Be Read by Mrs. Patricia Hutar," undated, Sheila Weidenfeld Files, box 47, folder "Women—International Women's Year Conference," Gerald R. Ford Presidential Library, https://www.fordlibrarymuseum.gov/library/document/0126/1489978.pdf.

8. See, for example, Olcott, *International Women's Year*, 82, 157, 159, 171, 201, 210, 218–19, 235; Ghodsee, *Second World, Second Sex*, chap. 6.

9. Hilkka Pietilä, *The Unfinished Story of Women and the United Nations* (New York: United Nations, UN Non-Governmental Liaison Service Development Dossier, 2007), 50–52; Fulton, "Copenhagen," 194–201.

10. Pietilä, *The Unfinished Story of Women and the United Nations*, 49.

11. Wainaina, comp., *HerStory: Our Journey*, 13.

12. See, for example, Hilbourne A. Watson, *Errol Barrow and the Postwar Transformation of Barbados: The Independence Period, 1966–1976* (Mona, Saint Andrew Parish, Jamaica: University of the West Indies Press, 2020).

13. Barrow's formal leadership roles ranged from the YWCA to the International Council of Adult Education, the Pan American Health Organization for the Caribbean, and the Christian Medical Commission of the World Council of Churches. Nita Barrow Collection, UNESCO, https://www.unesco.org/en/memory-world/lac/nita-barrow-collection; Nita Barrow Collection, UNESCO Women in History Project, Collections on HERstory, http://mowherstory.org/items/show/7.

14. Virginia Hazzard's obituary lists New York University as the institution from which she earned her MA degree. However, a UNICEF publication from 1987 that Hazzard wrote lists Columbia as the institution from which she earned her MA. Because Hazzard was the author of the UNICEF publication (and, likely, of her own biography that appeared in its front matter), and because this biography contained more precise details of her career than the obituary, I am listing Columbia as her graduate degree-granting institution. Virginia Hazzard, *UNICEF and Women: The Long Voyage, A Historical Perspective*, History Series Monograph VII (New York: UNICEF, 1987), http://www.cf-hst.net/UNICEF-TEMP/mon/CF-HST-MON-1986-007-women-long-voyage-mono-VII.pdf, front matter, and "E. Virginia Hazzard Obituary," *Star-Ledger*, November 4, 2007, https://obits.nj.com/us/obituaries/starledger/name/e-hazzard-obituary?id=13667023.

15. *NGO Forum on Women, Beijing 95: Look at the World through Women's Eyes* (New York: UN Department of Public Information, 1995), 74, https://archivio.women.it/wp-content/uploads/sites/5/2023/05/forum_95_final_report_web_OCR.pdf.

16. "Editorial," *FEMNET News* 1.1 (May–July 1989): 2, FEMNET Archive.

17. Gachukia, "Dr. Eddah Gachukia," 47.

18. "History of the Riara Group of Schools," Riara Group of Schools Facebook Post, August 22, 2022, https://www.facebook.com/riaragroupofschools/posts/5241423902572327; Joshua Malii, "Gachukias: Meet Little Known Billionaire Who Own the Riara Group of Schools," *Bizna*, November 27, 2023, https://biznakenya.com/owners-of-riara-group-of-schools; and Gachukia, "Dr. Eddah Gachukia," 47–49.

19. Gachukia, "Dr. Eddah Gachukia," 47.

20. "FEMNET's Advance into the Future," *FEMNET News* 2.1 (December 1992–March 1993): 4.

21. Eddah Gachukia, "Chairman's Address," in *Towards an African Women's Network: A Report of the African Women's Task Force Meeting Held in Nairobi on 11–15th April 1988*, comp. by Sara Hlupekile Longwe (Nairobi: African Women's Task Force, 1988), 116–18, FEMNET Archive.

22. Njoki Wainaina, "Njoki Wainaina, FEMNET Founding Member and Chairperson (1992–1996)," interview by Fatma Alloo and Carlyn Hambuba, in Wainaina, comp., *HerStory: Our Journey*, 51.

23. Wainaina, comp., *HerStory: Our Journey*, 14.

24. *Forum '85 Report* (Nairobi: Kenya NGO Organizing Committee, September 1987), 17, FEMNET Archive.

25. Dorothy Kweyu, "The Kenyan Feminist Praised by President of Malawi as a Friend," *Nation*, December 14, 2013, https://nation.africa/kenya/news/the-kenyan-feminist-praised-by-president-of-malawi-as-a-friend--927012.

26. Wainaina, "Njoki Wainaina," 50.

27. Wainaina, "Njoki Wainaina," 49.

28. Wainaina, "Njoki Wainaina," 50.

29. Wainaina, "Njoki Wainaina," 50–51.

30. Wainaina, comp., *HerStory: Our Journey*, 14–15; Gachukia, "Dr. Eddah Gachukia," 48.

31. Wainaina, "Njoki Wainaina," 52.

32. Longwe, comp., *Towards an African Women's Network*, 2; Gachukia, "Chairman's Address," 119; "FEMNET's Advance into the Future," *FEMNET News* 2.1 (December 1992–March 1993): 4; Olembo, ed., "African Women's Development and Communication Network (FEMNET) Report on First Programming Conference," iii, 3; Gachukia, "Dr. Eddah Gachukia," 48; Wainaina, comp., *HerStory: Our Journey*, 22–23. Most editions of *FEMNET News* between 1989 and 1994 thank UNICEF for funding their publication.

33. Wainaina, comp., *HerStory: Our Journey*, 22.

34. Wainaina, "Njoki Wainaina," 52.

35. Wainaina, comp., *HerStory: Our Journey*, 14–15.

36. "The Birth of a Network," *FEMNET News* 1.1 (May–July 1989): 1, FEMNET Archive.

37. Wainaina, comp., *HerStory: Our Journey*, 14–15.

38. "Editorial," *FEMNET News* 1.1 (May–July 1989): 2, FEMNET Archive.

39. *Forum '85 Report*, 1.

40. Olcott, *International Women's Year*, 1.

41. "The Spirit of Nairobi," *Los Angeles Times*, July 23, 1985, https://www.latimes.com/archives/la-xpm-1985-07-23-me-7459-story.html.

42. Wainaina, comp., *HerStory: Our Journey*, 16.

43. For a discussion of AAWORD and a broader history African feminist organizing, see Amina Mama, "African Feminist Thought," in *The Oxford Research Encyclopedia of African History* (Oxford: Oxford University Press, 2020), https://doi.org/10.1093/acrefore/9780190277734.013.504.

44. Fulton, "Copenhagen," 196–97.

45. Fulton, "Peace Is the Way to Peace," *Canadian Woman Studies / Les Cahiers de la Femme* 7, no. 1 & 2 (1986): 159–62.

46. Karen Maters, "The Nairobi World Conference," Supplement No. 24 to *Women of Europe* (Brussels: Commission of the European Communities, Directorate-General Information, Communication, Culture, Women's Information Service, 1986), 56.

47. Wainaina, comp., *HerStory: Our Journey*, 16.

48. Works that use various terminology to describe female circumcision and explain the reasoning behind the chosen terms include Hodgson, *Gender, Justice, and the Problem of Culture*, 233; Anna Winterbottom, Jonneke Koomen, and Gemma Burford, "Female Genital Cutting: Cultural Rights and Rites of Defiance in Northern Tanzania," *African Studies Review* 52, no. 1 (April 2009): 47–71; Jonneke Koomen, "Global Governance and the Politics of Culture: Campaigns against Female Circumcision in East Africa," *Gender, Place & Culture: A Journal of Feminist Geography* 21, no. 2 (2014): 244–61; Carla Makhlouf Obermeyer, "Female Genital Surgeries: The Known, the Unknown, and the Unknowable," *Medical Anthropology Quarterly* 13, no. 1 (March 1999): 79–106; Fran P. Hosken, *The Hosken Report: Genital and Sexual Mutilation of Females* (Lexington, MA: Women's International Network News, 1979).

49. Martine Gibert, "Les Nations Unies et les femmes. A propos de la Conférence de Nairobi (10-27 juillet 1985)," *Politique africaine* 20 (1985): 117.

50. See, for example, John Tochukwu Okwubanego, "Female Circumcision and the Girl Child in Africa and the Middle East: The Eyes of the World Are Blind to the Conquered," *International Lawyer* 33, no. 1 (Spring 1999): 173. Footnote 131 references "reporting that at the 1980 U.N. Mid-Decade Conference for Women in Copenhagen, a group of African women deliberately shouted down the author while she was presenting a paper on female circumcision."

51. Gachukia, "Dr. Eddah Gachukia," 48.

52. Bekers, ed., *Rising Anthills*.

53. Bekers, ed., *Rising Anthills*; L. Amede Obiora, "The Little Foxes That Spoil the Vine: Revisiting the Feminist Critique of Female Circumcision," *Canadian Journal of Women and the Law* 9, no. 46 (1997): 46–73; Nnaemeka, ed., *Female Circumcision and the Politics of Knowledge*. For a discussion of divides between African and Black American women at the UN Third World Conference on Women in Nairobi, see Mandana Hendessi, "Fourteen Thousand Women Meet: Report from Nairobi, July 1985," *Feminist Review* 23 (Summer 1986): 147–56.

54. Edwin A. Gimode, "The Role of the Police in Kenya's Democratization Process," in *Kenya: The Struggle for Democracy*, ed. Godwin R. Murunga and Shadrack Wanjala Nasong'o, 227–60 (Dakar: Codesria in association with Zed, 2007); Jennifer Widner, *The Rise of a Party-State in Kenya: From 'Harambee!' to 'Nyayo!'* (Berkeley: University of California Press, 1993), chap. 5, https://publishing.cdlib.org/ucpressebooks/view?docId=ft9h4nb6fv.

55. Gimode, "The Role of the Police in Kenya's Democratization Process," 227–60.

56. Wainaina, "Njoki Wainaina," 52.

57. Wainaina, "Njoki Wainaina," 52.

58. Wainaina, comp., *HerStory: Our Journey*, 16.

59. Wainaina, "Njoki Wainaina," 52.

60. Dominique Mazire, "Une organization de femmes au Kenya: Maendeleo ya Wanawake," *Politique africaine* 53 (1994): 141, https://www.persee.fr/doc/polaf_0244-7827_1994_num_53_1_5752.

61. Maureen Ajiambo Muleka and Pontian Godfrey Okoth, "The Role of the Maendeleo ya Wanawake Organization in Women's Economic Empowerment: The Case of Abakhayo Women, Busia County (1978–2002)," *Pathways to African Feminism and Development: Women's Economic Empowerment* 7, no. 1 (2022): 60.

62. Muleka and Okoth, "The Role of the Maendeleo ya Wanawake Organization in Women's Economic Empowerment," 65. See also Anne Namatsi Lutomia, Brenda Nyandiko Sanya, and Dorothy Owino Rombo, "Examining and Contextualizing Kenya's *Maendeleo ya Wanawake Organization* (MYWO) through an African Feminist Lens," in *Women's Emancipation and Civil Society Organizations: Challenging or Maintaining the Status Quo?*, ed. Christina Schwabenland, Chris Lange, Jenny Onyx, and Sachiko Nakagawa (Bristol, UK: Policy, 2016), 321–42, https://academic.oup.com/policy-press-scholarship-online/book/18631/chapter/176825521.

63. Rosemary Wanjiku Mbugua, "Women's Organizations and Collective Action in Kenya: Opportunities and Challenges—The Case of the Maendeleo ya Wanawake Organization," *Pathways to African Feminism and Development* 1, no. 5 (May 2017): 8–9.

64. Wainaina, "Njoki Wainaina," 52.

65. Gachukia, "Dr. Eddah Gachukia," 48.

66. "Tribute to Prof. Norah Olembo, One of Kenya's Finest Biochemists," *Science Africa*, last modified March 19, 2021, https://news.scienceafrica.co.ke/tribute-to-prof-norah-olembo-one-of-kenyas-finest-biochemists/.

67. Dorothy Kweyu, "End of Era as Prof. Norah Olembo is Laid to Rest," *Nation*, March 20, 2021, https://nation.africa/kenya/blogs-opinion/opinion/end-of-era-as-prof-norah-olembo-is-laid-to-rest-3329880.

68. Nora Olembo, "Prof. Nora Olembo, Founding Member of FEMNET (1985–1992)," interview by Fatma Alloo and Carlyn Hambuba, in Wainaina, comp., *HerStory: Our Journey*, 64.

69. Gachukia, "Chairman's Address," 2; M'Sodzi G. Mutukwa, "Implementation of the U.N. Convention on the Elimination of All Forms of Discrimination against Women: The African Experience," in Longwe, comp., *Towards an African Women's Network*, 45–70; and Sara Hlupekile Longwe, "From Welfare to Empowerment: The Situation of Women in Africa; A Post UN Women's Decade Update and Future Directions," in Longwe, comp., *Towards an African Women's Network*, 71–111.

70. Gachukia, "Chairman's Address," 2.

Chapter Three

1. Agnes Aidoo, *The Girl Child: An Investment in the Future* (New York: UNICEF, 1990), 14, 7.

2. UNICEF, "'The Girl Child': An Investment in the Future," in *Draft: Children and Development in the 1990s: A UNICEF Sourcebook on the Occasion of the World Summit for Children, 29–30 September 1990* (New York: UNICEF, 1990). Agnes Aidoo is listed as a "contributor" to the UNICEF sourcebook that initially contained the pamphlet in 1990. The stand-alone publication from 1990 states in the first pages that Aidoo prepared it.

3. Lawrence Summers, "The Most Influential Investment," *Scientific American*, August 1992, 132.

4. Carl Hartman, "Third World Urged to Educate Girls: Development: World Bank Study Concludes That Women with Even an Elementary Education Raise a Poor Nation's Living Standard," Associated Press, in *Los Angeles Times*, September 19, 1993; Elizabeth M. King and M. Anne Hill, eds., *Women's Education in Developing Countries: Barriers, Benefits, and Policies* (Baltimore: Published for the World Bank by the Johns Hopkins University Press, 1993), v.

5. Claudia Goldin, "Human Capital," in *Handbook of Cliometrics*, ed. Claude Diebolt and Michael Haupert, 55–86 (Heidelberg: Springer, 2016), https://dash.harvard.edu/bitstream/handle/1/34309590/human_capital_handbook_of_cliometrics_0.pdf?sequence=1&isAllowed=y.

6. Calkin, *Human Capital in Gender and Development*, 3.

7. Esther Boserup, *Woman's Role in Economic Development* (London: George Allen & Unwin, 1970).

8. Moeller, *The Gender Effect*, chap. 1 and 2; Moeller, "Girls as New Frontiers: Corporatized Development and the Politics of Investing in Girls," in *Girls in Global Development*, ed. Heather Switzer, Karishma Desai, and Emily Bent (Oxford: Berghahn, 2024), 41–56; Murphy, *The Economization of Life*, chap. 10; Calkin, *Human Capital in Gender and Development*; Calkin, "Human Capital Theory and Girlhoods in Development," in *Girls in Global Development*, 21–40; Meyerowitz, *A War on Global Poverty*.

9. For a few of many examples, see Malgorzata Fidelis, *Women, Communism, and Industrialization in Postwar Poland* (Cambridge: Cambridge University Press, 2010); Stefka Koeva and Sally Bould, "Women as Workers and Carers under Communism and After: The Case of Bulgaria," *International Review of Sociology* 17 (2007): 303–18; Minru Mo, "Women and Development: Aspects of the Chinese Case under Communism," Retrospective Theses and Dissertations, 1919–2007, University of British Columbia (1994), https://open.library.ubc.ca/soa/cIRcle/collections/ubctheses/831/items/1.0087526.

10. James P. Grant, *The State of the World's Children 1984* (Oxford: Published for UNICEF by Oxford University Press, 1983), 59.

11. A classic text on the history of neoliberal capitalism is David Harvey, *A Brief History of Neoliberalism* (Oxford: Oxford University Press, 2005).

12. Kristen Ghodsee has argued that neoliberal feminism became dominant at the UN Fourth World Conference on Women and within the mainstream of the broader global women's movement because the end of the Cold War removed socialist and other leftist economic counterpressures on the United States and its allies. This, she posits, allowed neoliberal visions of feminism to go unchecked at the final UN World Conference on Women in Beijing and beyond (Ghodsee, *Second World, Second Sex*, introduction and conclusion). Nancy Fraser, meanwhile, has claimed that feminism was unwittingly complicit in the creation of neoliberal feminism, largely due to five intellectual and political stances embedded within "second wave" feminism since the late 1960s. In this line of argumentation, Fraser almost exclusively focuses on actors in and ideologies supposedly stemming from the Global North, reproducing a broader trend in feminist historiography to trace the Western origins of feminist and woman-focused activism at the expense of linked and separate movements in other parts of the world (Nancy Fraser, "Feminism, Capitalism, and the Cunning of History," *New Left Review* 56 [2009]: 97–117).

13. For a few of many examples, see John Ashton, "Alma Ata and Primary Health Care, 40 Years On," *Journal of the Royal Society of Medicine* 111, no. 12 (2018): 462–63, https://journals.sagepub.com/doi/full/10.1177/0141076818818367; Laura Gottlieb, "Learning from Alma Ata: The Medical Home and Comprehensive Primary Health Care," *Journal of the American Board of Family Medicine* 22, no. 3 (May–June 2009): 242–46, https://www.jabfm.org/content/jabfp/22/3/242.full.pdf; Zulfiqar Ahmed Bhutta, Rifat Atun, Navjoyt Ladher, and Kamran Abbasi, "Alma Ata and Primary Healthcare: Back to the Future," *BMJ* 363 (2018).

14. *Alma-Ata 1978 Primary Health Care: Report of the International Conference on Primary Health Care, Alma-Ata, USSR, 6–12 September 1978* (Geneva: World Health Organization, 1978), 2, https://www.who.int/publications/i/item/9241800011; Fernando Antonio Pires-Alves and Marcos Cueto, "The Alma-Ata Decade: The Crisis of Development and International Health," *Ciencia & Saude Coletiva* 22 (2017): 2135–44.

15. "Declaration on the Establishment of a New International Economic Order," 4.

16. "Declaration on the Establishment of a New International Economic Order," 1.

17. *Alma-Ata 1978 Primary Health Care*, 4.

18. *Alma-Ata 1978 Primary Health Care*, 4, 6.

19. Zhou Xun, "From China's 'Barefoot Doctor' to Alma Ata: The Primary Health Care Movement of the Long 1970s," in *China, Hong Kong, and the Long 1970s: Global Perspectives*, ed. Priscilla Roberts and Odd Arne Westad (Cham, Switzerland: Palgrave Macmillan, 2017), 135–57; Youngsub Lee and Hyoungsup Kim, "The Turning Point of China's Rural Public Health during the Cultural Revolution Period: Barefoot Doctors: A Narrative," *Iranian Journal of Public Health* 47, suppl. 1 (2018): 1–8.

20. "Dr. Halfdan Mahler's Address to the 61st World Health Assembly: Former Director-General of WHO," World Health Organization Director-General Speeches, last modified May 20, 2008, https://www.who.int/director-general/speeches/detail/dr-halfdan-mahler-s-address-to-the-61st-world-health-assembly.

21. Maggie Black, *Children First: The Story of UNICEF, Past and Present* (Oxford: Published for UNICEF by Oxford University Press, 1996), 37.

22. Direct quotation from James P. Grant in Edward H. Berman, *The Influence of the Carnegie, Ford, and Rockefeller Foundations on American Foreign Policy: The Ideology of Philanthropy* (Albany: State University of New York Press, 1983), 140–41.

23. James P. Grant, *The State of the World's Children 1982–83* (Oxford: Published for UNICEF by Oxford University Press, 1982), 4.

24. Grant, *The State of the World's Children 1982–83*, 3.

25. James P. Grant, *The State of the World's Children 1984* (Oxford: Published for UNICEF by Oxford University Press, 1983), 4; Richard Jolly and Giovanni Cornia, eds., *The Impact of World Recession on Children* (New York: Pergamon, 1984).

26. Giovanni Andrea Cornia, Richard Jolly, and Frances Stewart, eds., *Adjustment with a Human Face, A UNICEF Study: Volume I, Protecting the Vulnerable and Promoting Growth* (Oxford: Oxford University Press and Clarendon, 1987), 3.

27. Grant, *The State of the World's Children 1982–83*; Jolly and Cornia, eds., *The Impact of World Recession on Children*. See also Meyerowitz, *A War on Global Poverty*, chap. 5, "Dangerous Debt."

28. David Harvey, *A Brief History of Neoliberalism* (Oxford: Oxford University Press, 2005), 23, 29–31, 99–100; Robert Lensink, *Structural Adjustment in Sub-Saharan Africa* (New York: Longman, 1996); Hodgson, *Being Maasai, Becoming Indigenous*, introduction and chap. 2; Walden Bello, Shea Cunningham, and Bill Rau, *Dark Victory: The United States and Global Poverty* (London: Pluto Press / Institute for Food and Development Policy, 1994); Henry Veltmeyer, James Petras, and Steve Vieux, *Neoliberalism and Class Conflict in Latin America: A Comparative Perspective on the Political Economy of Structural Adjustment* (London: Macmillan, 1997); George Clement Bond, "Introduction: Globalization, Neoliberalism, and Historical Conditionalities," *Journal of African American History* 88, no. 4 (2003): 330–38; Franz Heidhues and Gideon A. Obare, "Lessons from Structural Adjustment Programmes and their Effects in Africa," *Quarterly Journal of International Agriculture* 50, no. 1 (2011): 55–64.

29. See, for example, Grant, *The State of the World's Children 1982–83*; Grant, *The State of the World's Children 1984*; Jolly and Cornia, eds., *The Impact of World Recession on Children*; Cornia, Jolly, and Stewart, eds., *Adjustment with a Human Face*.

30. Jolly and Cornia, eds., *The Impact of World Recession on Children*, 4.

31. Giovanni Andrea Cornia, "A Summary and Interpretation of the Evidence," in *The Impact of World Recession on Children*, ed. Richard Jolly and Giovanni Andrea Cornia (New York: Pergamon, 1984), 211–12.

32. Reginald Herbold Green and Hans Singer, "Sub-Saharan Africa in Depression: The Impact on the Welfare of Children," in *The Impact of World Recession on Children*, ed. Jolly and Cornia, 122.

33. Green and Singer, "Sub-Saharan Africa in Depression," 123.

34. Green and Singer, "Sub-Saharan Africa in Depression," 124.

35. Grant, *The State of the World's Children 1984*, 67.

36. Cornia, "A Summary and Interpretation of the Evidence," 211.

37. See, for example, Raul Prebisch, "Introduction: The Economic Development of Latin America and Its Principal Problems," *Economic Survey of Latin America 1948* (Santiago: ECLAC); Raul Prebisch, "Growth, Disequilibrium and Disparities: Interpretation of the Process of Economic Development," *Estudio Económico de América Latina y el Caribe*, Naciones Unidas Comisión Económica para América Latina y el Caribe (CEPAL) 1105 (1949); Hans Singer, "Economic Progress in Underdeveloped Countries," *Social Research* 16, no. 1 (1949): 1–11;

Walter Rodney, *How Europe Underdeveloped Africa* (London: Bogle-L'Ouverture, 1972); and B. N. Ghosh, *Dependency Theory Revisited* (London: Routledge, 2001).

38. Grant, *The State of the World's Children 1984*, 10, 67.

39. Grant, *The State of the World's Children 1984*, 15.

40. Grant, *The State of the World's Children 1984*, 10, 49, 67.

41. Grant, *The State of the World's Children 1982–83*, 3.

42. Grant, *The State of the World's Children 1982–83*, 6–21.

43. Marcos Cueto, "The Origins of Primary Health Care and Selective Primary Health Care," *American Journal of Public Health* 94, no. 11 (2004): 1864–74; Grant, *The State of the World's Children 1982–83*, 21.

44. *UNICEF Annual Report* (New York: UNICEF, 1982), 3.

45. Grant, *The State of the World's Children 1982–83*, 21.

46. *UNICEF Annual Report* (New York: UNICEF, 1983), 5.

47. Ben Wisner, "GOBI versus PHC? Some Dangers of Selective Primary Health Care," *Social Science and Medicine* 26, no. 9 (1988): 963–69.

48. Grant, *The State of the World's Children 1984*, 5, 7.

49. Grant, *The State of the World's Children 1984*, 49, 59.

50. Grant, *The State of the World's Children 1984*, 49.

51. Grant, *The State of the World's Children 1984*, 51–53.

52. Grant, *The State of the World's Children 1984*, 53–57.

53. Black, *Children First*, 191–92.

54. Grant, *The State of the World's Children 1984*, 57–59.

55. Grant, *The State of the World's Children 1984*, 59.

56. Grant, *The State of the World's Children 1984*, 60–61.

57. Black, *Children First*, 191.

58. *UNICEF Annual Report 1984* (New York: UNICEF, 1984), 43; *UNICEF Annual Report 1988* (New York: UNICEF, 1988), 46. It is important to note that UNICEF's annual reports cover the financial year before they were published. So, the 1984 and 1988 reports cover 1983 and 1987, respectively.

59. Black, *Children First*, 191.

60. Black, *Children First*, version available at https://www.unicef.org/documents/children-first.

61. Grant, *The State of the World's Children 1984*, 23.

62. Grant, *The State of the World's Children 1984*, 45–47.

63. Grant, *The State of the World's Children 1984*, 59.

64. *World Bank Development Report* (Washington, DC: World Bank, 1980), 50; Catherine Herfeld, "Between Mathematical Formalism, Normative Choice Rules, and the Behavioural Sciences: The Emergence of Rational Choice Theories in the Late 1940s and Early 1950s," *European Journal of the History of Economic Thought* 24, no. 6 (2017): 1277–1317; Catherine Herfeld, "From Theories of Human Behavior to Rules of Rational Choice: Tracing a Normative Turn at the Cowles Commission, 1943–54," *History of Political Economy* 50, no. 1 (2018): 1–48; Giandomenica Becchio and Giovanni Leghissa, *The Origins of Neoliberalism*, chap. 3.

65. A number of studies on sex differentiation in colonial education policy had been published when UNICEF formulated its child revolution in the early 1980s. For a few examples, see Niara Sudarkasa, "Sex Roles, Education, and Development in Africa," *Anthropology & Education Quarterly* 13 (September 1982): 279–88; Barbara A. Yates, "Colonialism, Education, and Work:

Sex Differentiation in Colonial Zaire," in *Women and Work in Africa*, ed. Edna Bay, 127–53 (Boulder, CO: Westview, 1982); Barbara A. Yates, "Church, State and Education in Belgian Africa: Implications for Contemporary Third World Women," in *Women's Education in the Third World: Comparative Perspectives*, ed. Gail P. Kelly and Carolyn M. Elliott, 127–51 (Albany: State University of New York Press, 1982); Esther Boserup, *Woman's Role in Economic Development* (London: George Allen & Unwin, 1970); Clive Whitehead, "Education in British Colonial Dependencies, 1919–39: a Re-Appraisal," *Comparative Education* 17, no. 1 (1981): 71–80.

66. Grant, *The State of the World's Children 1984*, 68.

67. Grant, *The State of the World's Children 1984*, 59.

68. Grant, *The State of the World's Children 1984*, 60, 68.

69. Wisner, "GOBI versus PHC?," 965.

70. Halfdan Mahler, "Healthy for All—Everyone's Concern," *World Health: The Magazine of the World Health Organization*, April–May 1983, 3.

71. For a few of many examples, see George, *Making Modern Girls*; Decker, *Mobilizing Zanzibari Women*; Thomas, *Politics of the Womb*; Rose Hunt, *A Colonial Lexicon*. See also the endnotes in this book's introduction.

72. John Toye, "The Achievements of an Optimistic Economist," in *Towards Human Development: New Approaches to Macroeconomics and Inequality*, ed. Giovanni Andrea Cornia and Frances Stewart, 27 (Oxford: Oxford University Press, 2014).

73. UNICEF History, Annual Reports (1972–1999), https://sites.unicef.org/about/history/index_annualreports.html. For more information on the complex and shifting Cold War politics involving international development, the UN system, and various national governments, see Sunil Amrith and Glenda Sluga, "New Histories of the United Nations," *Journal of World History* (2008): 251–74; Glenda Sluga, *Internationalism in the Age of Nationalism* (Philadelphia: University of Pennsylvania Press, 2015); Marc Frey, Sönke Kunkel, and Corinna R. Unger, eds., *International Organizations and Development, 1945–1990* (London: Palgrave Macmillan, 2014); Ghodsee, *Second World, Second Sex*; Getachew, *Worldmaking after Empire*.

74. Courtney Hercus, *The Struggle over Human Rights: The Non-Aligned Movement, Jimmy Carter, and Neoliberalism* (London: Lexington, 2019), 4, 53–54, 123; Meyerowitz, *A War on Global Poverty*, chap. 2.

75. UNICEF, "The Female Child Today," NGO Forum Convened in Conjunction with the Board Meeting, 1985; Alba Zizzamia, *NGO/UNICEF Cooperation: A Historical Perspective*, UNICEF History Series: Monograph V (New York: UNICEF, 1987), 36.

76. UN Commission on the Status of Women, *The Role of Women in the Economic and Social Development of Their Countries: Report of the Secretary-General* (New York: United Nations, 1968); Frederick Harbison, "The Strategy of Human Resource Development in Modernizing Economies," November 17, 1961, agenda item 6b, UN Economic Commission for Africa, Working Party on Economic and Social Development, Addis Ababa, January 15–27, 1962 (E/CN.14/ESD/5); Frederick Harbison and Charles Andrew Myers, *Education, Manpower, and Economic Growth: Strategies of Human Resource Development* (New York: Tata McGraw-Hill Education, 1964); Frederick Harbison, *Human Resources as the Wealth of Nations* (New York: Oxford University Press, 1973); UN Economic Commission for Africa, Social Development Section, *The Status and Role of Women in East Africa* (New York: United Nations, 1967); Boserup, *Woman's Role in Economic Development*; "Factors Affecting Education, Training and Work Opportunities for Girls and Women within the Context of Development," April 30, 1971, UN Economic and Social Council, Regional Conference on Education, Vocational Training and Work Opportunities

for Girls and Women in African Countries, Rabat, Morocco, May 20-30, 1971 (E/CN.14/SW/36); UN Economic Commission for Africa, Human Resources Development Division, "Women: The Neglected Human Resource for African Development," *Canadian Journal of African Studies* 6, no. 2 (1972): 359; Maureen Woodhall, "Investment in Women: A Reappraisal of the Concept of Human Capital," *International Review of Education* 19, no. 1 (1973): 9-29.

77. Boserup, *Women's Role in Economic Development*; Rai, *Gender and the Political Economy of Development*; Rai, "The History of International Development"; Rai, "Gender and Development."

78. "United Nations Children's Fund, Report of the Executive Board, 15-26 April 1985," UN Economic and Social Council Official Records, 1985, Supplement No. 10, 4, 36, 43-44 (E/ICEF /1985/12), https://digitallibrary.un.org/record/105876?ln=en; Zizzamia, *NGO/UNICEF Cooperation*, 35-37.

79. "UNICEF Response to Women's Concerns" (E/ICEF/1985/12), in *A Compilation of Excerpts from Reports of the Board, 1980-1985*, UN Economic and Social Council, UN Children's Fund Executive Board, Executive Board Policy Decisions, November 23, 1992, 51 (E/ICEF /L.1309/Add.3), https://www.unicef.org/executiveboard/media/1251/file/1992-L1309-Add3-Com pendium_of_decisions_1980-1985-EN.pdf.

80. "Women, Children, and Development" (E/ICEF/673), in *A Compilation of Excerpts from Reports of the Board, 1980-1985*, 54.

81. "Women, Children and Development," 55.

82. Hazzard, *UNICEF and Women*, 104-5.

83. Hazzard, *UNICEF and Women*, 105; Zizzamia, *NGO/UNICEF Cooperation*, 37, 91, endnotes 64 and 65.

84. Hazzard, *UNICEF and Women*, 106-7.

85. "UNICEF Response to Women's Concerns," 50.

86. Ashwini Tambe, *Defining Girlhood in India: A Transnational History of Sexual Maturity Laws* (Urbana: University of Illinois Press, 2019), chap. 6. An extensive bibliography of girl child-related publications and events in South Asia during the 1980s and since appears in Dinesh Das, "A Study on Conditions of Child Labour with Special Reference to Kokrajhar District in Assam" (PhD diss., University of North Bengal, July 2011), 258-69, https://ir.nbu.ac.in /bitstream/123456789/1467/14/241114.pdf.

87. A. Battacharjee, "The Girl Child: A Being That Does Not Exist for the Media," paper presented at the NMC-UNICEF Media Workshop on the Girl Child, New Delhi, October 12-14, 1985; M. Chaudhury, "Sex Bias in Child Nutrition," paper presented at the NMC-UNICEF Media Workshop on the Girl Child New Delhi, October 12-14, 1985. An extensive bibliography of girl child-related publications and events in South Asia during the 1980s, including the 1985 conference that the Indian National Media Center and UNICEF cohosted, appears in Dinesh Das, "A Study on Conditions of Child Labour."

88. *Report of the National Workshop on the Girl Child, 27-29 December 1987, India International Center*, New Delhi: Women's Development Division, National Institute of Public Cooperation and Child Development, 1987.

89. Capoor Indu, "Nutrition and Health Discrimination against Girls from 0-20 Years of Age," in *Report of the National Workshop on the Girl Child*.

90. Neera Burra, "Sight Unseen: Reflections on Female Working Child," in *Report of the National Workshop on the Girl Child*.

91. Neera Burra, "A Report on Child Labour in Lock Industry of Aligarh, Uttar Pradesh, India," New Delhi: UNICEF, 1987. Published as "Exploitation of Child Workers in Lock Industry

of Aligarh," *Economic and Political Weekly* (1987): 1117–21; and "A Report on Child Labor in the Gem Polishing Industry of Jaipur Rajasthan, India," New Delhi: UNICEF, 1987.

92. For a summary of the workshop, see Shanti Ghosh, "Girl Child in the SAARC Countries," *Indian Journal of Pediatrics* 57 (1990): 15–19. Papers presented at the workshop (divided by country) include: Government of India, "Message for the Girl Child: A Discussion Paper on Media of Communication," SAARC Workshop on the Girl Child, New Delhi, 1988; "Country Paper on the Girl Child, Presented by Dr. (Mrs.) Norbo, Ms. Nangayom, Kingdom of Bhutan," SAARC Workshop on the Girl Child, New Delhi, 1988; "Nepal Country Paper for Workshop on the Girl Child, Women Development SAARC Division, Ministry of Labour and Social Welfare, His Majesty's Government of Nepal, Katmandu," New Delhi, 1988; and "Pakistan Country Paper for SAARC Workshop on the Girl Child, Government of Pakistan, Ministry of Health, Special Education & Social Welfare," New Delhi, 1988.

93. Neera Bura, "Out of Sight, Out of Mind: Working Girls in India," *International Labour Review* 128, no. 5 (1989): 651–60; Devaki Jain, "Improving the Lot of Working Girl Child," *Kurukshetra* 30, no. 2 (1990): 10–14.

94. Amartya Sen, "More Than 100 Million Women Are Missing," *New York Review of Books*, December 20, 1990, https://www.nybooks.com/articles/1990/12/20/more-than-100-million-women-are-missing.

95. Aaron O'Neill, "Gender Ratios in Select Countries after the Second World War 1950," *Statista*, June 21, 2022, https://www.statista.com/statistics/1261433/post-wwii-gender-ratios-in-select-countries/.

96. Sen, "More Than 100 Million Women Are Missing."

97. Amartya Sen and Sunil Sengupta, "Malnutrition of Rural Children and the Sex Bias," *Economic and Political Weekly* 18, no. 19/21 (May 1983): 864.

98. Sen and Sengupta, "Malnutrition of Rural Children and the Sex Bias," 855–64.

99. Rafiqul Huda Chaudhury, "Adequacy of Child Dietary Intake Relative to that of Other Family Members," *Food and Nutrition Bulletin* 10, no. 2 (1998): 5.

100. Alaka Malwade Basu, "Is Discrimination in Food Really Necessary for Explaining Sex Differentials in Childhood Mortality?," *Population Studies* 43, no. 2 (1989): 193–210.

101. Basu, "Is Discrimination in Food Really Necessary," 199.

102. Basu, "Is Discrimination in Food Really Necessary," 209.

103. Basu, "Is Discrimination in Food Really Necessary," 194.

104. Basu, "Is Discrimination in Food Really Necessary," 204.

105. Basu, "Is Discrimination in Food Really Necessary," 204.

106. Basu, "Is Discrimination in Food Really Necessary," 205.

107. *Children and Development in the 1990s: A UNICEF Sourcebook on the Occasion of the World Summit for Children, 29–30 September, United Nations, New York, 1990* (New York: UNICEF, 1990).

108. Tambe, *Defining Girlhood in India*, chap. 6.

109. Aidoo, *The Girl Child: An Investment in the Future*, 7.

110. Aidoo, *The Girl Child: An Investment in the Future*, 7, 9.

111. Aidoo, *The Girl Child: An Investment in the Future*, 14, 20, 23.

112. Aidoo, *The Girl Child: An Investment in the Future*, 18.

113. Aidoo, *The Girl Child: An Investment in the Future*, 25.

114. Aidoo, *The Girl Child: An Investment in the Future*, 32.

115. Aidoo, *The Girl Child: An Investment in the Future*, 14.

116. Aidoo, *The Girl Child: An Investment in the Future*, 24.

117. Aidoo, *The Girl Child: An Investment in the Future*, 7.

118. "Statement of UNICEF Director, 'Focus on the Girl Child,'" in "Executive Board Policy Decisions: A Compilation of Decisions Taken by the Executive Board, 1986–1990," UN Economic and Social Council, UNICEF Executive Board, November 26, 1993, 5; "1990/17: Focus on the Girl Child," in "Executive Board Policy Decisions," UNICEF Executive Board, November 26, 1993, 50, accessed April 29, 2017, https://www.unicef.org/about/execboard/files/86-90-L1309-Add4-Compilation_English.pdf; Algeria et al., "Focus on the Girl Child: Implementation of UNICEF Policy on Women in Development: Draft Proposal," 1990, UN Economic and Social Council, International Children's Emergency Fund (UNICEF), accessed March 28, 2023, https://digitallibrary.un.org/record/89585?ln=en.

119. "Statement of UNICEF Director, 'Focus on the Girl Child,'" 5; "1990/17: Focus on the Girl Child," 50.

120. "Statement of UNICEF Director, 'Focus on the Girl Child,'" 5.

121. "1990/17: Focus on the Girl Child," 50.

122. Calkin, *Human Capital in Gender and Development*, 135.

123. Karin A. L. Hyde, "Improving Women's Education in Sub-Saharan Africa: A Review of the Literature," Population and Human Resources Department, Education and Employment Division Background Series no. PHREE 89/15 (Washington, DC: World Bank, 1989), accessed April 27, 2017, http://documents.worldbank.org/curated/en/534621468741591475/Improving-womens-education-in-sub-Saharan-Africa-a-review-of-the-literature; *Improving Girls' School Attendance and Achievement in Developing Countries: A Guide to Research Tools* (Washington, DC: USAID, October 1989), accessed April 29, 2017, http://pdf.usaid.gov/pdf_docs/PNABE782.pdf.

124. "Statement of UNICEF Director, 'Focus on the Girl Child,'" UNICEF Executive Board Meeting, 1990, 5, in "Executive Board Policy Decisions," UNICEF Executive Board, November 26, 1993, 50.

125. Summers, "The Most Influential Investment," 132.

126. Hartman, "Third World Urged to Educate Girls"; King and Hill, eds., *Women's Education in Developing Countries*, v.

127. "The Girl Child," in *Children and Development in the 1990s*, 214.

Chapter Four

1. "Information and Communication Program: Annual Progress and Financial Report, Reporting Period May 1, 1998, Grant No: B6657, Grant Maker: Carnegie Corporation of New York, Purpose: Towards Strengthening FEMNET's Communication Activities, Staff on Program, One Communication Officer, One Secretary/Translator, One Documentalist" (Nairobi: FEMNET, Undated), 4–5, FEMNET Archive; "2010 Annual Report: Twenty-Two Years of Harnessing the Collective Leadership of African Women" (Nairobi: FEMNET, 2011), 9, FEMNET Archive.

2. Longwe, comp., *Towards an African Women's Network*, 15.

3. "Of Pythons and Young Girls," *FEMNET News* 1.3 (April–June 1990): 8–9.

4. "Of Pythons and Young Girls," 8–9.

5. "Editorial: Literacy: The Light for Mankind," *FEMNET News* 1.4 (June–September 1990): 2.

6. Colman McCarthy, "Opinion: Hunger Hangs On," *Washington Post*, November 23, 1989, https://www.washingtonpost.com/archive/opinions/1989/11/23/hunger-hangs-on/07c0ae04-53f3-447c-b68e-eb147bbb04ce.

7. Ann Damaiya Usher and Evelyne Girardet, "Rhetoric over Women's Education," *FEMNET News* 1.4 (June–September 1990): 9.

8. "Africa's 'Pillars' Marginalized: A Summary of FEMNET's Statement Circulated at the Jomtien Meeting," *FEMNET News* 1.4 (June–September 1990): 6.

9. "Africa's 'Pillars' Marginalized," 6.

10. "Voice of the Children," *FEMNET News* 1.4 (June–September 1990): 12.

11. "Voice of the Children," 12.

12. "Decade for Survival," *FEMNET News* 1.8 (January–April 1992): 10.

13. "Lessons for Africa," *FEMNET News* 1.8 (January–April 1992): 20.

14. "No Excuse . . . ," *FEMNET News* 1.4 (June–September 1990): 7.

15. Winnie Ogana, "Rights on a Silver Platter?," *FEMNET News* 1.9 (May–August 1992): 1.

16. "Options for a Better Life for Young Women and Girls," *FEMNET News* 1.1 (May–July 1989): 5.

17. "Options for a Better Life for Young Women and Girls," 5.

18. "Conquering the World through Science," *FEMNET News* 1.2 (August–October 1989): 9.

19. "Conquering the World through Science," 9.

20. Action for Development (ACFODE), Kampala, Uganda, "Credentials of the African Woman," *FEMNET News* 1.6 (April–June 1991): 20.

21. Helen Twongyeirwe, comp., Regina Bafaki and Nassali Sandra, eds., and Julius Ocwinyo, contributing ed., *A Partnership of 28 Years in Uganda: Stories of Transformed Lives and Communities* (Kampala, Uganda: Action for Development, 2017), 23, https://www.acfode.or.ug/sites/default/files/Publication/Community%20Transformation.pdf.

22. Action for Development (ACFODE), "Credentials of the African Woman."

23. Mukaba Koba Sheila, "The Hazards Faced by Women in Pursuit of Education," *FEMNET News* 1.4 (June–September 1990): 14.

24. See, for example, Gertrude Mianda, "Colonialism, Education, and Gender Relations in the Belgian Congo: The *Evolue* Case," in *Women in African Colonial Histories*, ed. Jean Allman, Susan Geiger, and Nakanyike Musisi (Bloomington: Indiana University Press, 2002), 144–63; Jane Parpart, "Wicked Women and Respectable Ladies: Reconfiguring Gender on the Zambian Copperbelt, 1936–1964," in *"Wicked" Women and the Reconfiguration of Gender in Africa*, ed. Dorothy L. Hodgson and Sheryl McCurdy, 274–92 (Portsmouth, NH: Heinemann Educational, 2001).

25. "Options for a Better Life for Young Women and Girls," 5–6.

26. "Options for a Better Life for Young Women and Girls," 5–6.

27. "Africa: Education Situation Critical," *FEMNET News* 1.4 (June–September 1990): 1, 3.

28. "Computers: How Ideal for Women?," *FEMNET News* 1.4 (June–September 1990): 16.

29. "The Unsung Heroines," *FEMNET News* 1.6 (April–June 1991): 8.

30. "Black Is Beautiful But . . . ," *FEMNET News* 1.3 (April–June 1990): 2. See also Lynn Thomas, *Beneath the Surface: A Transnational History of Skin Lighteners* (Durham, NC: Duke University Press, 2020).

31. "The Need for Education on Pesticides, Skin Lighteners," *FEMNET News* 1.3 (April–June 1990): 1–2.

32. "Technocrats Slammed," *Herala Reporter* in *FEMNET News* 1.8 (January–April 1992): 7.

33. "The Girl Child," *FEMNET News* 1.8 (January–April 1992): 24.

34. Wandera-Chagenda, "Roots," *FEMNET News* 1.8 (January–April 1992): 24.

35. Tereziah Njoki, "The African Child," *FEMNET News* 1.8 (January–April 1992): 24.

Chapter Five

1. See, for example, Sally Engle Merry, *Human Rights and Gender Violence: Translating International Law into Local Justice* (Chicago: University of Chicago Press, 2006); Ghodsee, *Second World, Second Sex*, conclusion; Charlotte Bunch and Susana Fried, "Beijing '95: Moving Women's Human Rights from Margin to Center," *Women's Human Rights* 22, no. 1 (Autumn 1996): 200–204; Elisabeth J. Friedman, "The Effects of 'Transnationalism Reversed' in Venezuela: Assessing the Impact of UN Global Conferences on the Women's Movement," *International Feminist Journal of Politics* 1, no. 3 (1999): 357–81; Tarr-Whelan, "The Impact of the Beijing Platform for Action."

2. Switzer, Desai, and Bent, *Girls in Global Development*, 8–9.

3. Tarr-Whelan, "The Impact of the Beijing Platform for Action." See also Dorothy O. Helly, "Beijing '95: The Fourth World Conference on Women," *NWSA Journal* 8, no. 1, Global Perspectives (Spring 1996): 171; and HRNet, "Women's Conference in Dakar."

4. For one of many examples of a contemporaneous account sensationalizing the "odd mixture of the sublime and the silly" at the Beijing conference, see Mary Ann Glendon, "What Happened at Beijing," *First Things*, January 1996, https://www.firstthings.com/article/1996/01/what-happened-at-beijing. See also Ghodsee, *Second World, Second Sex*; Olcott, *International Women's Year*; Olcott, "Cold War Conflicts and Cheap Cabaret: Sexual Politics at the 1975 United Nations International Women's Year Conference," *Gender & History* 22, no. 3 (2010): 733–54.

5. Olembo, ed., "African Women's Development and Communication Network (FEMNET) Report on First Programming Conference," 28.

6. "FEMNET's Advance into the Future," *FEMNET News* 2.1 (December 1992–March 1993): 4.

7. The African Regional Steering Committee (ARSC)/Le Comité Organisateur Régional d'Afrique (CORA), "Proceedings of African Regional Steering Committee in Preparation for Dakar 1994 & Beijing 1995 NGO Meetings," New Stanley Hotel, Nairobi, January 4–7, 1994 (Nairobi: FEMNET, February 1994), i, 1, 11, FEMNET Archive; "Report of the Fourteenth Meeting of the African Regional Co-ordinating Committee for the Integration of Women in Development," April 19–21, 1993 (E/ECA/ATRCW/ARCC.XIV/93/10) (Addis Ababa, Ethiopia: UN Economic and Social Council, Economic Commission for Africa, April 26, 1993), 21–22, http://repository.uneca.org/bitstream/handle/10855/936/Bib-12680.pdf?sequence=1.

8. "Report of the Fourteenth Meeting of the African Regional Co-ordinating Committee," 1.

9. "Report of the Fourteenth Meeting of the African Regional Co-ordinating Committee," 6, 14–16.

10. "Draft Platform for Action: African Common Position for the Advancement of Women," undated, in UN Economic Commission for Africa, African Center for Women, *Volume 3: Draft African Platform for Action*, Fifth African Regional Conference on Women, Dakar, Senegal, November 16–23, 1994, 7 (E/ECA/ACW/RC.V/EXP/WP.6).

11. "Draft Platform for Action: African Common Position for the Advancement of Women," 16.

12. "Draft Platform for Action: African Common Position for the Advancement of Women."

13. "Draft Platform for Action: African Common Position for the Advancement of Women," 19.

14. "Draft Platform for Action: African Common Position for the Advancement of Women," 8.

15. "Draft Platform for Action: African Common Position for the Advancement of Women," 8, 34.

16. "Draft Platform for Action: African Common Position for the Advancement of Women," 4, 7, 8, 9, 34.

17. "Draft Platform for Action: African Common Position for the Advancement of Women," 34.

18. "Draft Platform for Action: African Common Position for the Advancement of Women," 10.

19. UNICEF, "The Situation of Girls in Africa," in *Volume 2: Conference Papers on Priority Issues, Part II B: Education, Health and Social Issues*, UN Economic Commission for Africa, African Centre for Women, Fifth African Regional Conference on Women, Dakar, Senegal, November 16–23, 1994, 58 (E/ECA/ACW/RC.V/EXP/WP.3B).

20. FEMNET, *Our Rights* 1.2 (January 1994): 8.

21. Different editions of *FEMNET News* covered the following topics as part of the NGO's advocacy campaign leading up to Dakar: Women and Democratization (*FEMNET News* 2.2, April–June 1993), Women for Peace (*FEMNET News* 2.3, July–September 1993), Women and Health (*FEMNET News* 2.4, October–December 1993), Women and AIDs (*FEMNET News* 3.1, January–March 1994), Women and the Media (*FEMNET News* 3.2, April–June 1994), Women in Crisis (*FEMNET News* 3.3, July–September 1994), and Women and Population (*FEMNET News* 3.4, October–December 1994—Dakar Conference, November 16–23). See also *1995 Annual Report* (Nairobi: FEMNET, February 1996), 10, FEMNET Archive.

22. "Report of the Ad Hoc Expert Group Meeting to Consider Strategies for Enhancement of Women's Skills in Mainstreaming and Decision Making," UN Economic Commission for Africa, Fifteenth Meeting of the African Regional Coordinating Committee for the Integration of Women in Development (ARCC), Addis Ababa, Ethiopia, April 20–22, 1994, 10 (E/ECA/ATRCW/ARCC.XV/94/8), https://repository.uneca.org/bitstream/handle/10855/3116/Bib-25975.pdf?sequence=1&isAllowed=y.

23. "Report of the Ad Hoc Expert Group Meeting," 10–11.

24. UNICEF, "The Situation of Girls in Africa," 43–75.

25. UNICEF, "The Situation of Girls in Africa," 45–46, 49–50.

26. Berhane Ras-Work, "Eradication of Harmful Traditional Practices for the Empowerment of Girls," paper presented at the UNICEF Inter-regional Consultation on the Girl Child, India, February 1994, in UNICEF, "The Situation of Girls in Africa," 51.

27. UNICEF, "The Situation of Girls in Africa," 51–56.

28. UNICEF, "The Situation of Girls in Africa," 63.

29. UNICEF, "The Situation of Girls in Africa," 45–46, 49–50.

30. UNICEF, "The Situation of Girls in Africa," 51.

31. UNICEF, "The Situation of Girls in Africa," 63.

32. UNICEF, "The Situation of Girls in Africa," 69.

33. Initially called the Kenya Alliance for the Advancement of Children's Rights, the NGO has since shortened its name to the Kenya Alliance for Advancement of Children. It still uses the same acronym, KAACR.

34. Salome Wairimu Muigai, "The African Girl Child: Our Multiple Challenge," African Preparatory Conference for the Fourth World Conference on Women: The NGO Forum, Dakar, November 12–15, 1994 (Nairobi: KAACR, 1994), 1, Alexander Street Archive, Document Cluster Women's Global Networks, 1883–2007. See also Salome Muigai, interview with Dorothy Kweyu, "All That a Disabled Child Needs Is Acceptance and Support," *Daily Nation*, July 12, 2016, accessed July 24, 2024, https://nation.africa/kenya/life-and-style/dn2/all-that-a-disabled-child-needs-is-acceptance-and-support-1216826.

35. Muigai, "The African Girl Child: Our Multiple Challenge," 5–6.

36. Muigai, "The African Girl Child: Our Multiple Challenge," 3.

37. Muigai, "The African Girl Child: Our Multiple Challenge," 12.

38. Tim Ekesa, ed., *Girls Are Not Passing Clouds*, illustrations by Peter Wambu and Daniel Lapa (Nairobi: KAACR, October 1994), FEMNET Archive.

39. "KAAR-Kenya," *Our Rights* 1.3 (March 1994): 6.

40. Madeline Njeri, interview with Robert M. Press, "More African Kids Take to the Streets," *Christian Science Monitor*, February 7, 1994, accessed April 29, 2017, http://www.csmonitor.com/1994/0207/07111.html; "About Us," Undugu Society of Kenya, accessed July 24, 2024, https://undugusociety.org/about-us/.

41. Ekesa, ed., *Girls Are Not Passing Clouds*, 20.

42. Ekesa, ed., *Girls Are Not Passing Clouds*, 19.

43. Ekesa, ed., *Girls Are Not Passing Clouds*, 14–16.

44. Ekesa, ed., *Girls Are Not Passing Clouds*, 18.

45. Ekesa, ed., *Girls Are Not Passing Clouds*, 2–5.

46. "KAAR-Kenya," *Our Rights* 1.3 (March 1994): 6.

47. D. Okumu, "Situation of the Girl Child in Kenya," prepared by the Child Welfare Society of Kenya and UNICEF, Nairobi, 1992, in UNICEF, "The Situation of Girls in Africa," 58.

48. UNICEF, "The Situation of Girls in Africa," 58.

49. Olembo, ed., "African Women's Development and Communication Network (FEMNET) Report on First Programming Conference," 48.

50. FEMNET, *1995 Annual Report*, 12.

51. Joyce Mangvwat and Joyce Umbima, comps., *Platform for Action on the African Girl Child* (New York and Nairobi: FEMNET, 1994), preface, 1, 8–9, FEMNET Archive.

52. Mangvwat and Umbima, comps., *Platform for Action on the African Girl Child*, preface, 1.

53. Mangvwat and Umbima, comps., *Platform for Action on the African Girl Child*, 5.

54. Mangvwat and Umbima, comps., *Platform for Action on the African Girl Child*, 5.

55. In "The Situation of Girls in Africa," UNICEF published, "Today's girls are tomorrow's women" and "today's girl grows into tomorrow's woman," 47.

56. "African Platform for Action," UN Economic and Social Council, Economic Commission for Africa, Fifth African Regional Conference on Women Ministerial Conference, Dakar, Senegal, November 21–23, 1994, 22 (E/ECA/ACW/RC.V/CM/3), published January 20, 1995, accessed April 29, 2017, http://repository.uneca.org/bitstream/handle/10855/6743/Bib-46785.pdf?sequence=1.

57. "African Platform for Action," 46–47.

58. "African Platform for Action," 2.

59. "African Platform for Action," 4.

60. "African Platform for Action," 47.

61. "African Platform for Action," 23.

62. FEMNET, *1995 Annual Report*, 14–15.

63. FEMNET, *1995 Annual Report*, 14–15. See also *Girls Speak Out* (Nairobi: FEMNET, 1995), FEMNET Archive.

64. US Department of State, "Overview of the Draft Platform for Action as Negotiated at the Final Preparatory Conference for the Fourth World Conference on Women," June 1995, University of Illinois at Chicago Online Repository, "1995 World Conference on Women: Press Releases and Statements," 4, accessed April 29, 2017, http://dosfan.lib.uic.edu/ERC/intlorg/conference_women/950601.html.

65. Martha Alter Chen, "Engendering World Conferences: The International Women's Movement and the United Nations," *Third World Quarterly* 16, no. 3 (September 1995): 486.

66. US Department of State, "Overview of the Draft Platform," 4.

67. "Beijing Declaration and Platform of Action, Adopted at the Fourth World Conference on Women, 15 September 1995," para. 59f. Numerous publications on the impact of structural

adjustment programs on women and girls came out before the Beijing World Conference on Women in 1995. For a few examples, see the works discussed in chapters 1 and 3 of this book. See also, for example, Pamela Sparr, ed., *Mortgaging Women's Lives: Feminist Critiques of Structural Adjustment* (London: Zed, 1994); Jean M. Due and Christina H. Gladwin, "Impacts of Structural Adjustment Programs on African Women Farmers and Female-Headed Households," *American Journal of Agricultural Economics* 73, no. 5 (December 1991): 1431–39; and Lourdes Benería and Shelley Feldman, eds., *Unequal Burden: Economic Crises, Persistent Poverty, and Women's Work* (Boulder, CO: Westview, 1992).

68. US Department of State, "Overview of the Draft Platform," 4; "Beijing Declaration and Platform of Action," paras. 62, 64, 83r, 165p, 166d, 166h, 167c, 169c, 170, and 258. Voluminous literature explores the links between microfinance lending and the growth of free-market or neoliberal feminisms. For a few examples, see Ananya Roy, *Poverty Capital: Microfinance and the Making of Development* (New York: Routledge, 2010); Christine Keating, Claire Rasmussen, and Pooja Rishi, "The Rationality of Empowerment: Microcredit, Accumulation by Dispossession, and the Gendered Economy," *Signs: Journal of Women in Culture and Society* 35, no. 1 (2010): 153–76; and Meyerowitz, *A War on Global Poverty*, chap. 5.

69. US Department of State Bureau of Public Affairs, "Focus on 4WCW Update on Preparations," June 16, 1995, electronic press release, accessed July 24, 2024, https://1997-2001.state.gov/picw/archives/foc1.html.

70. US Department of State Bureau of Public Affairs, "Focus on 4WCW Update on Preparations."

71. Charles Hirschkind and Saba Mahmood, "Feminism, the Taliban, and Politics of Counter-insurgency," *Anthropological Quarterly* 75, no. 2 (2002): 339–54; Lila Abu-Lughod, "Do Muslim Women Really Need Saving? Anthropological Reflections on Cultural Relativism and Its Others," *American Anthropologist* 104, no. 3 (2002): 783–90; Omar Dahbour, "Hegemony and Rights: On the Liberal Justification for Empire," in *Exceptional State: Contemporary U.S. Culture and the New Imperialism*, ed. Ashley Dawson and Malini Johar Schueller (Durham, NC: Duke University Press, 2007), 105–32; Gargi Bhattacharyya, *Dangerous Brown Men: Exploiting Sex, Violence and Feminism in the War on Terror* (London: Zed, 2013); Nicole Nguyen, "Education as Warfare? Mapping Securitised Education Interventions as War on Terror Strategy," *Geopolitics* 19, no. 1 (2014): 109–39; Nicola Pratt, "Weaponising Feminism for the 'War on Terror,' versus Employing Strategic Silence," *Critical Studies on Terrorism* 6, no. 2 (2013): 327–31; Sunera Thobani, "White Wars: Western Feminisms and the 'War on Terror,'" *Feminist Theory* 8, no. 2 (2007): 169–85.

72. FEMNET, *1995 Annual Report*, 16–18.

73. "Beijing Declaration and Platform of Action," para. 70.

74. "Beijing Declaration and Platform of Action," para. 39.

75. "Beijing Declaration and Platform of Action," para. 10.

76. "Beijing Declaration and Platform of Action," para. 118.

77. "Beijing Declaration and Platform of Action," paras. 4, 110.

78. "Beijing Declaration and Platform of Action," para. 117.

79. Carol Bellamy, "Letter to the Co-ordinator," and Emmanuel Dierckx de Casterle, "Letter to the Co-ordinator," *Our Rights* 2.3 (July–September 1995): 12–13.

80. Helly, "Beijing '95: The Fourth World Conference on Women."

81. Wainaina, comp., *HerStory: Our Journey*, 25.

82. Safiatu Kassim Singhateh and Njoki Wainaina, "Commentary on NGO Forum 95 and

the UN Fourth World Conference on Women Held in Beijing," *1995 Annual Report* (Nairobi: FEMNET, 1996), front matter, FEMNET Archive.

83. FEMNET, *1995 Annual Report*, 22.
84. FEMNET, *1995 Annual Report*, 24.
85. FEMNET, *1995 Annual Report*, 25–26.
86. FEMNET, *1995 Annual Report*, 27–30.
87. Wainaina, comp., *HerStory: Our Journey*, 48.
88. Wainaina, comp., *HerStory: Our Journey*, 48.
89. Tarr-Whelan, "The Impact of the Beijing Platform for Action: 1995 to 2010."
90. Ghodsee, *Second World, Second Sex*, conclusion.

Chapter Six

1. Mercy Musomi (Executive Director of the Girl Child Network), interviewed by author, October 3, 2013.

2. Switzer, *When the Light Is Fire*, conclusion and footnote 7 to the conclusion. See also Switzer, Desai, and Bent, *Girls in Global Development*, 9; Purewal, "Interrogating the Rights Discourse on Girls' Education"; Tambe, *Defining Girlhood in India*, chap. 6; Moeller, *The Gender Effect*; Croll, "From the Girl Child to Girls' Rights."

3. "Girl Child Network General Meeting Held on 13th January 1998 at the British Council, Nairobi," Meeting Minute 4/98, Girl Child Network (GCN) Archive, Nairobi.

4. For scholarship on spaces in Africa as laboratories in which development and other forms of social scientific thought have been worked out, contested, appropriated, and otherwise creatively engaged with, see Helen Tilley, *Africa as a Living Laboratory: Empire, Development, and the Problem of Scientific Knowledge, 1870–1950* (Chicago: University of Chicago Press, 2011) and Omnia El Shakry, *The Great Social Laboratory: Subjects of Knowledge in Colonial and Postcolonial Egypt* (Stanford, CA: Stanford University Press, 2007). For scholarship on African spaces as hubs of thought related to histories of science and education, see Abena Dove Osseo-Asare, *Bitter Roots: The Search for Healing Plants in Africa* (Chicago: University of Chicago Press, 2014); and Ousmane Oumar Kane, *Beyond Timbuktu: An Intellectual History of Muslim West Africa* (Cambridge, MA: Harvard University Press, 2016).

5. A strong case study of some of this creative engagement can be found in Switzer, *When the Light Is Fire* and "Disruptive Discourses: Kenyan Maasai Schoolgirls Make Themselves." See also Kirk, Mitchell, and Reid-Walsh, "Toward Political Agency for Girls."

6. See Johnson, "On Agency"; Wilson, *Race, Racism and Development*, 45–68; Madhok and Rai, "Agency, Injury, and Transgressive Politics in Neoliberal Times"; Madhok, Phillips, and Wilson, eds., *Gender, Agency and Coercion*; Madhok, *Rethinking Agency*; Thomas, "Historicising Agency"; and Bellows-Blakely, "Review Essay: Disentangling Feminisms from the Cold War."

7. Overviews of many of these girl-focused campaigns can be found in Switzer, "(Post)Feminist Development Fables"; Shain, "'The Girl Effect'"; Bent, "Girl Rising and the Problematic Other"; Mann, "Latina Girls, Sexual Agency, and the Contradictions of Neoliberalism"; Murphy, *The Economization of Life*; Moeller, *The Gender Effect*; and Chant, "Galvanizing Girls for Development?"

8. Hodgson, *Being Maasai, Becoming Indigenous*, introduction. I also draw here on the concept of friction put forth by a number of scholars, most notably for my own thinking Tsing, *Friction* and Burton, *Africa in the Indian Imagination*, introduction, chap. 4, and epilogue.

9. "Access to Education, Reaching the Unreached," UNESCO online article, November 3, 2020, accessed July 26, 2024, https://gcedclearinghouse.org/news/access-education-reaching-unreached; "Our History," Girl Child Network, accessed July 7, 2022, https://girlchildnetwork.org/about-us/our-history.

10. "Overview," Girl Child Network Kenya, LinkedIn, accessed July 7, 2022, https://www.linkedin.com/company/girl-child-network-kenya/about.

11. "Access to Education."

12. "Minutes of the Girl Child Networking Group Meeting on 27th February, 1996 at CARE Kenya Offices"; "Minutes of the Girl Child Network Meeting on 5th March 1996, at CARE Kenya Conference Room, 08:00 to 12:00 HRS"; "Minutes of the Girl-Child Network Meeting on 2nd April, 1996, at CARE Kenya Conference Room, 09:99 to 12:00 HRS"; "Minutes of the Girl-Child Network Meeting on 7th May 1996"; "Minutes of Girl-Child Network Meeting Held on 6th August 1996"; "Minutes of Girl Child Network Meeting Held on 12.11.96 at CARE Conference Room," GCN Minutes File: Minutes from 1996 to Date, GCN Archive, Nairobi.

13. "Minutes of the Girl Child Network Meeting on 5th March 1996," agenda item 4, Presentation of Working Committee's Report.

14. "Minutes of the Girl Child Network General Meeting held on 19th May 1998 at FAWE," Minute 8/98, FAWE Presentation, GCN Archive, Nairobi.

15. "Minutes of the Girl-Child Network Meeting on 2nd April, 1996," agenda; "Minutes of the Girl Child Network Meeting on 5th March 1996," agenda item 5, Sources of Funds for Network Activities; "Minutes of Girl Child Network Meeting Held on 12.11.96," Present/List of Attendees.

16. For more on the NGO boom, the political history of NGOs, and neoliberal capitalism, see Sonia E. Alvarez, "Advocating Feminism: The Latin American Feminist NGO 'Boom,'" *International Feminist Journal of Politics* 1, no. 2 (1999): 181–209; Sonia E. Alvarez, "Beyond NGO-ization? Reflections from Latin America," *Development* 52, no. 2 (2009): 175–84; Arundhati Roy, "The NGO-ization of Resistance," *Massalijin News* (2014), http://www.queensneighborhoodsunited.org/wp-content/uploads/2014/12/NGOization-1.pdf; D. L. Sheth, "Democracy and Globalization in India: Post–Cold War Discourse," *Annals of the American Academy of Political and Social Science* 540, no. 1 (1995): 24–39; Thomas Davies, *NGOs: A New History of Transnational Civil Society* (Oxford: Oxford University Press, 2014); Akira Iriye, "A Century of NGOs," *Diplomatic History* 23, no. 3 (1999): 421–35.

17. "Minutes of the Girl Child Network Meeting on 5th March 1996," Members Present.

18. "75 Years of Care," Care International, accessed July 7, 2022, https://www.care-international.org/who-we-are/75-years-care.

19. "Minutes of the Girl-Child Network Meeting on 7th May 1996," Core Team.

20. "Minutes of the Girl-Child Network Meeting on 2nd April, 1996," Members Present; "Minutes of the Girl-Child Network Meeting on 7th May 1996," Core Team.

21. "Minutes of the Girl-Child Network Meeting on 7th May 1996," Present and Core Team.

22. "Minutes of the Girl Child Network General Meeting held on 15th September 1998 at the Hilton Hotel Nairobi," Minute 22/98, Canadian International Development Agency (CIDA), GCN Archive, Nairobi; "Minutes of the Girl Child Network General Meeting held on 19th May 1998 at FAWE," Minute 10/98, Research Committee.

23. "Minutes of the Girl Child Network Meeting on 5th March 1996," agenda item 4, Presentation of Working Committee's Report.

24. "Minutes of the Girl Child Network Meeting on 5th March 1996," agenda item 5, Source of Funds for Network Activities; "Minutes of Girl-Child Network Meeting Held on 6th August 1996," Review of Memorandum of Understanding between GCN and the Hosting Organization.

25. Ester Boserup, *Woman's Role in Economic Development* (London: Earthscan, 1970). See also Gina Koczberski, "Women in Development: A Critical Analysis," *Third World Quarterly* 19, no. 3 (1998): 395–410; Joanne Meyerowitz, *A War on Global Poverty*.

26. Carol Miller and Shahra Razavi, *From WID to GAD: Conceptual Shifts in the Women and Development Discourse*, No. 1, UNRISD Occasional Paper, No. 1, United Nations Research Institute for Social Development (UNRISD), Geneva, 1995, https://www.econstor.eu/bitstream/10419/148819/1/863101828.pdf; Eva M. Rathgeber, "WID, WAD, GAD: Trends in Research and Practice," *Journal of Developing Areas* 24, no. 4 (1990): 489–502; Kalpana Wilson, "Towards a Radical Re-appropriation: Gender, Development and Neoliberal Feminism," *Development and Change* 46, no. 4 (2015): 803–32.

27. "Minutes of the Girl Child Network Meeting on 5th March 1996," agenda item 5, Source of Funds for Network Activities. For a discussion of the relationships between Women in Development, Gender and Development, Girls in Development, and neoliberal capitalism, see Switzer, *When the Light Is Fire*, conclusion; Moeller, *The Gender Effect*, chap. 1 and 2; and Murphy, *The Economization of Life*, chap. 10.

28. "Minutes of Girl Child Network Meeting Held on 12.11.96," Minute 2, Update on Progress in Support of the GCN.

29. Wanjiru Carolyne Kamau, "Kenya and the War on Terrorism," *Review of African Political Economy* 33, no. 107 (2006): 133–41; Edward Mogire and Kennedy Mkutu Agade, "Counter-Terrorism in Kenya," *Journal of Contemporary African Studies* 29, no. 4 (2011): 473–91; John Davis, ed., *Africa and the War on Terrorism* (London: Routledge, 2007).

30. Laura Zanotti, "Governmentalizing the Post–Cold War International Regime: The UN Debate on Democratization and Good Governance," *Alternatives* 30, no. 4 (2005): 461–87; Laura Zanotti, *Governing Disorder: UN Peace Operations, International Security, and Democratization in the Post–Cold War Era* (University Park: Pennsylvania State University Press, 2011).

31. For one of many examples of scholarship on how NGOs have undermined state sovereignty in Kenya and beyond, see Maurice N. Amutabi, *The NGO Factor in Africa: The Case of Arrested Development in Kenya* (New York: Routledge, 2013).

32. Patricia Kameri-Mbote, "The Operational Environment and Constraints for NGOs in Kenya: Strategies for Good Policy and Practice," *International Environmental Law Research Centre Working Paper* 2 (2000): 1–31, http://erepository.uonbi.ac.ke/bitstream/handle/11295/41169/full%20text%20.pdf;sequence=1; Michael Bratton, "The Politics of Government-NGO Relations in Africa," *World Development* 17, no. 4 (1989): 569–87; and "Nonprofit Law in Kenya: Country Notes," Council on Foundations online article, July 2023, accessed July 26, 2024, https://cof.org/content/nonprofit-law-kenya#Applicable_Laws#Applicable_Laws.

33. "Our History."

34. "Human Rights Watch Report 1996—Kenya," *Human Rights Watch*, January 1, 1996, https://www.refworld.org/docid/3ae6a8a318.html.

35. Amutabi, *The NGO Factor in Africa*; Bratton, "The Politics of Government-NGO Relations in Africa"; Jennifer N. Brass, "Blurring Boundaries: The Integration of NGOs into Governance in Kenya," *Governance* 25, no. 2 (2012): 209–35; Jennifer Bass, "Surrogates for Government? NGOs and the State in Kenya" (PhD diss., University of California Berkeley, 2010), https://es

cholarship.org/uc/item/6b4157cd; Gwendolin Joan Bandi, "Non-Governmental Organizations in Kenya's Education Sector" (PhD diss., University of Pittsburgh, 2011); Lisa Aubrey, *The Politics of Development Co-operation: NGOs, Gender and Partnership in Kenya* (New York: Routledge, 1997).

36. "Launching Pad to Greatness," *Binti: The Newsletter for Girl Child Programming in Kenya*, no. 44 (July–September 2007): 8, GCN Archive, Nairobi.

37. *Girl Child Network Annual Report: Narrative and Financial Report for the Year 2005/2006* (Nairobi: Girl Child Network, 2006), 19.

38. Miriam N. Gichohi, "Report of the Sanitary Towels Campaign at Nakumatt Lifestyle Supermarket, Nairobi, 3rd–18th Sept. 2005," submitted to the Senior Program Officer at the Girl Child Network, October 26, 2005; "Report of Sanitary Towels Campaign Held at Nairobi International Trade Fair, 26th Sep to 2nd Oct. 2005," submitted to the Senior Program Officer at the Girl Child Network, October 26, 2005, GCN Archive, Nairobi.

39. Eliud Kinuthia, "Message from the National Chairperson," *Girl Child Network Annual Report 2005/2006*, 4; "The Sanitary Towels Project," *Girl Child Network Annual Report 2005/2006*, 10–11; "Income from Donors," *Girl Child Network Annual Report 2005/2006*, 26; "Minutes for the GCN Staff Meeting Held on 12/06/06 at GCN Offices from 9:00 am–11:00 am," Minute 3/06, Program Reports, (e) The Binti Challenge, GCN Archive, Nairobi.

40. John Muiruri, "Treasurer's Report for July 2005–June 2006," *Girl Child Network Annual Report 2005/2006*, 19.

41. See, for example, Switzer, Desai, and Bent, *Girls in Global Development*, 4–13.

42. Ciku Kimeria, "The Story of How Kenyan Women Are Bringing P&G to Task over the Always 'Burning Pads' Saga," *Quartz*, February 26, 2020, https://qz.com/africa/1807045/kenyan-women-take-pg-to-task-over-always-burning-pads.

43. Beth Gardiner, "The Plastics Pipeline: A Surge of New Production is on the Way," *Yale Environment 360* (2019), https://www.biologicaldiversity.org/news/media-archive/a2019/plasticpollution_yale360_12.19.19.pdf; Hiroko Tabuchi, Michael Corkery, and Carlos Mureithi, "Big Oil Is in Trouble. Its Plan: Flood Africa with Plastic," *New York Times*, August 30, 2020, https://nyti.ms/3lyqqIg.

44. Moeller, *The Gender Effect*; Murphy, *The Economization of Life*; Switzer, "(Post)Feminist Development Fables"; Shain, "'The Girl Effect'"; Bent, "Girl Rising and the Problematic Other"; Chant, "Galvanizing Girls for Development?"; Jason Hickel, "The 'Girl Effect': Liberalism, Empowerment and the Contradictions of Development," *Third World Quarterly* 35, no. 8 (2014): 1355–73.

45. Hodgson, *Being Maasai, Becoming Indigenous*, introduction.

46. Moeller, *The Gender Effect*; Murphy, *The Economization of Life*; Switzer, "(Post)Feminist Development Fables"; Switzer, *When the Light Is Fire*; Shain, "'The Girl Effect'"; Bent, "Girl Rising and the Problematic Other"; Chant, "Galvanizing Girls for Development?"; Purewal, "Interrogating the Rights Discourse on Girls' Education"; Mann, "Latina Girls, Sexual Agency, and the Contradictions of Neoliberalism"; Cynthia M. Caron and Shelby A. Margolin, "Rescuing Girls, Investing in Girls: A Critique of Development Fantasies," *Journal of International Development* 27, no. 7 (2015): 881–97; Sydney Calkin, "Disrupting Disempowerment: Feminism, Co-optation, and the Privatised Governance of Gender and Development," *New Formations* 91 (2017): 69–86; Hickel, "The 'Girl Effect.'"

Conclusion

1. "Staff in UNICEF Offices (December 1994)," *UNICEF Annual Report* (New York: UNICEF, 1995), 48–49; Christopher S. Wren, "Unicef Says Fraud Cost $10 Million," *New York Times*, May 26, 1995, https://www.nytimes.com/1995/05/26/world/unicef-says-fraud-cost-10-million.html.

2. Switzer, "(Post)Feminist Development Fables"; Switzer, "Disruptive Discourses"; Shain, "'The Girl Effect'"; Pruitt, "'Fixing the Girls'"; Bent, "Girl Rising and the Problematic Other"; Purewal, "Interrogating the Rights Discourse on Girls' Education"; Mann, "Latina Girls, Sexual Agency, and the Contradictions of Neoliberalism"; Chant, "Galvanizing Girls for Development?"; Kirk, Mitchell, and Reid-Walsh, "Toward Political Agency for Girls"; Moeller, *The Gender Effect*; Murphy, *The Economization of Life*; Banet-Weiser, "'Confidence Can Carry!'"; and Switzer, Desai, and Bent, *Girls in Global Development*.

3. Shain, "'The Girl Effect'"; Moeller, *The Gender Effect*, chap. 3; Sydney Calkin, "'Tapping' Women for Post-crisis Capitalism: Evidence from the 2012 World Development Report," *International Feminist Journal of Politics* 17, no. 4 (2015): 611–29.

4. Wilson, *Race, Racism and Development*, 45–68; Madhok and Rai, "Agency, Injury, and Transgressive Politics in Neoliberal Times"; Madhok, Phillips, and Wilson, eds., *Gender, Agency and Coercion*; Madhok, *Rethinking Agency*.

5. Johnson, "On Agency," 120–21.

6. Thomas, "Historicising Agency," 324. See also Sarah Bellows-Blakely, "Review Essay: Disentangling Feminisms from the Cold War," *Gender & History* 32, no. 1 (2020): 247–58.

7. Tsing, *Friction*; Burton, *Africa in the Indian Imagination*, introduction, chap. 4, epilogue.

8. Trouillot, *Silencing the Past*.

9. Amina Mama, "What Does It Mean to do Feminist Research in African Contexts?," *Feminist Review* 98, no. 1 suppl. (2011): e13.

10. Hodgson, *Being Maasai, Becoming Indigenous*, introduction.

11. This quotation is from Antoinette Burton as she builds on the work of Sara Ahmed in "Killing Joy: Feminism and the History of Happiness," *Signs: Journal of Women in Culture and Society* 35, no. 3 (2010): 571–74. *Africa in the Indian Imagination*, introduction.

Index

AAWORD/AFARD (Association of African Women for Research and Development), 62–63, 137, 192n43
abortion, 85, 115, 116
ACFODE (Action for Development), 114, 202nn20–22
Action Aid Kenya, 152
Action for Development (ACFODE), 114, 202nn20–22
Adebayo, Bisi, 152
African Charter on the Rights and Welfare of the Child (1990), 100
African Network for the Prevention and Protection against Child Abuse and Neglect (ANPPCAN), 152
African Platform for Action (1994), 128–29, 130, 131, 132, 136–37, 138
African regional conference (Arusha, Tanzania, 1984), 50, 51–52, 53–57, 58, 60, 107, 127
African Regional Coordinating Committee (ARCC), 128, 130, 131, 132, 137
African Women's Communication and Development Network (FEMNET): and children's rights, 111–12; and girl-focused advocacy, 18–20, 22, 45, 101, 104–23, 132–36, 165; history of, 1–4, 10–11, 41–45, 51, 53–54, 56, 58–60, 64, 67–71, 106–7, 109–11, 142–43, 154, 156, 169, 182n28; lobbying campaigns, 127–41, 145–46, 165, 170; reports of, 2–3, 21, 23, 32–35, 38–39, 41, 99, 143–44; and UNICEF, 4, 6–7, 10, 12–14, 16–18, 38–39, 44, 47, 53–64, 66, 69–72, 105, 124–25, 165–66, 168–71; and UN World Conference on Women in Beijing, 11–12, 19, 47–48, 64, 70–71, 104, 105–6, 127–28, 130, 133, 137, 141–45. *See also* African Women's Task Force; *FEMNET News* (newsletter)

African Women's Encounter (Nairobi, 1985), 59–60
African Women's Task Force: history of, 17–18, 46–47, 50–53, 56, 58–60, 61, 106, 109, 165; and Kenyan state, 64, 67–68; as Pan-African organization, 69–70, 106, 109, 121, 127–28; and UN World Conference on Women in Nairobi, 46, 59–60, 68–70, 165
Agency for Technical Cooperation, German, 22
agnotology, 8, 166, 179n14
Aidlink, 156, 158, 159–60
Aidoo, Agnes Akosua, 73, 75; and *The Girl Child*, 100–101, 102
Aidoo, Ama Ata, 10, 179n12, 182n25
Ajiambo, Maureen Muleka, 67, 193n61
Anjiah, Lydiah, 152
ANPPCAN (African Network for the Prevention and Protection against Child Abuse and Neglect), 152
apartheid, 28, 48, 131, 143, 182n26
ARCC. *See* African Regional Coordinating Committee (ARCC)
Association of African Women for Research and Development (AAWORD/AFARD), 62–63, 137, 192n43
austerity: economic, 18, 41, 72–73, 75, 80–82, 86, 164; and effects on girl-focused development, 2, 14, 19–21, 29, 33, 35–36, 40, 105, 107–8, 164–65

Bacon, Ruth, 48–49, 190n3
"barefoot doctors," 77, 195n19
Barrow, Dame Nita, 51–55, 61, 67, 127, 191n13
Beijing, China. *See* World Conference on Women: 1995 (Beijing)

Beijing Platform for Action, 4–5, 121, 124–26, 137–42, 144–49, 150–51, 153, 164, 165, 167, 169
Bellamy, Carol, 141, 206n79
Binti (magazine), 156, 157, 210n36
Black, Maggie, 85, 86
Blackness, 112, 118
boys: access to education, 1, 2, 22, 23–25, 27–28, 29, 30, 36; access to health care, 96, 98, 100; access to nutrition, 96, 97, 98; disadvantaging, 28; gender roles of, 21, 26–27, 30, 32, 34, 35, 37, 57; imprisonment of, 28; mortality rates, 96; violence of, 31, 131
bracketing, 138–39
breastfeeding, 82, 84, 133
Burra, Neera, 94, 95

Canadian International Development Agency (CIDA), 113, 122, 153
capitalism: in crisis, 18, 19–20, 72, 76, 105, 150, 166; critique of, 27, 32; effects on girl-focused development, 3, 14, 17, 18, 24, 34, 36, 37, 45, 61, 93, 103, 143, 150, 160; free-market, 25–26, 76, 122; global expansion of, 15–16, 161–62; neoliberal, 2, 5, 6–7, 9, 19, 21, 33, 34, 74–75, 79, 145, 160, 162, 165, 168–71; and racism, 117
CARE Kenya, 152, 153–54, 156
Carnegie Corporation, 130
caste, 98, 99
Center for the Study of Adolescence, 152
Chicago school of economics, 74
Childline Kenya, 13
children: and health, 78–79, 80, 84–87, 88, 89, 91, 94, 98, 100, 101, 116, 141; immunization of, 80, 82; labor of, 15, 28, 32, 34, 87, 94–95, 97; marriage (*see* marriage: early); mortality rates, 78–79, 80–82, 84, 85, 86, 87, 88, 96, 98, 99, 164; organizations with focus on, 7, 75; programs for, 80; rearing of, 16; rights of, 100, 111–12, 119; UNICEF "children's revolution," 78, 82–91, 102, 112, 116–17, 118, 121, 165. *See also* boys; girls
Child Welfare Society of Kenya, 13, 134–35, 152
CIDA. *See* Canadian International Development Agency (CIDA)
Clinton, Bill, 4, 124
Clinton, Hillary Rodham, 4, 124, 168
Clinton Global Initiative, 74, 150, 167, 168
clitoridectomy, 64
Collaborative Center for Gender and Development, 152
colonialism, 2–3, 5, 7, 14, 25, 54, 81, 118; in Africa, 15, 115, 152, 160–61; British, 32–34, 52, 57; French, 26, 34; and gender roles, 36, 45, 116; and globalization, 13, 16; and NIEO, 48, 106, 108, 120, 150, 165, 168, 171

Conference on Primary Health Care (Alma Ata, Kazakh Soviet Socialist Republic, 1978), 76–78, 83, 84, 85, 89, 99, 103
contraception, 85
Copenhagen, Denmark. *See* World Conference on Women: 1980 (Copenhagen)
corporal punishment, 28
Council for Economic Empowerment of Women in Africa, 137
Credit Suisse, 74
crisis: in capitalism, 7, 18, 20, 72, 166; climate, 161; debt, in Africa, 111; debt, in Tanzania, 80; economic, in Africa, 40; economic, in Kenya, 25; global, 72, 76, 79, 83, 86, 88, 102, 103, 108, 117, 129, 150, 164
cultures, local, 3, 18, 21, 37, 94, 105, 129, 131, 146, 164; and family, 88, 89, 91, 101, 103, 164; and patriarchy, 41, 45, 91, 103
curriculum: French norms of, 27; gender-biased, 27, 37–38
custody, 15, 114

debt: adjustment programs, 25, 79, 84; crisis, global, 18, 79, 128–29; crisis in Africa, 111, 128; crisis in Tanzania, 80; foreign, 111–13, 128–29, 136–37, 138–39, 143, 146; forgiveness of, 6, 113, 116, 137, 138–39, 162–63; state-owned, 14, 106, 109, 111, 143, 146
decolonization: of academia, 170; debates over, 7, 9, 10, 14, 21, 48, 50, 52, 105, 126, 166; of education, 55, 57, 117; of policymaking, 1, 3, 17, 22, 28, 34–35, 37, 46–47, 62, 70, 76, 83, 120, 122
democratization, 34, 42, 66–67, 130, 138, 154–55
de-Westernization, 35–37
DFID. *See* United Kingdom's Department for International Development (DFID)
Dierckx de Casterle, Emmanuel, 141
discrimination: gender-based, 36, 57, 94, 96–97, 110, 118, 130, 131, 167; of girls, 22, 36, 88, 91, 101, 108, 131, 132, 136, 140–41, 164; intra-family, 36, 45, 99, 135, 141, 164; racial, 48, 57
disempowerment. *See* empowerment
domesticity, courses in, 16, 26, 34
donations: and African Women's Task Force, 13, 19, 68, 69; via corporate sponsorships, 149, 156, 168; from Eastern Bloc, 90, 145; and Girl Child Network, 149, 155–59, 162; and UNICEF, 42, 44, 45, 77, 83, 85, 89–90, 106

Eastern and Southern Africa Regional Office (ESARO), UNICEF, 22, 35–42, 112, 121–22, 134
Eastern Bloc, 62, 74–75; donations from, 90, 145
education: access to, 2, 6, 17, 22, 24, 28, 32–33, 36, 72–73, 74, 88, 129, 137, 150–51, 160, 167; colonial, 25, 26, 30, 34, 37, 54–55, 88; financing, 25, 26, 29,

30, 132; formal, 2, 15, 22, 23–24, 26, 28, 41, 88, 111, 117, 130, 157; of girls, 1, 3, 16, 18, 21–26, 31–38, 40, 42, 44, 53, 73, 75, 84–88, 93, 99–103, 107–17, 122–23, 132, 134, 137, 144–45, 164; primary, 23–24, 29, 30, 33, 34, 36; public, 16, 25, 33, 34, 35, 75, 90, 108, 114–16, 132; reforms, 25, 30–31, 34; secondary, 23, 27, 28, 29, 30; state expenditure on, 2, 33, 79, 80, 129, 155; tertiary, 29, 30, 31

Educational Research Network in Eastern and Southern Africa (ERNESA), 22–24, 26

empowerment: bottom-up, 3, 116, 121, 165; emotional, 18, 103, 146; forms of, 103, 132, 159–60; gender-based, 161–62; of girls, 15, 19, 73, 102–3, 121, 128, 132, 137, 146, 149; of parents, 86–87, 149; principles of, 9, 83, 144; of women, 69, 86, 129, 137, 139

equality. *See* inequality

ERNESA (Educational Research Network in Eastern and Southern Africa), 22–24, 26

ESARO. *See* Eastern and Southern Africa Regional Office (ESARO), UNICEF

Eurocentrism, 10, 36, 170

family: economic decisions of, 25–26, 28, 36, 88, 132; gendered discrimination and roles in, 32, 36, 72, 84, 86, 88–89, 91, 97–99, 103, 116, 132–33, 141, 153, 164, 167; planning, 15, 84–85, 116, 137; work of, 26–27, 66, 92

FAWE (Forum for African Women Educationalists), 109, 151, 157

Federation of Women Lawyers (FIDA), 13

feminism: free-market, 5–7, 10, 14, 19–20, 76, 127, 149, 150, 167, 170, 171; Marxist, 7; neoliberal, 5, 6, 8, 46, 64, 69–70, 76, 127, 145–46, 168–69, 170, 195n12, 206n68; racialized, 150

FEMNET. *See* African Women's Communication and Development Network (FEMNET)

FEMNET News (newsletter): and advocacy for girls, 106–10, 120–21; and criticism of GOBI-FFF, 119; and education for girls, 113, 117–18; and FGM, 116; and gender equality, 118; and Girl Child Project, 41–42, 45, 119, 141–42; and *Our Rights* newsletter, 11, 130, 133–34; and patriarchy, 114–15; and rights of children, 111–12

fertility, control of, 15, 85, 89, 100, 115–16

FGM (female genital mutilation): discussion of, 64–66, 91, 142; and *FEMNET News*, 116; and Girl Child Project, 150–51; regulation of, 15; in UNICEF's lobbying campaign, 131–33, 140–42, 144

FIDA (Federation of Women Lawyers), 13

Fifth African Regional Conference on Women (Dakar, Senegal, 1994), 11, 126, 127, 128, 130–37, 189n72

First UN World Conference on Women. *See* World Conference on Women: 1975 (Mexico City)

food: for children, 80, 84; and gender inequality, 96, 99, 100; for pregnant women, 84; security, 6, 63, 77. *See also* nutrition

Ford, Betty, 49, 50

Ford, Gerald, 49

Ford Foundation, 78

Forum for African Women Educationalists (FAWE), 109, 151, 157

Fourth UN World Conference on Women. *See* World Conference on Women: 1995 (Beijing)

Fulton, Margaret, 62–63

Gachukia, Daniel, 55

Gachukia, Eddah (née Wacheke): and African Women's Task Force, 58–60, 67, 69; biography of, 16–17, 54–55; and *FEMNET News*, 53, 109, 115–16; functions of, 43, 47, 55–57, 58, 109, 110, 127, 128; and girl-focused policy, 10, 149, 151–52, 157, 170; and Maendeleo ya Wanawake, 67–68; and UN World Conference on Women in Nairobi, 61, 63, 65, 67, 69, 144

Gandhi, Indira, 83

Gandhi, Rajiv, 94

GCN. *See* Girl Child Network (GCN)

gender: bias, 27, 37–38, 96–97, 157; and development programs, 17, 93, 125, 161–62; and education, 2–3, 23, 24, 26–31, 33–35, 87–88, 108; inequality, 1, 4, 6, 15, 26, 30–36, 41, 45, 57, 94, 97–98, 101, 107–9, 118, 131, 167; justice, 6–7, 99, 104, 117, 135–36, 143, 153, 164, 166–67; roles, 21, 24, 25, 27, 34, 37, 96, 108, 115–16, 132, 153; sensitivity trainings, 37–38, 122, 138; and violence, 24, 31–32, 33, 98, 129, 131, 133, 135, 140–41, 144–45, 150–51, 157

Gender and Development framework (GAD), 153

genital mutilation. *See* FGM (female genital mutilation)

Gindy, Aida, 1, 59, 110

Girl Child Network (GCN): campaigns of, 148–49, 152, 156–60, 168, 170; documentation of, 12–13; donors of, 19, 149–51, 156–58, 161; history of, 150–60, 162, 167–68; and UN World Conference on Women in Beijing, 13, 19, 148–53, 162, 164, 166–71

girl-focused action: advocacy, 18, 44, 106, 120–21, 138; development, 75, 94, 119; developmentalism, 15, 17, 105, 120, 168; economic programming, 45, 126; initiatives, 138, 139, 140, 141–44, 147; policymaking, 2, 10, 32, 39–40, 45, 58, 86; programs, 40, 100, 168. *See also* Girls in Development (program)

girlhood: African, 14, 21, 24; social history of, 14; studies of, 73, 167

Girl Rising, 150
girls: agency of, 102, 103; concept of the "girl child," 94–95, 97–99, 119; and development planning, 4, 6, 17–19, 21–22, 26–27, 33, 36, 37–38, 40–41, 70–71, 73, 75, 100–103, 121–22, 124–26, 128–30, 131–46, 148, 150, 153, 167; discrimination against, 26, 33, 36, 37, 94, 97, 99, 130, 132, 135, 136, 140, 149–51; empowering, 38, 132; rights of, 38, 41, 95, 139, 147; socialization of, 26, 128, 132; victimization of, 123, 131–32, 162
Girls in Development (program), 6–7, 9–13, 15–20, 21, 45, 64, 66, 71, 73–76, 95, 100–104, 105, 107, 113, 117, 121–23, 148–50, 159, 164–67, 169; lobbying of, 15–16, 19, 72, 94, 147–48, 152, 165, 170; and multinational corporations, 160–61, 162, 168–69; and neoliberal feminism, 18, 19–20, 46, 69, 149, 170
"girl turn," 71, 76, 103–4, 105
Global North: and decolonization, 51–52, 169; and gender inequality, 97–98, 144; and global capitalism, 79, 88, 143, 144, 161; and NIEO, 48, 49, 144, 162; positions at UN World Conferences on Women, 61–62, 63–65, 141–42
GOBI initiatives, 82–89, 91, 119
Grant, James P.: biography of, 77–78; and GOBI-FFF, 82–83, 84–90; and NIEO, 81–82, 90; and selective primary health care, 77–78; and UNICEF, 40, 75, 78, 79, 92–93, 101, 102

Haggag Youssef, Nadia, 56
handicrafts, 16
Hazzard, Virginia: biography of, 51, 52–53, 191n14; and FEMNET, 59; functions of, 55; and UN World Conference on Women in Nairobi, 54, 55, 61, 92–93, 127
health care: basic, 82; general, 2, 6, 36, 75, 76, 78, 79, 80, 85, 86, 87, 90, 96, 99, 100, 108, 128, 129, 137, 141, 155; norms, 83; primary, 77, 83–84, 88; and protection from disease, 78, 82, 131; selective, 77–78, 84, 91
history of science, 8, 207n4; feminist, 166
HIV/AIDS, 37, 130, 145
housing, 77, 79, 80, 90; security, 6
human capital: girls and women as, 18, 74, 82, 86, 113, 116, 153, 157, 164; theory of, 74, 95
humanitarianism, 15, 149; for-profit, 6, 7
human resource theory, 74
human rights: with focus on girls, 95, 101, 136, 147, 151, 155; movements, 66, 67, 155; norms of, 4, 121, 124, 144–45, 170
hygiene, 15, 16; products for, 156–59, 161. See also Sanitary Pads Campaign

Idowu, Genga, 152
ILO. See International Labour Organization (ILO)

IMF. See International Monetary Fund (IMF)
inequality: economic, 72, 87–88, 118, 130, 144; global, 1, 3, 6, 19, 62, 72, 87, 105, 107, 123, 125, 136, 143, 144, 167; of women and children, 1, 4, 26–28, 32, 62–63, 66, 72, 87–88, 101–2, 118, 130, 136–37, 140
infibulation, 64. See also FGM (female genital mutilation)
intellectual history, global, 8–9, 166
International Development Research Centre (Canada), 22
International Labour Organization (ILO), 94, 95
International Monetary Fund (IMF), 7, 25, 31, 75, 79–80, 132
International Planned Parenthood Federation, 58

Jolly, Richard, 16–17, 40, 79, 80, 89, 185n43, 186n46

KAACR. See Kenya Alliance for the Advancement of Children's Rights (KAACR)
Kamweru, Esther, 42, 43
Kenya, government of: and public education, 25, 29–31, 34; relations to NGOs, 18, 20, 42–45, 64, 66–69, 70–71, 153, 155; and UNICEF, 11–13, 39, 95
Kenya African National Union (KANU), 44, 66, 67–68
Kenya Alliance for the Advancement of Children's Rights (KAACR), 124–25, 132–35, 136–37, 140, 142, 146, 151
Kenyatta, Jomo, 55, 66
knowledge: forms of, 45, 69–70; history of, 8, 45; production and erasure of, 1, 2, 7, 8, 17, 19–20, 21–22, 36, 41, 45, 46, 62, 70, 85–86, 101, 102, 105–7, 125–27, 138, 157, 162, 166–67, 170–71

labor: gender roles and division of, 21, 24–33, 35–37, 66, 92, 97–98, 115, 132; paid, 5–6, 15, 22, 34–35, 90–93, 102, 103, 117, 122, 157, 162–63, 164, 167; unpaid domestic, 27, 30, 34, 57, 70, 87, 94, 114
Labouisse, Henry R., 78
lacemaking, 26
Lekyo, Christopher, 119
lobbying: campaigns, 4, 126, 141, 145–46, 151–52; of FEMNET-UNICEF, 4, 6, 10–14, 19, 48, 64, 72, 124–25, 130–36, 140, 142, 165–67, 170–71; strategies, 50–51, 53, 59, 136, 139, 148, 168
Longwe, Sara Hlupekile, 109–10
Longwe Framework for Gender Analysis, 109
Lutheran World Federation, 134
Lwanga-Okwenje, Elizabeth, 109–10

Maathai, Wangari, 42–43, 44
Maendeleo ya Wanawake (Progress of Women), 44, 55, 67–68
Mahler, Halfdan, 76, 77, 83, 89

malnutrition, 78, 81, 82, 84, 87, 98. *See also* nutrition
Mangvwat, Joyce, 135
Mao Zedong, 77
Marenah, Coumba Ceesay, 110
marriage, 15; early, 116, 131, 133, 140, 151, 157
Marvel Five, 157–58, 161
Matsepe-Casaburri, Ivy, 56
Mau Mau Emergency, 16, 66, 153
Mauroy, Pierre, 83
Mboya, Tom, 66
Mbugua, Jane, 152
Mbugua, Rosemary Wanjiku, 68, 152
men: advantages of, 96; as oppressors, 15, 21, 37, 131–32; sensitization of, 37–38, 41, 63, 136; social and gender roles of, 9, 28, 30, 34–35, 115, 136; and violence, 31, 114–15. *See also* boys
menstruation, 157–60. *See also* Sanitary Pads Campaign
Mexico City, Mexico. *See* World Conference on Women: 1975 (Mexico City)
microcredit, 72–73, 84, 139, 144–45, 185n43, 206n68
microfinance. *See* microcredit
missionaries, Christian, 26–27
Moi, Daniel arap, 42, 66, 154
Moi administration, 42, 44, 66, 67–69, 154–55
Molotsi, Prisca, 56
Mombeshora, Swithun, 119
Mongella, Gertrude, 124, 139
Mpungu, Jennifer, 152
Musomi, Mercy, 147–48, 149, 150–51, 156, 160, 161, 167
Muthoni Kamuru, Marilyn, 44
Mutukwa, Gladys M'Sodzi, 110
MYWO. *See* Maendeleo ya Wanawake (Progress of Women)

Nairobi, Kenya. *See* World Conference on Women: 1985 (Nairobi)
Nairobi Women's Hospital, Gender Violence Recovery Center at, 13
Nakumatt, 157, 160
National Council of Women of Kenya, 55
nationalism, 9, 160
neoliberalism, 5–10, 14–19, 21–22, 72–76, 82–83, 103–104, 150, 161, 167–168
neoliberal turn, 72, 74, 76, 83–84
New International Economic Order (NIEO), 48–50, 63, 76–78, 81, 83, 89, 103; and health care, 77–78, 83; and UN World Conferences on Women, 46–50, 63–64, 122, 140
NGO Forum: 1975 (Mexico City), 62; 1980 (Copenhagen), 51, 62; 1985 (Nairobi), 51, 56, 59–61, 64, 67–68, 144; 1995 (Beijing), 60, 126, 137–38, 140, 142, 143, 147

NIEO. *See* New International Economic Order (NIEO)
Nike Foundation, 15, 74, 150, 167
NoVo Foundation, 150, 167
Nsekela, Christina, 56
nutrition: of children, 15, 101; girls' access to, 94, 95, 96–97, 102; of mothers, 15
Nyagah, Grace, 25, 29–32
Nyerere, Julius, 80

Obura, Anna, 23, 32–39
Ogana, Winnie, 112
oil shocks, 72, 79
Okoth, Pontian Godfrey, 67
Olembo, Norah Khadzini, 68–69, 110
Onyancha, Edwin, 152
Opondo, Fred, 25, 29–32

Palme, Olof, 83
Pan-Africanism: as concept, 1, 7, 9, 10, 62, 80; and FEMNET, 10, 38, 42, 46–71; and women's movement, 66, 69, 109, 110, 128, 165, 169, 170
patriarchy, 3, 4, 6, 7, 11, 19, 21, 25, 27, 32, 39, 66, 72, 87–88, 91, 93, 97–99, 103, 114, 121, 125, 126–27, 142, 144, 146, 150, 164, 167; universality of, 35, 36, 45, 99, 100, 167
Plan International, 13, 74
Platt, Nana, 56
population: control of, 15, 85; growth of, 82, 88–89, 96, 113, 130
poverty: feminization of, 2, 33, 35, 41, 129; of girls and women, 7, 10, 11, 14, 16, 18–19, 39, 41, 73, 107, 112, 122, 124–27, 131–32, 135–36, 141, 143, 150, 167; and patriarchy, 3, 7, 11, 21, 39, 72, 87–88, 93, 100, 103, 125, 126–27, 150, 167
pregnancy: of girls, 28, 85, 115, 116, 131; nutrition during, 84
Procter & Gamble, 156, 157, 158, 160–61. *See also* Sanitary Pads Campaign

Rabb Weidenfeld, Sheila, 49
racism: fight against, 50, 57, 121, 122, 144; as form of oppression, 3, 7, 65, 117, 144; personal experiences of, 16, 55, 57
Ramamonjisoa, Suzy, 26
reading, 26
Reagan, Ronald, 18, 79, 90
Rockefeller Foundation, 22, 78, 82

SAARC (South Asian Association for Regional Cooperation), 95
Sanitary Pads Campaign, 156–61, 168
Save the Children, 152
Second UN World Conference on Women. *See* World Conference on Women: 1980 (Copenhagen)

Sen, Amartya, 96, 97, 99
Sengupta, Sunil, 97
sewing, 26
sexuality, 115, 131, 168
Singer, Hans, 81
Skowcroft, Brent, 49
SNV Netherlands Development Organization, 153
Sohoni, Neera, 100
South Asian Association for Regional Cooperation (SAARC), 95
sponsorships, corporate. *See* donations: via corporate sponsorships
Steady, Filomina, 10
STEM education, 30–31, 37, 114, 117
stereotypes, 37, 40
structural adjustment programs (SAPs): and development, 3, 34–35, 80, 83, 86, 90, 109–10, 112, 114, 116–17, 132, 136, 139, 141, 143, 146; effects of, 2, 18, 21, 25, 32–33, 35, 42, 45, 79, 108, 110–11, 114, 138, 141, 145, 164
student movement of 1968, 55
Summers, Lawrence "Larry," 73–74, 75, 101, 102

Tarr-Whelan, Linda, 124, 146
Thahane, Timothy, 113
Thatcher, Margaret, 18, 79, 82–83
Thika Secondary School, 16
Third UN World Conference on Women. *See* World Conference on Women: 1985 (Nairobi)
Third World Organization for Women in Science, 113
traditions, cultural, 36, 115, 120
Twiga Chemicals, 157

Uchumi, 157, 160
Umbima, Joyce, 134–35
UN Charter on Economic Rights and Duties of States, 48
UN Commission on the Status of Women, 2, 12, 48–49, 137, 141, 177n1, 198n76
UN Convention on the Rights of the Child, 111–12, 119
UN Decade for Women (1976–1985), 1, 46, 47–48, 50–52, 54–58, 60, 62, 64, 67, 70, 90–92, 106, 145
UN Development Program, 12, 82, 110, 128
Undugu Society of Kenya, 133
UN Economic Commission for Africa, 91, 110
UNESCO. *See* United Nations Educational, Scientific and Cultural Organization (UNESCO)
UN General Assembly, 12, 48, 76, 127
UNICEF. *See* United Nations Children's Fund (UNICEF)
UNICEF's Forum on the Female Child Today (New York City, 1985), 91, 92, 93
UN International Women's Year (1975), 47–49, 55
United Kingdom's Department for International Development (DFID), 153
United Nations Children's Fund (UNICEF), 1, 53, 72–73, 75–78, 80–85, 87–95, 99–104, 132–33, 152, 154; archives of, 11–12; case studies, 26, 35–41, 79, 80, 81, 99; criticism of, 83, 85–86; and FEMNET, 2–7, 10–11, 12–22, 38, 41–42, 44–45, 47–48, 59, 64, 66, 69–71, 72, 105–6, 112–14, 116, 120–25, 127–30, 134–36, 142, 146, 164–171; Kenya Country Office of, 11–12, 22, 39, 42, 53, 60, 69, 70–71, 110, 112, 134, 154, 165; reports, 22, 82, 91–92, 131, 134; Somalia headquarters of, 11. *See also* Eastern and Southern Africa Regional Office (ESARO), UNICEF
United Nations Educational, Scientific and Cultural Organization (UNESCO), 12, 26, 52, 151
United States Agency for International Development (USAID), 18, 74, 78, 95, 102, 103, 157
UN Women's Movement, 50, 125
UN World Conference on Education for All (Jomtien, Thailand, 1990), 110
UN World Conference on Women. *See* World Conference on Women
UN World Summit for Children (1990), 73, 100, 119–20

violence: colonial, 48, 110, 121; corporal, 28; gender-based, 32, 157; against girls and women, 31, 33, 98, 128–29, 130, 131, 133, 135, 140–41, 150–51; sexual, 24, 31, 33, 135; of state, 33, 66, 69; of war, 24, 25

Wainaina, Njoki, 1, 10, 42, 43–44, 47, 51, 53–54, 56–60, 61, 67–69, 109, 110–11, 127, 128, 149, 170, 182n28
Wamahiu, Sheila, 25, 29, 30, 31, 32
War on Terror, 139, 154, 159, 162, 168, 171
wealth: inequality, 1, 6, 14, 28, 72, 81–82, 88, 98, 105, 129, 136; redistribution of, 49, 63, 66, 116, 163
welfare: during colonialism, 15–16, 159; and neoliberalism, 5–7, 9, 14, 18, 20, 72, 76, 78–81, 86, 88, 90, 105, 108, 111, 125, 129, 166; programming based on, 9, 93, 96, 98–99, 103, 116, 160; and public education, 24, 53, 72, 77, 116–17
Were, Miriam Khamadi, 107, 110
WHO. *See* World Health Organization (WHO)
WiLDAF (Women in Law and Development in Africa), 110
Wisner, Ben, 83, 88
women: liberation of, 5–6, 57, 141; literacy of, 16, 99, 109, 111; rights of, 57–58, 69, 85, 110, 126, 130, 139, 140, 141–42, 147, 168–69. *See also* girls
Women in Development (WID), 55, 58, 63, 73–75, 91–95, 103–4, 153
Women in Law and Development in Africa (WiLDAF), 110

World Bank: as agent, 12, 18, 80, 82, 85, 87, 111, 128, 132, 167; and Kenyan state, 25, 31; and neoliberal capitalism, 7, 73–75, 79, 95, 101–3, 168

World Conference on Women

—1975 (Mexico City), 47–48, 55–56; and NIEO, 48–50; and public reception, 61; topics of, 62

—1980 (Copenhagen), 47, 51, 55, 56; topics of, 62, 64–65, 142, 145

—1985 (Nairobi): and African Women's Task Force, 46, 50, 59–60, 68–70, 165; event of, 43, 60–64, 70; and Kenyan state, 66–67, 70–71; and NIEO, 46–50, 63–64, 122; and representation, 52–57, 127–28, 165; topics of, 61, 64–66, 70, 91–92, 103–4, 142, 144, 148–49, 162–63, 165

—1995 (Beijing): and FEMNET, 4, 11–12, 19, 47–48, 64, 70–71, 104, 105–6, 127–28, 130, 133, 137, 141–45; and Girl Child Network, 13, 19, 148–53, 162, 164, 166–71; and NIEO, 47–48, 50, 70; topics of, 3, 4–5, 6, 10, 19, 66, 70–71, 72, 104, 106, 121–27, 139, 145–48, 164, 167

World Health Organization (WHO), 12, 76, 77, 81, 82, 83, 85, 89, 99

writing, 26